World Wisdom
The Library of Perennial Philosophy

The Library of Perennial Philosophy is dedicated to the exposition of the timeless Truth underlying the diverse religions. This Truth, often referred to as the Sophia Perennis—or Perennial Wisdom—finds its expression in the revealed Scriptures as well as the writings of the great sages and the artistic creations of the traditional worlds.

Touchstones of the Spirit appears as one of our selections in the Perennial Philosophy series.

The Perennial Philosophy Series

In the beginning of the twentieth century, a school of thought arose which has focused on the enunciation and explanation of the Perennial Philosophy. Deeply rooted in the sense of the sacred, the writings of its leading exponents establish an indispensable foundation for understanding the timeless Truth and spiritual practices which live in the heart of all religions. Some of these titles are companion volumes to the Treasures of the World's Religions series, which allows a comparison of the writings of the great sages of the past with the perennialist authors of our time.

Other Books by the Same Author

Traditionalism: Religion in the Light of the Perennial Philosophy (2000)

Journeys East: Twentieth Century Western Encounters with Eastern Religious Traditions (2004)

A Christian Pilgrim in India: The Spiritual Journey of Swami Abhishikt-ananda (Henri Le Saux) (2008)

Mediations: Essays on Religious Pluralism and the Perennial Philosophy (2008)

Frithjof Schuon and the Perennial Philosophy (2010)

Books Edited

The Betrayal of Tradition: Essays on the Spiritual Crisis of Modernity (2005)

Light from the East: Eastern Wisdom for the Modern West (2007)

Crossing Religious Frontiers: Studies in Comparative Religion (2010)

Touchstones
of the Spirit

Essays on Religion, Tradition & Modernity

Harry Oldmeadow

World Wisdom

Touchstones of the Spirit:
Essays on Religion, Tradition, and Modernity
© 2012 World Wisdom, Inc.

Cover:
Rain God Mesa,
Monument Valley, Utah.
Photo by Harry Oldmeadow

Library of Congress Cataloging-in-Publication Data

Oldmeadow, Harry, 1947-
Touchstones of the spirit : essays on religion, tradition & modernity /
Harry Oldmeadow.
    p. cm. -- (The library of perennial philosophy)
Includes bibliographical references and index.
ISBN 978-1-936597-03-1 (pbk. : alk. paper) 1. Religions. I. Title.
BL87.O43 2012
200--dc23

                                                      2012002609

Printed on acid-free paper in the United States of America.

For information address World Wisdom, Inc.
P.O. Box 2682, Bloomington, Indiana 47402-2682
www.worldwisdom.com

CONTENTS

PREFACE

This compilation of essays is structured around three themes: the timeless messages of Tradition; the obscuration of this perennial wisdom in the modern world; and the spiritual intercourse between East and West which holds out some hope that we may yet recover something of what we have lost. These subjects have preoccupied me in the thirty-five years since I first discovered the great traditionalist writers—René Guénon, Ananda Coomaraswamy, Frithjof Schuon, and Titus Burckhardt, and those who came after. In other works I have dealt with both the perennialist outlook and the spiritual encounter of East and West in more systematic and comprehensive fashion. The present, somewhat unruly collection brings together scattered writings from the last thirty years. Previously isolated fragments are here strung, so to speak, on a single cord. Despite the diversity of subjects, readers will discern a persistent set of underlying concerns, related to the themes already mentioned. Taken as a whole, these essays comprise so many attempts, no doubt with varying degrees of success, to consider a variety of phenomena in the light of the principles so magisterially affirmed by the traditionalists. I do not, of course, suggest that all of my findings would meet with their approval.

Most of the pieces gathered here have been previously published, most often in scholarly journals. They remain substantially as they were on first appearance. In essays composed over so many years there will inevitably be some unevenness in tone and style, some inconsistencies and incongruities. I have made no effort to harmonize either the content or style of these essays, preferring, for better or worse, to leave them more or less intact. However, I have removed a few anachronisms, rectified some of the more conspicuous stylistic inadvertencies, standardized some terminology and made some minor changes to the text, mainly to avoid undue repetition. In several cases footnotes have been severely culled; readers wanting fuller documentation are directed back to the originals which are listed in the Sources section at the end of this book. In some instances I have substituted more recent editions than those originally cited, particularly with respect to the writings of Frithjof Schuon, and here and there I have added a reference to a work which had not appeared at the time of first writing.

Harry Oldmeadow

1. Echoes of Tradition

The sense of the sacred is fundamental for every civilization because fundamental for man; the sacred—that which is immutable, inviolable, and thus infinitely majestic—is in the very substance of our spirit and of our existence.

FRITHJOF SCHUON

CHAPTER 1

"Melodies from the Beyond":
The Spiritual Heritage of the Australian Aborigines

> In all epochs and in all countries there have been revelations, religions, wisdoms; tradition is a part of mankind just as man is a part of tradition.
>
> *Frithjof Schuon*[1]

In *The Reign of Quantity* (1945) René Guénon observes that it is only in these latter days of the accelerating "solidification" of the world, that "Cain finally and really slays Abel"[2]—which is to say that the sedentary civilizations destroy the nomadic cultures. Moreover, Guénon remarks,

> It could be said in a general way that the works of sedentary peoples are works of time: these people are fixed in space within a strictly limited domain, and develop their activities in a temporal continuity that appears to them to be indefinite. On the other hand, nomadic and pastoral peoples build nothing durable, and do not work for a future that escapes them; but they have space before them, not facing them with any limitation, but on the contrary always offering them new possibilities.[3]

No doubt it was with such considerations in mind that Frithjof Schuon declared that "traditions having a prehistoric origin are, symbolically speaking, made for 'space' and not for 'time'. . . ."[4] It follows from these general observations that the slaying of Abel—the violent extirpation of the primordial nomadic cultures—not only constitutes a drastic contraction of human possibilities but is actually a cosmic

---

1 F. Schuon, *Light on the Ancient Worlds: A New Translation with Selected Letters* (Bloomington, IN: World Wisdom, 2006), p. 25.

2 R. Guénon, *The Reign of Quantity & The Signs of the Times* (Ghent, NY: Sophia Perennis et Universalis, 1995), p. 178.

3 R. Guénon, *Reign of Quantity*, p. 180.

4 F. Schuon, *Light on the Ancient Worlds*, p. 8.

desecration. Recall the words of Marco Pallis, on the destruction of the traditional and largely nomadic culture of Tibet:

> One can truly say that this remote land behind the snowy rampart of the Himalaya had become like the chosen sanctuary for all those things whereof the historical discarding had caused our present profane civilization, the first of its kind, to come into being. . . . [T]he violation of this sanctuary and the dissipation of the sacred influences hitherto concentrated there becomes an event of properly cosmic significance, of which the ulterior consequences for a world that tacitly condoned the outrage or, in many cases, openly countenanced it on the plea that it brought "progress" to a reluctant people have yet to ripen fully.[5]

Similar considerations may be applied to more or less analogous cases, whether we think of the fate of the American Indians, the Australian Aborigines, the Inuit, the Bedouin, the Gypsies, the Bushmen of the Kalahari, the Maori, or any other peoples who have been trampled by the juggernaut of modernity.

Since the genocidal ravages of the nineteenth century a great deal has been written about the destruction of the Indian cultures of North America. There have also been many attempts, with varying success, to reanimate at least some aspects of the ancestral way of life. It need hardly be stated that many of the writers on these subjects are altogether impervious to the deeper significance of the events and processes which they seek to explain. On the other hand, Frithjof Schuon's *oeuvre* comprises a peerless explication of the *sophia perennis* which informs all integral traditions, including those of primordial origin. His writings, along with those of Guénon and Ananda Coomaraswamy, have fulfilled a providential function by answering to certain spiritual necessities arising from the peculiar cyclic conditions of the time. Amongst Schuon's most poignant writings are those on the American Plains Indians, many of which were gathered together in *The Feathered Sun* (1990),[6] accompanied by reproductions of his luminous paintings on Indian themes. The metaphysical and cosmological doctrines of the

---

5 M. Pallis, review of *The New Religions*, by Jacob Needleman, *Studies in Comparative Religion*, 5:3, 1971, pp. 189-190.

6 F. Schuon, *The Feathered Sun: Plains Indians in Art and Philosophy* (Bloomington, IN: World Wisdom Books, 1990).

Indians, the symbolic language of their myths, rituals, and art, the arcane practices of shamanism, and many other aspects of their religious life are elucidated with great clarity, profundity, and beauty. Schuon's writings on the religious heritage of the American Indians furnish us with an exemplary account of a mythologically-based spiritual economy; what follows is an application of the principles expounded by Schuon to another spiritual heritage, that of the Australian Aborigines.

Background

Since the arrival of the Europeans, late in the eighteenth century, attitudes to Australia's indigenous inhabitants have ranged from sentimental romanticism, to deep hostility and contempt, to misguided paternalism. The Aborigine has been cast in various roles: the "Noble Savage"; a harmless and infantile figure of fun; an embodiment of all that is morally repugnant in man's nature; an anthropological relic of the Stone Age; a biological curio; a victim of a divine curse; a social misfit incapable of living a responsible and productive life. The stereotypes have changed under the pressure of circumstances and the shifting ideological presuppositions of the observers but throughout them all runs the persistent European failure to understand Aboriginal culture, in particular that network of beliefs, values, relationships, and patterned behaviors which we can loosely assemble under the canopy of "Aboriginal religion." The factors which have shaped European attitudes are precisely those which have fuelled the ongoing cultural vandalism of modern industrial societies against indigenous peoples across the globe. To name a few: ignorance about the culture in question; assumptions about the cultural superiority of modern, industrial civilization, often buttressed by evolutionism of both a biological and social kind; an aggressive Christian exclusivism, operating as an accomplice to European colonialism; the reductive conceptual apparatus brought to the study of "primitive" cultures. The attitude to Aboriginal religion of most European observers has been "a melancholy mixture of neglect, condescension, and misunderstanding."[7]

From the outset there was a tenacious, often willful, refusal to acknowledge that the Aborigines had any religion at all. In 1798, for instance, an early colonist wrote:

7 M. Charlesworth et al. (ed.), *Religion in Aboriginal Australia: An Anthology* (St Lucia: University of Queensland Press, 1984), p. 1.

It has been asserted by an eminent divine, that no country has yet been discovered where some trace of religion was not to be found. From every observation and inquiry that I could make among these people, from the first to the last of my acquaintance with them, I can safely pronounce them an exception to this opinion.[8]

The recognition that the Aborigines had a vibrant spiritual life came slowly and was never more than partial. Such nineteenth century scholarship as there was concerning Aboriginal religion often rested on rotten foundations, namely, those vague but potent Victorian prejudices and cultural valuations which assumed the biological and cultural superiority of the white man, the belief that British institutions marked the apotheosis of civilization, and the notion that the extinction of the indigenous peoples of Australia was not only inevitable but divinely appointed.[9] Notions of cultural superiority had a long and sordid pedigree in Europe, refurbished by evolutionism in both its scientific and sociological guises. The global decline of the darker races was a theme which enjoyed widespread currency in the Victorian era. Thus a late nineteenth century writer:

It seems a law of nature where two races whose stages of progression differ greatly are brought into contact, the inferior race is doomed to disappear. . . . The process seems to be in accordance with a natural law which . . . is clearly beneficial to mankind at large by providing for the survival of the fittest. Human progress has all been achieved by the spread of the progressive race and the squeezing out of the inferior ones. . . . It may be doubted that the Australian aborigine would ever have advanced much beyond the status of the neo-lithic races . . . and we need not therefore lament his disappearance.[10]

8 D. Collins, *An Account of the English Colony in New South Wales* (1798), quoted in W.E.H. Stanner, "Religion, Totemism and Symbolism" in *Religion in Aboriginal Australia*, p. 138. Such a view is echoed in the words of an otherwise sympathetic missionary, writing in the mid-nineteenth century: "The Aborigines of New Holland, in this part of the Colony, have no priesthood, no altar, no sacrifice, nor any religious service, strictly so-called; their superstitious observances can scarcely be designated as divine rites being only mysterious works of darkness, revelings, and suchlike" (L.E. Threlkeld quoted in *Religion in Aboriginal Australia*, p. 2).

9 See the historical survey of European attitudes in T. Swain, *Interpreting Aboriginal Religion: An Historical Account* (Adelaide: Australian Association for the Study of Religion, 1985).

10 *The Age*, January 11, 1889, quoted in H. Reynolds (ed.), *Dispossession: Black Austral-*

A militant Christian evangelism helped to erode the early Romantic image of the Noble Savage which had been derived, largely, from the writings of Rousseau. (We should note in passing Schuon's remark that although the Noble Savage motif was no doubt largely sentimental, it was not drawn entirely "out of thin air."[11]) With widespread missionizing activity in Australia and the Pacific came a reaction against romantic primitivism: to churchmen of evangelical persuasion it was less than proper that "pagan savages" should be idealized as either noble or innocent.[12] The theme of the Aborigines' moral abasement was in vogue by mid-century and all manner of pseudo-Biblical rationales were invoked to legitimize racialist and self-interested prejudices.

The story of how the whites made the Aborigines exiles in their own land is, to say the least, a dismal one. The introduction of European diseases such as tuberculosis, influenza, and syphilis, the appropriation of Aboriginal hunting grounds, the spreading of malign influences such as alcohol and gunpowder, the sexual exploitation of Aboriginal women, brutal physical violence escalating into a program of genocidal extermination in parts of the continent,[13] institutionalized racial discrimination ranging from vicious repression to ill-conceived paternalism, the legal fiction of *terra nullius*, and governmental policies of "assimilation" and "integration," all played a role in this tragic story.[14] More crucial perhaps than any of these depredations was the

---

ians and White Invaders (Sydney: Allen & Unwin, 1989), p. 9.

11 F. Schuon, *Feathered Sun*, p. 77.

12 The complex role of Christian missionaries and their impact on Aboriginal culture has been vastly oversimplified by apologists on both sides of the fence. It would certainly be misleading to suggest that the role of the missionaries was entirely destructive. In some areas the missionaries provided a refuge in which Aboriginal people were able to survive physically and in which at least some remnants of traditional culture were preserved. Nonetheless, a good deal of evil was perpetrated in the name of Christianity. For a discussion of this issue see M. Furlong, *The Flight of the Kingfisher: Journey Among the Kukatja Aborigines* (London: Harper Collins, 1996), esp. Ch. 4.

13 As late as 1902 white commentators were still justifying the deliberate killing of Aborigines in terms such as these: "The substitution of more than a million of industrious and peaceful people for a roaming, fighting contingent of six thousand cannot be said to be dearly purchased even at the cost of the violent deaths of a fraction of the most aggressive among them" (H.A. Turner, *History of the Colony of Victoria*, Vol. 1, [London, 1902], p. 239, quoted in *Dispossession: Black Australians and White Invaders*, p. 9).

14 As well as the work by Reynolds already cited see H. Reynolds, *The Other Side of*

desecration of sacred sites without which Aboriginal religious life could not survive.

Certainly, recent anthropologists have abandoned many of the cruder racist assumptions of their predecessors but all too often have succeeded only in replacing Victorian prejudices with those more characteristic of our own age whilst still retaining a childish faith in the capacity of a rationalistic and materialistic pseudo-science to grasp the mysteries of a complex spiritual tradition. Nothing more dramatically betokens the failure of Durkheimian anthropology than its continuing insistence that Aboriginal "religion" is, essentially, a system for sanctioning certain social functions and relationships. Not without reason has Mircea Eliade written of the "religious illiteracy" of many scholars of so-called "primitive" religious traditions.[15] Whilst intellectual fashions amongst ethnologists and anthropologists have changed over the last two hundred years the one constant factor has been an intransigent reductionism which refuses to treat Aboriginal religion in its own terms or, indeed, in terms appropriate to *any* religious tradition. The theories of Freud, Durkheim, and Levy-Bruhl, for instance, are all variations on the reductionist theme.[16] But as Whitall Perry once observed, "the scientific pursuit of religion puts the saddle on the wrong horse, since it is the domain of religion to evaluate science, and not vice versa."[17] Nothing so characterizes the mentality of modernism as the naive belief that the greater can be contained in the lesser, which is precisely the impossibility attempted when a profane scholarship, immune to anything of a spiritual order, tries to force a living tradition into the sterile categories of a quasi-scientific reductionism—no matter whether it be Durkheimian, Freudian, Marxist, or structuralist! In the words of W.E.H. Stanner, one of Australia's more sensitive anthropologists,

the *Frontier: Aboriginal Resistance to the European Invasion of Australia* (Ringwood: Penguin, 1982), and C.D. Rowley, *The Destruction of Aboriginal Society* (Ringwood: Penguin, 1972).

15 M. Eliade, *Australian Religions: An Introduction* (Ithaca: Cornell University Press, 1971), pp. xiii-xiv.

16 See E.E. Evans-Pritchard, *Theories of Primitive Religion* (Oxford: Clarendon Press, 1965), and M. Eliade, *Australian Religions*, p. xvii.

17 W. Perry, review of *The Phenomena of Religion*, by Ninian Smart, *Studies in Comparative Religion*, 7:2, 1973, p. 127.

It is preposterous that something like a century of study, because of rationalism, positivism, and materialism, should have produced two options: that Aboriginal religion is either (to follow Durkheim) what someone called "the mirage of society" or (to follow Freud) "the neurosis of society."[18]

Such a situation should alert us to the dangers and impostures of modernism in its many different "scholarly" guises. From a religious viewpoint, we cannot too often recall Schuon's reminder that, "it is the spiritual, not the temporal, which culturally, socially, and politically is the criterion of all other values."[19]

Aboriginal Culture

In terms of its socio-economic organization Aboriginal culture, over most of the continent, was a hunter-gatherer society in which tribal members were highly mobile within clearly understood geographical boundaries, and in which the social dynamics were governed by complex kinship and totemic systems, and by principles of reciprocity and exchange. The web of beliefs and practices, which might loosely be labeled "religious," is best described as mythologically-based and embedded in a ritual-ceremonial complex centering on a sacramental relationship with the land itself. (If it be asked what is meant by the term "sacramental" one can hardly do better than the traditional Christian formulation that a sacrament is "an outer and visible sign of an inner

---

18 W. E. H. Stanner, "Religion, Totemism and Symbolism," p. 155. One must, in fairness, concede that anthropology has produced some imaginative, sensitive, and sympathetic scholars who have alerted us to the many misdemeanors of their predecessors and who have helped to foster a more respectful approach which tries to understand Aboriginal religion in its own terms. The late Professor Stanner, for instance, insisted that Aboriginal religion must be studied "*as religion and not as the mirror of something else*" and strenuously refuted the fallacy that "the social order is primary and in some sense causal, and the religious order secondary and in some sense consequential" (W.E.H. Stanner, *On Aboriginal Religion*, The Oceania Monographs, No. 11 [Sydney: University of Sydney, 1963], quoted in M. Eliade, *Australian Religions*, pp. 196-197). See also W.E.H. Stanner, *White Man Got No Dreaming: Essays 1938-1973* (Canberra: Australian National University Press, 1979). For a fascinating recent account of some of the controversies in Australian anthropology see Barry Hill, *Broken Song: T.G.H. Strehlow and Aboriginal Possession* (Sydney: Vintage, 2002).

19 F. Schuon, *The Transfiguration of Man* (Bloomington, IN: World Wisdom Books), 1995, p. 28.

and invisible grace.") Aboriginal religion can also be described as "primal" which is to say that it is prehistoric in origin, non-literate, tribal, and one in which the distinction between "religion" and "culture" at large has no meaning. The qualities which Hilton Deakin has identified as characteristic of primal cultures apply specifically to Aboriginal society: such cultures are ethnocentric, non-universal, non-missionizing; they are intimately related to the natural world by a perceived spiritual kinship; they emphasize the existence of supernatural powers which are accessible to the human world; and they experience the world as saturated with spiritual power.[20] Schuon's words concerning the American Indians apply equally well to the Aborigines:

> The Indian is predisposed towards the suprasensible and strives to penetrate the hard wall of the sensible world, seeks openings where he can, and finds them chiefly in phenomena themselves, which indeed, in their contents, are nothing other than signposts to the suprasensible. Things are hard-frozen melodies from the Beyond.[21]

Such cultures are also governed by sacred mythic accounts which leave them indifferent to the linear and horizontal conception of history as it is understood in the modern West.[22] Of course, we here use "myth" not in its pejorative modern sense of a fanciful fabrication but rather in its perennial sense as a narrative account carrying metaphysical and spiritual messages—the sense in which Coomaraswamy used the word when he wrote,

> The myth is the penultimate truth, of which all experience is the temporal reflection. The mythical narrative is of timeless and placeless validity, true nowhere and everywhere. . . . Myth embodies the nearest approach to absolute truth that can be stated in words.[23]

The Aboriginal worldview is also underpinned by a "visionary

---

20 See H. Deakin, "Some Thoughts on Transcendence in Tribal Societies" in *Ways of Transcendence: Insights from Major Religions and Modern Thought*, ed. E. Dowdy (Adelaide: Australian Association for the Study of Religion, 1982), pp. 95-109.

21 F. Schuon, *Feathered Sun*, p. 154.

22 M. Eliade, *Australian Religions*, pp. xvff.

23 A.K. Coomaraswamy, *Hinduism and Buddhism* (New Delhi: Munshiram Manoharlal, 1995), p. 6.

geography" which constitutes an ordered and meaningful world and, indeed, which situates both the community and individual in relation to the whole cosmos.[24]

The Religious Heritage

Let us turn to several highly significant and suggestive manifestations of the Aboriginal religious heritage: the central conception of the Dreaming; beliefs about transcendental powers and the soul; the metaphysics of their sacred geography; the role of the *karadji*, or "medicine man." The Dreaming is a "plurivocal term with a number of distinct though connected meanings," expressed variously as *altjiranga, wongar,* and *bugari.*

> First, it is a narrative mythical account of the foundation and shaping of the entire world by the ancestor heroes who are uncreated and eternal. Second, "the Dreaming" refers to the embodiment of the spiritual power of the ancestor heroes in the land in certain sites, and in species of fauna and flora, so that this power is available to people today. Indeed, one might say that for the Aboriginal his land is a kind of religious icon, since it both represents the power of the Dreamtime beings and also effects and transmits that power. Third, "the Dreaming" denotes the general way of life or "Law"—moral and social precepts, ritual and ceremonial practices, etc.—based upon these mythical foundations. Fourth, "the Dreaming" may refer to the personal "way" or vocation that an individual Aboriginal might have by virtue of his membership of a clan, or by virtue of his spirit conception relating him to particular sites.[25]

The Dreaming is an ever-present reality, not only "a long-past period in a time when life filled the void. It is rather the ever-present, unseen, ground of being—of existence." As A.P. Elkin has also said, "The concept is not of a 'horizontal' line extending back chronologically through a series of pasts, but rather a 'vertical' line in which the past underlies and is within the present."[26] The landscape as a whole,

24 On this general subject see M. Eliade, *The Sacred and the Profane: The Nature of Religion* (New York: Harcourt Brace Jovanovich, 1959). The phrase "visionary geography" is from Henri Corbin.

25 M. Charlesworth, *Religion in Aboriginal Australia*, p. 10.

26 A.P. Elkin quoted in M. Charlesworth, *Religion in Aboriginal Australia*, p. 10.

particular sites, objects, myths, rituals, and human groups and individuals are all inter-related within the Dreaming which is "the most real and concrete and fundamental aspect of Aboriginal life and has nothing to do with the Western concept of dreaming as an imaginary, fantastic, and illusory state of consciousness."[27]

All the cardinal features of Aboriginal society are derived from the Dreaming:

> The most momentous communication is the plan of life itself, the all-encompassing scope of which is shown in the shapes of the landscape, the events narrated in myth, the acts performed in rites, the codes observed in conduct, and the habits and characteristics of other forms of life.

We find here a feature characteristic of all religions: the notion of a Revelation of supra-human origins which lays down the "will of heaven," and which invites but does not compel conformity to its dictates. As a recent anthropologist has noted,

> The way in which the plan was "passed on" to humans as the powers withdrew above or below the earth is left obscure . . . but at least it is certain that men are not constrained to fidelity by their nature. The Aborigines know that they can fall away from what their traditional culture requires. . . . [28]

This is to say that they were no strangers to that fundamental freedom which constitutes the human estate, its dignity and its most terrible responsibility. The Dreaming constitutes a revealed mythology whilst the ongoing ritual and ceremonial life can be seen as the cord which joins Aboriginal society to its supernatural origins. Indeed, as Lord Northbourne observed, "Tradition, in the rightful sense of the word, is the chain that joins civilization to Revelation."[29] Or again, tra-

---

27 M. Charlesworth, *Religion in Aboriginal Australia*, p. 11. See also M. Eliade, *Australian Religions*, pp. 1-3.

28 K. Maddock, "The World Creative Powers" in M. Charlesworth, *Religion in Aboriginal Australia*, pp. 86-87. The immediately preceding quotation is from the same source.

29 Lord Northbourne, *Religion in the Modern World* (London: J.M. Dent, 1963), p. 34. In this context we might also recall Marco Pallis' definition of tradition as "an effective communication of principles of more-than-human origin . . . through use of forms

dition might also usefully be thought of as "the mediator between time and eternity." Each of these definitions is perfectly apposite in the Aboriginal context.

The transcendental, world-creative power is known under a variety of names (*Baiame, Bunjil, Daramulan, Nurelli, Mangela*) and is anthropomorphic, masculine, creative, sky-dwelling, ethical, immutable, and eternal, existing before all things and paternally related to all of humankind—perhaps best translated in English as the "All-Father." Indeed, the belief in the divinity who created both man and the world and then ascended into heaven after bestowing on humankind the rudiments of culture, "is attested in many other archaic cultures."[30] The same kind of transcendent, world-creative power is portrayed in some tribes, particularly those of Northern Australia, as feminine— the "All-Mother."[31] Between the supreme being and more parochial and so-called "totemic" spirits and powers are supernatural beings, "sky heroes," with whom much of the mythology is concerned. The Rainbow Serpent, representing the generative force, is one of the most widespread of such figures.[32]

As to the Aboriginal relationship with the natural world, what Joseph Epes Brown has said of the American Indians is also, in large measure, true of the Australian Aborigines:

[T]he world of nature itself was their temple, and within this sanctuary they showed great respect to every form, function, and power. That the Indians held as sacred all the natural forms around them is

that will have arisen by applying those principles to contingent needs. . ." (M. Pallis, *The Way and the Mountain* [London: Peter Owen, 1960], p. 203).

30 M. Eliade, *Australian Religions*, p. 7. The early ethnologists, especially those of an evolutionist bent, were unable to grasp the possibility of any religious conception amongst the Aborigines which might be comparable to the belief in a supreme, benevolent, and ethical Deity such as was to be found in the great Occidental monotheisms; it ran counter to their assumptions about the intellectual and spiritual inferiority of the Aborigines. Nevertheless, as Eliade has remarked, "There is no doubt that the belief in such a celestial Supreme Being belongs among the most archaic and genuine traditions of the southeastern Aborigines." The ethnologists likewise had difficulty in coming to terms with Aboriginal notions about the pre-existent and eternal soul in which most tribes believed. Again, Eliade has emphasized that "the indestructibility of the human spirit seems to be a fundamental and pan-Australian conception" (p. 172).

31 K. Maddock, "World Creative Powers," pp. 88-92.

32 M. Eliade, *Australian Religions*, pp. 79ff.

not unique. . . . But what is almost unique in the Indians' attitude is that their reverence for nature and for life is *central* to their religion: each form in the world around them bears such a host of precise values and meanings that taken all together they constitute what one would call their "doctrine."[33]

It is not too much to say that for the Aborigines, as for the Indians, not only is nature their temple but also their Scripture. In the case of the Aborigines we have already seen how a mythic and sacred geography is derived from the Dreaming itself. Indeed, "in the end, the land is no more than a bridge between [them] and the sacred realm of the Dreaming."[34] Much of their sacred art was directed towards the preservation of the tribal knowledge of that mythic geography. It is also worth remembering a point frequently stressed by Eliade: for *homo religiosus*, who is also necessarily *homo symbolicus*, everything in nature is capable of revealing itself as a "cosmic sacrality," as a hierophany, in contrast to the profane outlook of modern man, an outlook which renders the universe "opaque, inert, mute," a swirling chaos of dead matter.[35]

The Aborigines' semi-nomadic lifestyle ensured that they remained immersed in the realm of nature. It is as well to remember that such a relationship, of itself, confers spiritual gifts. As Schuon so eloquently puts it,

> Virgin Nature is at one with holy poverty and also with spiritual childlikeness; she is an open book containing an inexhaustible teaching of truth and beauty. It is in the midst of his own artifices that man most easily becomes corrupted, it is they that make him covetous and impious; close to virgin Nature, who knows neither agitation nor falsehood, he has the hope of remaining contemplative like Nature herself.[36]

Elsewhere he reminds us that in our own time "the timeless message of

33 J.E. Brown, *The Spiritual Legacy of the American Indian* (New York: Crossroad, 1972), p. 37.

34 J. Cowan, "The Dream Journey: Ritual Renewal among Australian Aborigines," *Temenos*, 7, 1986, p. 181.

35 M. Eliade, *Sacred and the Profane*, pp. 12, 178.

36 F. Schuon, *Feathered Sun*, p. 41.

Nature constitutes a spiritual viaticum of the first importance."[37]

Aboriginal ritual life was largely given over to a re-entry into the *illud tempus* of the Dreaming, a time which is sacred

> because it [is] sanctified by the real presence and activity of the Supernatural Beings. But like all other species of "sacred time," although infinitely remote, it is not inaccessible. It can be reactualized through ritual.[38]

Through ritual life the members of the tribe not only recuperated sacred time but by reiterating the paradigmatic acts of the supernatural powers they helped to regenerate life by "recreating the world."[39] To neglect these awesome cosmic responsibilities would be to allow the world to regress into darkness and chaos. Indeed, here we have one of the keys to the demoralization of those survivors who must live in a world made meaningless by their separation from the land and the consequent annihilation of their ritual life. They are no longer able to participate in the Dreamtime nor to fulfill those ritual obligations which gave life dignity and purpose. The substitutes and palliatives the modern white world offers are, of course, tawdry and trivial in comparison, whether they be sinister, as in the case of alcohol, or comparatively benign and well-intentioned—a Western "education" for instance, or "proper housing."

The spiritual integrity of the Aboriginal tradition was preserved by individuals variously called *karadjis*, "medicine men," "clever men," or, in Elkin's terms, "men of high degree." It was their role to cure the sick, defend the community against "black" magic, perform vital functions in the communal ritual life, especially in initiation rituals, and to serve as cultural and spiritual exemplars by way of their access to occult powers and their custody of the mythological and ceremonial heritage. These men were viaducts, so to speak, between the supernatural and mundane worlds.[40] The initiation ceremonies (invariably

---

37 F. Schuon, *Feathered Sun*, p. 13.

38 M. Eliade, *Australian Religions*, p. 43.

39 M. Eliade, *Australian Religions*, p. 61.

40 See M. Eliade, *Australian Religions*, pp. 128ff, 156ff; A. P. Elkin, *Aboriginal Men of High Degree* (St Lucia: University of Queensland Press, 1977); and J. Cowan, *The Elements of the Aborigine Tradition* (Shaftesbury: Element Books, 1992), Ch. 6.

entailing a death and rebirth experience), the central role of visions and other ecstatic experiences, and the healing functions of the men of high degree are reminiscent of shamanic practices in Tibet, Siberia, and amongst the Indians of both North and South America.[41] Nevertheless, the Aboriginal tradition developed its own esoteric spiritual practices and metaphysical wisdom to which the medicine men conformed themselves and by which they were sanctified.[42] We should also note that in recent decades the "secret business" of women, their role in ceremonial life and in esoteric religious practices, has become more widely appreciated in the non-Aboriginal world.

The Marks of Tradition

Aboriginal culture exhibited four emblems of *all* religious traditions. Firstly, *a divine source*. As we have seen, the origins of this tradition are primordial, stretching back into time immemorial. We cannot anchor its origins in historical time nor tie it to any place, person, event, or book. Nonetheless, we can declare that this mythological-ritual complex was not and could not have been of merely human provenance though doubtless its spiritual economy providentially reflected the psychic receptivities of the Aboriginal peoples. As Schuon has affirmed, "Traditions emerge from the Infinite like flowers; they can no more be fabricated than can the sacred art which is their witness and their proof."[43]

Secondly the Aboriginal tradition enshrined *a doctrine* about the nature and "relationship" of the Absolute and the relative, the Real and the relatively or provisionally real. In the case of the Aborigines, as with the American Indians, the doctrines were not cast in the mold of a book or a collection of canonical writings, nor formulated in abstract dogmatic language but, rather, inhered in the relationship of the Aboriginal to the whole cosmos. As Schuon remarked, metaphysical doctrines do not of necessity find their expression only in verbal forms but can be expressed visually and ritually. Furthermore,

---

41 See M. Eliade, *Shamanism: Archaic Techniques of Ecstasy* (New York: Pantheon Books, 1964), and *Australian Religions*, pp. 128-164, and A. P. Elkin, *Aboriginal Men of High Degree*, pp. 57-58, 60-64.

42 See J. Cowan, *Mysteries of the Dreaming: The Spiritual Life of Australian Aborigines* (Bridport: Prism Press, 1989), Ch. 1.

43 F. Schuon, *Treasures of Buddhism* (Bangalore: Select Books, 1993), p. 8.

[T]he criterion of metaphysical truth or of its depth lies, not in the complexity or difficulty of its expression, but in the quality and effectiveness of its symbolism, allowing for a particular capacity of understanding or style of thinking. Wisdom does not lie in any complication of words but in the profundity of the intention. . . .[44]

The doctrine of the Aborigines is ingrained in their mythology, ritual life, and sacred art, each of these dimensions of Aboriginal culture hinging, so to speak, on a sacramental relationship with the land itself; their sense of the sacred expresses itself most readily in spatial rather than temporal terms. A failure to understand this principle lies behind the evident anthropological incomprehension in the face of the Dreaming, a category of the sacred which escapes completely the grip of all profane and linear notions of time, not to say of "history."

The third mark of any integral tradition, inseparable from the doctrine, is *a spiritual method*, a way which enables its practitioners to cleave to the Absolute, to conform their being to the demands of Eternity. Aboriginal spirituality was expressed primarily through rites and ceremonies. Indeed, one commentator has remarked that there can have been few cultures so dominated by ritual life.[45] Contrary to anthropologists' claims about the social "functions" of these rituals the crucial purpose of ceremonial life was to put both the tribe and the individual into right relationship with the Dreaming and with the natural world, the material vestment in which the Eternal was clothed.

Fourthly we find *the formal embodiment of tradition* in the sacred arts and sciences which determine the character of a civilization and which give it its own spiritual "personality," if one might so express it. Here we need look no further than Aboriginal art: far from being the "childish scratchings" of "ignorant savages" this art constitutes a rich symbolic vocabulary, always rooted in the natural order but comprising a vehicle for the most complex metaphysical ideas and the most resonant spiritual messages. Here we find an art that conforms to Schuon's claim that,

Traditional art derives from a creativity which combines heavenly inspiration with ethnic genius, and which does so in the manner of a

44 F. Schuon, *Understanding Islam* (Bloomington, IN: World Wisdom Books, 1998), p. 133.

45 J. Cowan, *Aborigine Tradition*, p. 53.

science endowed with rules and not by way of individual improvisa-
tion: *ars sine scientia nihil.*[46]

Aboriginal art assumed many different forms: sand sculptures,
rock wall art, body painting and decoration, ritual objects, and, in later
times, bark paintings. Many of these incorporated pictorial designs
and all were symbolic, not in the superficial modern sense whereby a
symbol "stands in" for something else, more or less arbitrarily, but in
the traditional sense which was re-articulated by Coleridge:

> A symbol is characterized . . . above all by the translucence of the
> Eternal through and in the Temporal. It always partakes of the Real-
> ity which it renders intelligible; and while it enunciates the whole,
> abides itself as a living part in that Unity of which it is the represen-
> tative.[47]

Traditional art is never arbitrary nor subjective but informed by a
language which rests on the analogies between spiritual realities and
transitory material phenomena which, by way of this relationship,
carry qualitative symbolic significances. It is in this context that we
must understand the indifference of Aboriginal art to the claims of
a naturalistic aesthetic which seeks to "imitate" nature, to accurately
reproduce the surfaces and appearances of the material world from the
viewpoint of the human spectator. As Schuon so often insisted, artistic
naturalism proceeds from an exteriorizing and materialistic mentality
which could not be normative in any traditional civilization.

Aboriginal art conveyed transcendental values and metaphysical
truths to the social collectivity. By-passing the pitfalls of abstract and
merely ratiocinative thought it was accessible to all mentalities and
through its symbolism addressed the whole person rather than the
mind only, thereby actualizing the teachings of tradition. The contrast
with our own modern art could hardly be more dramatic, confronted
as we so often are by an "art" which is boastfully anti-traditional, fuelled by a rampant individualism and an insatiable appetite for novelty,

---

46 F. Schuon, *Art from the Sacred to the Profane: East and West,* ed. C. Schuon (Bloomington, IN: World Wisdom, 2007), p. 5.

47 Coleridge quoted in A. Snodgrass, *Time, Architecture and Eternity: The Stellar and
Temporal Symbolism of Traditional Buildings,* Vol. 1 (New Delhi: Aditya Prakashan,
1990), p. 44.

preoccupied with an aestheticism attuned to the fashions of the day, directed towards little more than the stimulation of the senses, and quite indifferent to any spiritual function, an art characterized by stylistic excesses veering from a pedantic naturalism on one side to the grotesqueries of an inhuman surrealism on the other. Aboriginal art which retains even some of its traditional character is like a mountain stream in contrast to the cesspit of much modern art.

It is true that in recent years Aboriginal art has been afforded a new respect and a rather fashionable status within both the Australian and the international art establishment. Unhappily this new attitude is often informed by altogether anti-traditional values whereby Aboriginal art is seen primarily in terms of aesthetically pleasing "craft" objects which are expressions of the material culture of the Aborigines. As one commentator has recently observed, "Australian Aboriginal art remains the last great non-European cultural form available to the voracious appetite of the European art machine."[48] A sacred art resonant with symbolic and spiritual messages is thus wrenched out of its ceremonial context, is culturally appropriated, and eventually becomes an art commodity on which the art market fixes a monetary value. Again, a familiar story in many parts of the globe.[49]

The Lessons of Aboriginal Tradition

The Aboriginal tradition enshrined *a sense of proportion and an ordered scheme of values and priorities* which gave precedence to the spiritual, which stamped everyday life with a sense of the imperishable, and which afforded humankind an ontological dignity all but impossible to recover in a world which is prepared to countenance talk of the human being as a "trousered ape." In our own culture, swayed by the sentimental prejudices of the age and dedicated to the pursuit of a selfish and barbarous "progress," Aboriginal culture can stand as a reminder of those human possibilities on which we have so often turned our backs. It can remind us anew that we live, in the fullest sense, only in relation to the Absolute.

In a culture tyrannized by time and imprisoned in historicism, the Aboriginal indifference to profane history can provide us with another perspective on our earthly existence. The messages implicit in

48 T. Smith, "Black Art: Its Genius Explained," *The Independent Monthly*, September 1989, p. 18.

49 See J.E. Brown, *Spiritual Legacy of the American Indians*, p. 134.

Aboriginal culture can, of course, have no meaning for those whose materialistic worldview banishes anything and everything of a spiritual order. As Eliade has remarked, many students of archaic religions ultimately "take refuge in a materialism or behaviorism impervious to every spiritual shock."[50]

Anyone not in the grip of preconceptions of this kind cannot study Aboriginal religion without being continually reawakened to *a sense of the sacred*. If we are to ask what precisely constitutes the "sacred" we can do no better than turn again to Schuon. That is sacred, he writes,

> which in the first place is attached to the transcendent order, secondly, possesses the character of absolute certainty, and, thirdly, eludes the comprehension and control of the ordinary human mind. . . . The sacred introduces a quality of the absolute into relativities and confers on perishable things a texture of eternity.[51]

To reanimate such a sense is one of the most invaluable services which cultures such as that of the Australian Aborigines might perform for the contemporary world. Without a sense of the sacred we are lost in the world of accidental contingencies. As Schuon again reminds us,

> civilization only represents a value provided it is supra-human in origin and implies for the "civilized" man a sense of the sacred. . . . A sense of the sacred is fundamental for every civilization because fundamental for man; the sacred—that which is immutable, inviolable, and thus infinitely majestic—is in the very substance of our spirit and of our existence.[52]

It is not without some irony that it is the so-called "primitive," quite free from any complicity in the pathologies of modernity, who recalls us to this sense of the sacred.

---

50 M. Eliade, *The Quest: Meaning and History in Religion* (Chicago: University of Chicago Press, 1969), p. 62. See also p. 36.

51 F. Schuon, *Understanding Islam*, p. 45.

52 F. Schuon, *Understanding Islam*, p. 26. Elsewhere Schuon writes, "It is one of the most pernicious of errors to believe that the human collectivity, on the one hand, or its well-being, on the other, represents an unconditional or absolute value and thus an end in itself" (*Light on the Ancient Worlds*, p. 32).

Aboriginal society was one in harmony with nature rather than one intent on conquest and plunder; the millennia during which the Aborigines lived alone on the continent left it in a more or less primordial state of Edenic innocence, if one might so express it. As Schuon has remarked of the American Indians, if there is an element of ineluctable fatality in the disappearance of this paradise, this in no wise excuses the villainies to which the Aborigines have been subjected over the last two centuries.[53]

The Aborigines found in the world about them not only beauty and harmony but signs of *divine intent* to which men could and should conform themselves. This lies at the heart of their relationship to the land. One of the many lessons we can learn is that a properly-constituted ecological awareness can only be built on the foundations of what is ultimately a *spiritual recognition* of the holiness of the world around us: furthermore, this sacredness is conferred by the immaterial and spiritual realities which the world of nature reflects. At the same time we can say that Aboriginal religion was life-affirming in the most down-to-earth fashion, or, to put it another way, for the Aboriginal outlook the sacred was always materially incarnated in the realm of nature.

No amount of fashionable concern about the evils of pollution, no amount of "socially responsible" science, nor of the idolization of "Nature" can in any way substitute for the spiritual intuition which lies at the heart of many primal cultures. For modern man,

> It is not a question of projecting a supersaturated and disillusioned individualism into a desecrated Nature—this would be a worldliness like any other—but, on the contrary, of rediscovering in Nature, on the basis of the traditional outlook, the divine substance which is inherent in it; in other words, to "see God everywhere"....[54]

Of course, the sacredness of the world is necessarily inaccessible to a view which sees the planet as nothing more than a configuration of physical properties, processes, and energies, and "knowledge" as a quantitative accumulation of data about these material phenomena. The symbolist outlook, exemplified by the Aborigines, eludes the grasp of "Single Vision" in absolute fashion.[55]

53 See F. Schuon, *Feathered Sun*, pp. 41-43.

54 F. Schuon, *Feathered Sun*, p. 13.

55 See F. Schuon, "The Symbolist Mind" in *Feathered Sun*, pp. 3-13. "Single Vision"—

Aboriginal man also offers us *an exemplum of spiritual responsibility and authenticity*. As Mircea Eliade has observed,

> [I]t would be wrong to believe that the religious man of primitive and archaic societies refuses to assume the responsibility for a genuine existence. On the contrary . . . he courageously assumes immense responsibilities—for example, that of collaborating in the creation of the cosmos, or of creating his own world, or of ensuring the life of plants and animals, and so on. But it is a different kind of responsibility from those that, to us moderns, appear to be the only genuine and valid responsibilities. It is a responsibility on the cosmic plane, in contradistinction to the moral, social, or historical responsibilities that are alone regarded as valid in modern civilizations. From the point of view of profane existence, man feels no responsibility except to himself and to society. . . .[56]

In his commanding study of the crisis of modern civilization, *The Reign of Quantity*, René Guénon refers to

> the darkest enigmas of the modern world, enigmas which that world itself denies because though it carries them in itself it is incapable of perceiving them, and because this denial is an indispensable condition for the maintenance of the special mentality whereby it exists.[57]

Those enigmas can only be unraveled by recourse to the wisdom which existed within the cadre of all integral traditions, including that of Australia's indigenous people. As Schuon reminds us, no people anywhere has been bereft of a religious tradition animated by spiritual insights and values. It is only we moderns who have invented a godless and spiritless world, a desacralized universe. The ultimately important lessons of any traditional culture do not invite any kind of "imitation," which would be quite fruitless, but a return to the sources of the perennial wisdom which can always be found within our own religious tradition if only we have the will to look.

William Blake's characterization of the scientistic mentality.

56 M. Eliade, *Sacred and the Profane*, p. 93.

57 R. Guénon, *Reign of Quantity*, p. 11.

CHAPTER 2

Metaphysics: East and West

The possession of all the sciences, if unaccompanied by the knowledge of the best, will more often than not injure the possessor.

Plato[1]

European philosophers have been guilty of the insularity which afflicts so many of their counterparts in other disciplines. Many studies purporting to give us a history of philosophical thought or some kind of conspectus of philosophical trends within a given period still assume that "philosophy" and "Western philosophy" are synonymous. Eastern philosophical thought is all too often ignored, marginalized, or treated as kind of fumbling proto-philosophy, hopelessly mired in religious superstition. As Wilhelm Halbfass has demonstrated, the dominant trend in Western histories of philosophy has been to disqualify the Orientals altogether. Early exceptions, such as can be found in the works of the German Sanskritist Paul Deussen and the Russian orientalist Theodore Stcherbatsky, only confirm the rule. Here is a characteristic nineteenth century formulation:

> Ancient philosophy is essentially Greek philosophy. . . . That which the mind of other peoples and especially the Orient has aspired to in a related direction has remained more or less at the stage of primeval phantasies of the peoples. Everywhere, they lack the freedom of thought and the concomitant nobility of thought which tolerates the thralldom of myth for only a certain length of time and only in the infant stage of experience and thought.[2]

These days philosophers might be more cautious in expressing such barefaced judgments, but the attitudes and values informing this cultural myopia remain alive and well amongst Western intellectuals.

---

1 Plato quoted in W. Perry (ed.), *A Treasury of Traditional Wisdom* (London: Allen & Unwin, 1971), p. 731.

2 E. Dühring quoted in W. Halbfass, *India and Europe: An Essay in Philosophical Understanding* (Delhi: Motilal Barnarsidass, 1990), p. 153.

Rationalist, positivist, materialist, and pragmatic philosophers have generally, insofar as Eastern thought comes within their purview at all, adopted an altogether predictable and somewhat condescending stance, reserving their meager approbations for those aspects of Eastern philosophy which are seen to be "rational," "humanistic," "empirical," and the like. Other influential modern philosophical movements, such as logical positivism and other schools in the analytic movement, have retreated into a rarefied and highly technical domain which has little connection with philosophy's traditional purpose, the study and pursuit of wisdom; indeed, they may be considered as proponents of "misosophy"—a hatred of wisdom.[3] They have also taken for granted that mysticism is necessarily antithetical to rationality and have thus thrown the Eastern traditions out of the court of philosophy.[4] One might also note in passing that African influences on the Western tradition are generally subsumed under the rubric of "Greek philosophy" (as if Hypatia, Augustine, Origen, Cyril, and Tertullian were surrogate Greeks—a point made by the African philosopher Innocent Onyewuenyi.[5])

But the picture is not completely bleak. Over the past two centuries there *have* been some creative philosophical engagements with the thought of the East, and some self-critical recognition of the intellectual parochialism of much Western thought. Although European Orientalism has remained, to a large extent, locked in the historico-philological scholarship of the nineteenth century, since the Second World War it is no longer unusual to find Anglophone philosophers teaching comparative philosophy—one may mention such names as Charles Moore (the moving force behind the East-West Philosophers' Conferences in Hawaii), Dale Riepe, Arthur Danto, Charles Hartshorne, Robert Nozick, Ninian Smart, and Eliot Deutsch as well as Asian scholars who have worked in Western universities—Chang Chung-yuan, Garma Chang, J.N. Mohanty, J.L. Mehta, Arvind Sharma, Purushottama Bilimoria, to name a few.[6]

---

3 See S.H. Nasr, *Knowledge and the Sacred* (New York: Crossroad, 1981), p. 43. See also I. Watson, "The Anti-Wisdom of Modern Philosophy," *Studies in Comparative Religion*, 6:4, Autumn 1972, pp. 221-224.

4 See R. King, *Orientalism and Religion: Postcolonial Theory, India and 'The Mystic East'* (London: Routledge, 1999), pp. 28-34.

5 R. King, *Orientalism and Religion*, p. 29.

6 See W. Halbfass, *India and Europe*, pp. 162-163.

Over the past fifty years the academic field of comparative philosophy has emerged as one of the intellectual sites where the East-West
encounter has produced some interesting results. Certainly the pros-
pects have improved considerably since 1964 when Thomas Merton
wrote,

> There have of course been spurious attempts to bring East and West
> together. One need not review all the infatuated theosophies of the
> nineteenth century. Nor need one bother to criticize the laughable
> syncretisms which have occupied the talents of publicists (more of-
> ten Eastern than Western) in which Jesus, Buddha, Confucius, Tol-
> stoy, Marx, Nietzsche, and anyone else you like join in the cosmic
> dance which turns out to be not Shiva's but just anybody's. How-
> ever, the comparison of Eastern and Western philosophy is, in our
> time, reaching a certain level of seriousness and this is one small and
> hopeful sign. The materials for a synthesis of science and wisdom
> are not lacking.[7]

Tokens of this development include the East-West Philosophers'
Conferences in Hawaii and the appearance of journals such as *Philosophy East and West,* and more recently, *Asian Philosophy.* Since the
'70s there has also been a steady output of scholarly monographs in
this field. A representative sample: Chris Gudmunsen's *Wittgenstein
and Buddhism* (1977), Masao Abe's *Zen and Western Thought* (1985),
Harold Coward's *Derrida and Indian Philosophy* (1990), and compilations such as *Heidegger and Asian Thought* and *Nietzsche and Asian
Thought,* both edited by Graham Parkes, and *Buddhism and Western
Philosophy* (1981), edited by Nathan Katz. In such books and in the
dozens of disciplinary journals carrying the work of comparative philosophers and religionists one nowadays comes across any number
of articles drawing connections and comparisons between the philosophical ideas, schools, and movements of East and West: here Nagarjuna is compared to Kant, there Shankara to Eckhart, and over there is
an inquiry into the relation between Hume's thought and Buddhism,
or perhaps a comparison of the Buddha's teaching of *dukkha* and Kierkegaard's *angst.*[8] Such comparative philosophy also encompasses

---

7 T. Merton (ed.), *Gandhi on Non-Violence: A Selection from the Writings of Mahatma
Gandhi* (New York: New Directions, 1963), p. 3.

8 Some of the parallels and comparisons have become commonplace: Confucius:

the impact on Eastern thought of Western philosophers. Scholars like Graham Parkes, for example, have traced the post-war Japanese and Chinese enthusiasm for both Nietzsche and Heidegger.[9] Less common is the analysis and evaluation of Western philosophical constructs in traditional Eastern terms. One of the salutary results of this kind of inquiry is to administer some shock-therapy to the over-valuation of a misperceived "originality" of this or that Western thinker: any scholar thoroughly familiar with Nagarjuna will be less likely to be seduced by claims along the lines of "Kant was the first to show. . ."

It is not our present purpose to survey these rapidly proliferating and occasionally fertile inquiries but rather to consider the assumptions which often underlie them. Some forty years ago Seyyed Hossein Nasr, at that time Dean and Professor of Philosophy at Tehran University, laid down the "conditions for a meaningful comparative philosophy." It is worth revisiting Nasr's important essay from which, one would have hoped, many more comparativists might have derived considerable profit.

Early in his analysis Nasr states the nature of the problem which bedevils many of the enterprises of those scholars, of both East and West, who attempt some manner of comparative philosophy (referred to henceforth simply as comparativists):

> The Western students of Oriental doctrines have usually tried to reduce these doctrines to "profane" philosophy; and modernized Orientals, often burdened by a half-hidden inferiority complex, have tried to give respectability to these doctrines and to "elevate" them by giving them the honor of being in harmony with the thought of whichever Western philosopher was in vogue. On both sides, usually the relation of the "philosophy" in question to the experience or direct knowledge of the Truth, which is the source of this "philosophy," is forgotten and levels of reality confused.[10]

Aristotle; Mencius: Aquinas; Shankara: Eckhart, Spinoza, Kant, Bradley; Nagarjuna: Hume, Nietzsche, Heidegger, Wittgenstein, Derrida; Dogen: Heidegger.

9 See G. Parkes, "Nietzsche and East Asian Thought: Influences, Impacts and Resonances" in *The Cambridge Companion to Nietzsche*, ed. B. Magnus & K.M. Higgins (Cambridge: Cambridge University Press, 1996).

10 S.H. Nasr, "Conditions for a Meaningful Comparative Philosophy," *Philosophy East and West*, 22:1, 1972, p. 53.

One of the principal sources of this confusion is a failure to understand the crucial distinctions between metaphysics as a *scientia sacra* on one hand, wedded to direct spiritual experience and complementing revealed religious doctrines, and what is usually meant in the modern West by "philosophy," an autonomous and essentially *rational* and *analytical* inquiry into a range of issues and problematics. As Nasr observes,

> What is usually called Oriental philosophy is for the most part the doctrinal aspect of a total spiritual way tied to a method of realization and is inseparable from the revelation or tradition which has given birth to the way in question.[11]

Thus there is little common measure between the sapiential doctrines of the East which form part of a total spiritual economy and which draw on the wellsprings of revelation, tradition, and direct experience, and those mental constructions of Western thinkers which are usually circumscribed by the various alliances of rationalism, materialism, empiricism, and humanism which so dominate the "philosophical" thinking of the modern West. As Agehananda Bharati noted in an acidic reference to various Western excursions into comparative philosophy,

> No effort, however valiant and well-meant, should disabuse us of the fact that nobody from Kant to Heidegger, Rorty and Derrida has been interested in *moksa* [liberation] while nobody from Nagarjuna to Bhartrhari and Samkara has not.[12]

The only philosophers of the Western tradition who can meaningfully be compared with their Eastern counterparts are those theologians and metaphysicians who were indeed elaborating "the doctrinal aspect of a total spiritual way"—Plato, Plotinus, Eckhart, Aquinas, Bonaventura, and the like. On the other hand,

> To speak of rationalistic philosophy and Chinese or Hindu philosophy in the same breath is a contradiction, unless the word philoso-

11 S.H. Nasr, "Conditions for a Meaningful Comparative Philosophy," p. 55 (italics mine).

12 A. Bharati, review of *Derrida and Indian Philosophy*, by H. Coward, *Philosophy East and West*, 42:2, 1992, p. 340.

phy is used in two different senses: first as a wisdom that is wed to spiritual experience, and second as mental construct, completely cut off from it. A lack of awareness of this basic distinction has made a complete sham of many studies of comparative philosophy and has helped to reduce to nil the real significance of Oriental metaphysics. This metaphysics, far from being the object of mental play, has the function of enabling men to transcend the mental plane.[13]

A meaningful comparative philosophy can only proceed on the basis of a proper understanding of the different levels on which metaphysics, theology, and philosophy (in the modern sense) are situated. To approach a Shankara, a Nagarjuna, a Chuang-tzu, through the categories of a profane and one-dimensional "philosophy," stripped of all reference to the transcendent and what this implies for the human destiny, is to fall prey to that most pernicious of modern prejudices—the notion that the greater can be reduced to, and "explained" by, the terms of the lesser:

> If a blind man were to develop a philosophy based upon his experience of the world derived from his four senses, surely it would differ from one based upon these four senses as well as upon sight. How much more would a "philosophy" based upon man's rational analysis of sense data differ from one that is the result of the experience of a world which transcends both reason and the sensible world? . . . One must always remember the dictum of Aristotle that knowledge depends upon the mode of the knower.[14]

It is not only possible but highly desirable that scholars, equipped with the proper tools and cognizant of the profound differences between any traditional civilization and the modern West, should illuminate the similarities and contrasts between the doctrines of the different religious traditions. In the case of comparative studies between traditional doctrines and the ideas of modern thinkers, such a task will necessarily foreground the chasm which separates them. It will also expose the hazards of glib formulations of similarities which exist only at relatively superficial levels. Furthermore,

---

13 S.H. Nasr, "Conditions for a Meaningful Comparative Philosophy," p. 55.

14 S.H. Nasr, "Conditions for a Meaningful Comparative Philosophy," p. 57.

Oriental doctrines can fulfill the most fundamental and urgent task of reminding the West of truths that have existed within its own tradition but which have been completely forgotten. . . . Today it is nearly impossible for Western man to rediscover the whole of his own tradition without the aid of Oriental metaphysics. This is because the sapiential doctrines and the appropriate spiritual techniques . . . are hardly accessible in the West, and "philosophy" has become totally divorced from the nature of the spiritual experience.[15]

Philosophy and Metaphysics in Perennialist Perspective

Thus far we have been considering the case against a profane comparative philosophy as stated in Nasr's short but forceful essay. Nasr himself belongs to a school of thought which has been called "traditionalism" or "perennialism," and which is closely associated with its three most pre-eminent exponents: René Guénon (1886-1951), Ananda Coomaraswamy (1877-1947), and Frithjof Schuon (1907-1998). Their work turns on an affirmation of a timeless wisdom which lies at the heart of all integral religious traditions and seeks to elucidate the metaphysical and cosmological principles which inform this perennial wisdom—hence the term "perennialism." However, it is crucial to distinguish this school from other forms of so-called perennialism found in Theosophy, some forms of neo-Hinduism, and in the works of people such as Aldous Huxley who did much to popularize the term the "the perennial philosophy."[16] What sets the traditionalists apart is their commitment to the preservation of the particular forms which give each religious heritage its *raison d'être* and ensure its spiritual efficacy. Traditionalists adamantly reject any notion of a "universal" religion or the suggestion that some sort of "essence" can be distilled from the different religions in such a way as to provide a new spiritual path. To Nasr's considerations we can now add an exposition of the traditionalist understanding of the relationship of metaphysics and philosophy, highly pertinent to the subject at hand.

"Metaphysics is the finding of bad reasons for what we believe upon instinct."[17] This Bradleian formulation, perhaps only half-serious,

---

15 S.H. Nasr, "Conditions for a Meaningful Comparative Philosophy," p. 59.

16 See Huxley's *The Perennial Philosophy* (first published 1944) (New York: Harper & Row, 1970).

17 From F.H. Bradley, *Appearance and Reality*, quoted by S. Radhakrishnan, "Reply to

signposts a modern conception of metaphysics shared by a good many people, philosophers and otherwise. There is, of course, no single modern philosophical posture on the nature and significance of metaphysics. Some see it as a kind of residual blight on the tree of philosophy, a feeding-ground for obscurantists and lovers of mumbo-jumbo. Others grant it a more dignified status.[18] It is one of those words, like "dogma" or "mystical," which has been pejorated by careless and ignorant usage. The word is so fraught with hazards, so hedged about with philosophical disputation, and so sullied by popular usage that we shall have to take some care if the proper sense in which the perennialists use the word is to become clear. Nasr: "Metaphysics, which in fact is one and should be named metaphysic . . . is the science of the Real, of the origin and end of things, of the Absolute and in its light, the relative."[19] Similarly "metaphysical": "concerned with universal realities considered objectively."[20] It will be readily apparent that we are here dealing with a conception of metaphysics which would not be shared by most modern Western philosophers.

As René Guénon observed more than once, metaphysics cannot properly and strictly be defined, for to define is to limit, while the domain of metaphysics is the Real and thus limitless. Consequently, metaphysics "is truly and absolutely unlimited and cannot be confined to any formula or any system."[21] Its subject, in the words of Johannes Tauler, is "that pure knowledge that knows no form or creaturely way."[22] As Nasr observes elsewhere,

This supreme science of the Real . . . is the only science that can dis-

My Critics" in *The Philosophy of Sarvepalli Radhakrishnan*, ed. P.A. Schilpp (New York: Tudor, 1952), p. 791.

18 For some discussion of this term by a modern philosopher see J. Hospers, *An Introduction to Philosophical Analysis* (London: Routledge & Kegan Paul, 1956), pp. 211ff.

19 S.H. Nasr, *Man and Nature: The Spiritual Crisis of Modern Man* (London: Allen & Unwin, 1976), p. 81.

20 F. Schuon, *Logic and Transcendence: A New Translation with Selected Letters* (Bloomington, IN: World Wisdom, 2009), p. 176n.

21 R. Guénon, "Oriental Metaphysics" in *The Sword of Gnosis*, ed. J. Needleman (Baltimore: Penguin, 1974), pp. 43-44.

22 Tauler quoted in C.F. Kelley, *Meister Eckhart on Divine Knowledge* (New Haven: Yale University Press, 1977), p. 4.

tinguish between the Absolute and the relative, appearance and reality. . . . Moreover, this science exists, as the esoteric dimension within every orthodox and integral tradition and is united with a spiritual method derived totally from the tradition in question.[23]

The ultimate reality of metaphysics is the Supreme Identity in which all oppositions and dualities are resolved, those of subject and object, knower and known, being and non-being; thus a Scriptural formulation such as "The things of God knoweth no man, but the Spirit of God."[24] As Ananda Coomaraswamy remarks, in traditional civilizations such as that of India, metaphysics provided the vision (or *theoria*) and religion the way to its effective verification and actualization in direct experience.[25] The early estrangement of metaphysics, philosophy, and religion in the West is a peculiar phenomenon.

Because the metaphysical realm lies "beyond" the phenomenal plane the validity of a metaphysical principle can be neither proved nor disproved by any kind of empirical demonstration, by reference to material realities.[26] The aim of metaphysics is not to prove anything whatsoever but to make doctrines intelligible and to demonstrate their consistency. Metaphysics is concerned with a direct apprehension of reality or, to put it differently, with a recognition of the Absolute and our relationship to it. It thus takes on an imperative character for those capable of metaphysical discernment.

The requirement for us to recognize the Absolute is itself an absolute one; it concerns man as such and not man under such and such con-

---

23 S.H. Nasr, *Man and Nature*, pp. 81-82. See also Coomaraswamy's undated letter to "M" in *Selected Letters of Ananda K. Coomaraswamy*, ed. R.P. Coomaraswamy & A. Moore Jr. (New Delhi: Oxford University Press, 1988), p. 10: "traditional Metaphysics is as much a single and invariable science as mathematics."

24 1 Corinthians 2:11. The Absolute may be called God, the Godhead, *nirguna-Brahman*, the *Tao*, and so on, according to the vocabulary at hand. See F. Schuon, *Light on the Ancient Worlds: A New Translation with Selected Letters* (Bloomington, IN: World Wisdom, 2006), p. 75n.

25 A.K. Coomaraswamy, "A Lecture on Comparative Religion," quoted in R. Lipsey, *Coomaraswamy, Vol. 3: His Life and Work* (Princeton: Princeton University Press, 1977), p. 275. Also see A.K. Coomaraswamy, "The Vedanta and Western Tradition" in *Coomaraswamy, Vol. 2: Selected Papers, Metaphysics*, ed. R. Lipsey (Princeton: Princeton University Press, 1977), p. 6.

26 See R. Guénon, "Oriental Metaphysics," p. 53.

ditions. It is a fundamental aspect of human dignity, and especially of that intelligence which denoted "the state of man hard to obtain," that we accept Truth because it is true and for no other reason.[27]

Metaphysics assumes man's capacity for absolute and certain knowledge:

> This capacity for objectivity and for absoluteness amounts to an existential—and "preventive"—refutation of all the ideologies of doubt: if man is able to doubt, it is because there is certainty; likewise the very notion of illusion proves that man has access to reality. . . . If doubt conformed to the real, human intelligence would be deprived of its sufficient reason, and man would be less than an animal, for the intelligence of animals does not doubt the reality to which it is proportioned.[28]

Metaphysics, therefore, is immutable and inexorable, and the "infallible standard by which not only religions, but still more 'philosophies' and 'sciences' must be 'corrected' . . . and interpreted."[29] Metaphysics can be ignored or forgotten but not refuted "precisely because it is immutable and not related to change *qua* change."[30] Metaphysical principles are true and valid once and for all and not for this particular age or mentality, and could not, in any sense, "evolve." They can be validated directly in the plenary and unitive experience of the mystic. Thus Martin Lings can write of Sufism—and one could say the same of any intrinsically orthodox esotericism—that it

> has the right to be inexorable because it is based on certainties and not on opinions. It has the obligation to be inexorable because mysticism is the sole repository of Truth, in the fullest sense, being above all concerned with the Absolute, the Infinite, and the Eternal; and "If the salt have lost its savor, wherewith shall it be salted?" Without mysticism, Reality would have no voice in the world. There would be

27 F. Schuon, *In the Tracks of Buddhism* (London: Allen & Unwin, 1968), p. 33.

28 F. Schuon, *Logic and Transcendence*, p. 11. See also F. Schuon, *Esoterism as Principle and as Way* (London: Perennial Books, 1981), pp. 15ff.

29 Letter to J.H. Muirhead, August 1935, in A.K. Coomaraswamy, *Selected Letters*, p. 37.

30 S.H. Nasr, *Sufi Essays* (London: Allen & Unwin, 1972), p. 86. See also F. Schuon, *Stations of Wisdom* (London: John Murray, 1961), p. 42.

no record of the true hierarchy, and no witness that it is continually being violated.[31]

One might easily substitute the word "metaphysics" for "mysticism" in this passage, the former being the formal and objective aspect of the "subjective" experience. However, this is not to lose sight of the fact that any and every metaphysical doctrine will take it as axiomatic that every formulation is, in the face of the Divine Reality itself, "a provisional, indispensable, salutary 'error,' containing and communicating the virtuality of Truth."[32]

Modern European philosophy is dialectical, which is to say analytical and rational in its modes. From a traditionalist point of view it might be said that modern philosophy is anchored in a misunderstanding of the nature and role of reason; indeed, the idolatry of reason could otherwise hardly have arisen. Schuon spotlights some of the strengths and deficiencies of the rational mode in these terms:

> Reason is formal by its nature and formalistic in its operations; it proceeds by "coagulations," by alternatives and by exclusions—or, it can be said, by partial truths. It is not, like pure intellect, formless and "fluid" "light"; true, it derives its implacability, or its validity in general, from the intellect, but it touches on essences only through drawing conclusions, not by direct vision; it is indispensable for verbal formulations but it does not involve immediate knowledge.[33]

Titus Burckhardt likens reason to "a convex lens which steers the intelligence in a particular direction and onto a limited field."[34] Like any other instrument it can be abused. Much European philosophy, adrift from its religious moorings, has surrendered to a totalitarian rationalism and in so doing has violated a principle which was respected

---

31 M. Lings, *What is Sufism?* (London: Allen & Unwin, 1975), p. 93.

32 F. Schuon, *Spiritual Perspectives and Human Facts: A New Translation with Selected Letters* (Bloomington, IN: World Wisdom, 2007), p173. Cf. A.K. Coomaraswamy: "every belief is a heresy if it be regarded as the truth, and not simply as a signpost of the truth" ("Sri Ramakrishna and Religious Tolerance" in *Selected Papers 2*, p. 38).

33 F. Schuon, *Understanding Islam* (Bloomington, IN: World Wisdom Books, 1998), p. 15. See also F. Schuon, *Stations of Wisdom*, pp. 18ff.

34 T. Burckhardt, *Alchemy: Science of the Cosmos, Science of the Soul* (Baltimore: Penguin, 1972), p. 36 n1.

wherever a metaphysical tradition and a religious framework for the pursuit of wisdom remained intact—the principle of adequation, articulated thus by Aquinas: "It is a sin against intelligence to want to proceed in an identical manner in typically different domains—physical, mathematical, metaphysical—of speculative knowledge."[35] This, it would seem, is precisely what modern philosophers are bent on. No less apposite in this context is Plotinus' well-known maxim "knowing demands the organ fitted to the object."[36] The grotesqueries of modern philosophy spring, in large measure, from an indifference to this principle. The situation is exacerbated further by the fact that many philosophers have been duped by the claims of a gross scientism and thus suffer from a drastically impoverished view of reality and of the avenues by which it might be apprehended.

The place of reason, of logic and dialectic, in metaphysics is altogether more subordinate as the following sample of quotes make clear. It is worth mobilizing several quotations as this issue is so often misunderstood, with bizarre results. From Schuon:

> In the intellectual order logical proof is no more than a thoroughly provisional crystallization of intuition, the modes of which are incalculable because of the complexity of the real.[37]

Or again:

> Metaphysics is not held to be true—by those who understand it—because it is expressed in a logical manner, but it can be expressed in a logical manner because it is true, without—obviously—its truth ever being compromised by the possible shortcomings of human reason.[38]

Similarly Guénon:

> [F]or metaphysics, the use of rational argument never represents more than a mode of external expression (necessarily imperfect and

35 Quoted in S.H. Nasr, *Man and Nature*, p. 35.

36 Quoted in E.F. Schumacher, *A Guide for the Perplexed* (London: Jonathan Cape, 1977), p. 49.

37 F. Schuon, *Spiritual Perspectives*, p. 3.

38 F. Schuon, *Esoterism as Principle and as Way*, p. 28.

inadequate as such) and in no way affects metaphysical knowledge itself, for the latter must always be kept essentially distinct from its formulation. . . .[39]

Metaphysical discernment proceeds more through contemplative intelligence than through ratiocination. Metaphysical formulations depend more on symbol and on analogy than on logical demonstration, though it is a grave error to suppose that metaphysics has any right to irrationality.[40] What many modern philosophers apparently fail to understand is that thought can become increasingly subtle and complex without approaching any nearer to the truth. An idea can be subdivided into a thousand ramifications, fenced about with every conceivable qualification and supported with the most intricate and rigorous logic but, for all that, remain purely external and quantitative for "no virtuosity of the potter will transform clay into gold."[41] Furthermore,

> it apparently never crosses the minds of pure logicians that a line of reasoning might simply be the logical and provisional description of something that is intellectually self-evident and that the function of this reasoning might be the actualization of a self-evidence in itself supralogical.[42]

Analytical rationality, no matter how useful a tool, will never, in itself, generate metaphysical understanding. Metaphysicians of all ages have said nothing other. Shankara, for instance: "[T]he pure truth of *Atman* . . . can be reached by meditation, contemplation and other spiritual disciplines such as a knower of *Brahman* may prescribe—but never by subtle argument."[43] The Promethean arrogance of much modernist thought, often bred by scientistic ideologies, is revealed in the refusal to acknowledge the boundaries beyond which reason has no competence or utility. This has, of course, prompted some quite ludicrous claims about religion. As Schuon remarks,

---

39 R. Guénon quoted in F. Schuon, *Stations of Wisdom*, p. 29n.

40 See F. Schuon, *Esoterism as Principle and as Way*, p. 28.

41 F. Schuon, *Understanding Islam*, p. 181.

42 F. Schuon, *Logic and Transcendence*, pp. 31-32.

43 *Shankara's Crest-Jewel of Discrimination*, ed. Swami Prabhananda & C. Isherwood (New York: Mentor, 1970), p. 73.

The equating of the supernatural with the irrational . . . amounts to claiming that the unknown or the incomprehensible is the same as the absurd. The rationalism of a frog living at the bottom of a well is to deny the existence of mountains: this is logic of a kind but it has nothing to do with reality.[44]

The intelligibility of a metaphysical doctrine may depend upon a measure of faith in the traditional Christian sense of "assent to a credible proposition." As Coomaraswamy observes,

One must believe in order to understand and understand in order to believe. These are not successive, however, but simultaneous acts of the mind. In other words, there can be no knowledge of anything to which the will refuses its consent. . . . [45]

This mode of apprehension is something quite other than the philosophical thought that

believes it can attain to an absolute contact with Reality by means of analyses, syntheses, arrangements, filtrations, and polishings— thought that is mundane because of this very ignorance and because it is a "vicious circle," which not only provides no escape from illusion, but even reinforces it through the lure of a progressive knowledge that is in fact nonexistent.[46]

It is in this context that we can speak of modern philosophy as "the codification of an acquired infirmity."[47] Unlike modern philosophy, metaphysics has nothing to do with personal opinion, originality, or creativity—quite the contrary. It is directed towards those realities which lie outside mental perimeters and which are unchanging. The most a metaphysician will ever want to do is to reformulate some timeless truth so that it becomes more intelligible in the prevailing cli-

---

44 F. Schuon, *Logic and Transcendence*, p. 37.

45 A.K. Coomaraswamy, "Vedanta and Western Tradition," p. 8. See also S.H. Nasr, *Knowledge and the Sacred*, p. 6.

46 F. Schuon, *Logic and Transcendence*, p. 174.

47 F. Schuon, *The Transfiguration of Man* (Bloomington, IN: World Wisdom Books, 1995), p. 4.

mate.[48] A profane system of thought, on the other hand, is never more than a portrait of the person who creates it, an "involuntary memoir," as Nietzsche put it.[49]

The metaphysician does not seek to invent or discover or prove a new system of thought but rather to crystallize direct apprehensions of Reality insofar as this is possible within the limited resources of human language, making use not only of logic but of symbol and analogy. Furthermore, the science of metaphysics must always proceed in the context of a revealed religion, protected by the tradition in question which also supplies the necessary supports for the full realization or actualization of metaphysical doctrines. The metaphysician seeks not only to formulate immutable principles and doctrines but to live by them, to conform his or her being to the truths they convey. In other words, there is nothing of the "art for art's sake" type of thinking about the pursuit of metaphysics: it engages the whole person or it is as nothing.[50] As Schuon states,

> The moral requirement of metaphysical discernment means that virtue is part of wisdom; a wisdom without virtue is in fact imposture and hypocrisy. . . . [P]lenary knowledge of Divine Reality presupposes or demands moral conformity to this Reality, as the eye necessarily conforms to light; since the object to be known is the Sovereign Good, the knowing subject must correspond to it analogically.[51]

A point often overlooked: metaphysics does not of necessity find its expression only in verbal forms. Metaphysics can be expressed visually and ritually as well as verbally. The Chinese and Red Indian traditions furnish pre-eminent examples of these possibilities.

Metaphysics and Theology
The relationship between metaphysics and theology, and theology and philosophy, invites a similar exposition. However, given that we are

---

48 Here we are at the opposite end of the spectrum not only from the philosophical relativists but from those who hold a "personalist" or "existentialist" view of truth.

49 F. Nietzsche, *Beyond Good and Evil* (1886), taken from Extract 13 in *A Nietzsche Reader*, ed. R.J. Hollingdale (Harmondsworth: Penguin, 1977), p. 39.

50 See A.K. Coomaraswamy, "Vedanta and Western Tradition," p. 9.

51 F. Schuon, *Roots of the Human Condition* (Bloomington, IN: World Wisdom Books, 1991), p. 86.

here primarily concerned with the practice of comparative philosophy we shall restrict ourselves to two passages from Schuon which go to the heart of the matter. From Schuon's *The Transcendent Unity of Religions* (1953):

> [I]ntellectual knowledge also transcends the specifically theological point of view, which is itself incomparably superior to the philosophical point of view, since, like metaphysical knowledge, it emanates from God and not from man; but whereas metaphysics proceeds wholly from intellectual intuition, religion proceeds from Revelation.... [I]n the case of intellectual intuition, knowledge is not possessed by the individual insofar as he is an individual, but insofar as in his innermost essence he is not distinct from the Divine Principle. ... [T]he theological point of view, because it is based in the minds of believers on a Revelation and not on a knowledge that is accessible to each one of them . . . will of necessity confuse the symbol or form with the naked and supraformal Truth, while metaphysics . . . will be able to make use of the same symbol or form as a means of expression while at the same time being aware of its relativity. . . . [R]eligion translates metaphysical or universal truths into dogmatic language. . . . What essentially distinguishes the metaphysical from the philosophical proposition is that the former is symbolical and descriptive . . . whereas philosophy . . . is never anything more than what it expresses. When philosophy uses reason to resolve a doubt, this proves precisely that its starting point is a doubt it is striving to overcome, whereas . . . the starting point of a metaphysical formulation is always essentially something intellectually evident or certain, which is communicated, to those able to receive it, by symbolical or dialectical means designed to awaken in them the latent knowledge which they bear unconsciously, and it may even be said, eternally within them.[52]

In this context it is worth recalling Bertrand Russell's assessment of St. Thomas Aquinas in *A History of Western Philosophy* (1946):

> There is little of the true philosophic spirit in Aquinas. . . . The finding of arguments for a conclusion given in advance is not philosophy but special pleading. I cannot, therefore, feel that he deserves to be

---

52 F. Schuon, *The Transcendent Unity of Religions* (Wheaton, IL: Quest Books, 1993), pp. xxx-xxxii.

put on a level with the best philosophers either of Greece or of modern times.[53]

How right George Steiner was to refer to Russell's history as "a vulgar but representative book"![54]

The distinctions elaborated above by Schuon should be qualified by an observation he made in a later work:

> In our first book, *The Transcendent Unity of Religions*, we adopted the point of view of Ghazzali regarding "philosophy": that is, bearing in mind the great impoverishment of modern philosophies, we simplified the problem as others have done before us by making "philosophy" synonymous with "rationalism."[55]

We have followed more or less the same procedure here and will only modify it with two brief points. Firstly, the term "philosophy" in itself "has nothing restrictive about it"; the restrictions which we have imposed on it in this discussion have been expedient rather than essential. Schuon has exposed some of the issues raised by both the ancient and modern use of the term in an essay entitled "Tracing the Notion of Philosophy."[56] Secondly, it must also be admitted that our discussion of the relationships of philosophy, theology, and metaphysics has been governed by some necessary simplifications. From certain points of view the distinctions are not as clear-cut nor as rigid as our discussion has suggested. As Schuon himself writes,

> In a certain respect the difference between philosophy, theology, and *gnosis* is total; in another respect it is relative. It is total when one understands by "philosophy" only rationalism, by "theology" only the explanation of religious teachings, and by *gnosis* only intuitive and intellective, thus supra-rational, knowledge; but the difference is only relative when one understands by "philosophy" the fact of

---

53 B. Russell, *A History of Western Philosophy* (first published 1949) (London: Allen & Unwin, 1989), pp. 453-54.

54 G. Steiner, *Heidegger* (Glasgow: Collins, 1978), p. 11.

55 F. Schuon, *Sufism: Veil and Quintessence, A New Translation with Selected Letters* (Bloomington, IN: World Wisdom, 2006), pp. 95-96n.

56 F. Schuon, *Sufism: Veil and Quintessence*, pp. 89-100. See also F. Schuon, *Transfiguration of Man*, p. 3.

thinking, by "theology" the fact of speaking dogmatically of God and religious things, and by *gnosis* the fact of presenting pure metaphysics, for then the categories interpenetrate.[57]

It is only in the context of the considerations elaborated above, admittedly at some length, that we can return to the question of East-West comparative philosophy.

Perennialism and Comparative Metaphysics

In the light of the preceding discussion it will come as no surprise that the scholars and thinkers whose comparative studies have produced the most impressive results are precisely those who have a firm purchase on traditional principles. Of the traditionalists themselves one must particularly mention the works of Ananda Coomaraswamy and Frithjof Schuon. This is not to ignore the pioneering role of René Guénon in explicating the metaphysical doctrines of the East in such works as *Man and His Becoming According to the Vedanta* (1925). In the present context, however, he recedes somewhat into the background for several reasons. Guénon proceeded on the basis of first principles with comparatively little concern for their historical manifestations and applications. His scholarship was sometimes precarious and he was entirely disdainful of modern thought in all its guises. To undertake comparative philosophy of the kind with which are here concerned requires some sensitivity to the historical milieux in which traditional doctrines were given expression. Schuon and Coomaraswamy were much better equipped to undertake this kind of task. Nasr himself has produced some of the most authoritative works in the field of comparative philosophy but these have been concerned primarily with the Islamic and Christian worlds.

Ananda Coomaraswamy was one of the few scholars of the century who was equally at home in the worlds of Eastern and Western philosophy. Recall his observation that "my indoctrination with the *Philosophia Perennis* is primarily Oriental, secondarily Mediaeval, and thirdly classic."[58] His later work is saturated with references to Plato and Plotinus, Augustine and Aquinas, Eckhart and the Rhenish

---

57 F. Schuon, *Sufism: Veil and Quintessence*, p. 97.

58 Letter to Artemus Packard, May 1941, in A.K. Coomaraswamy, *Selected Letters*, p. 299.

mystics, to Shankara and Lao-tse and Nagarjuna. Amongst his most profound studies in the field of comparative philosophy we find "The Vedanta and Western Tradition" (1939), "Recollection, Indian and Platonic" (1944), "*Akimcanna*: Self-Naughting" (1940), and "*Atmayajna*: Self-Sacrifice" (1942)—but one can turn to almost any of his later writings to find profound comparative exegeses. He was, of course, keenly interested in the philosophical underpinnings of traditional art, and produced two dazzling comparative works in *The Transformation of Nature in Art* (1934) and *The Christian and Oriental, or True, Philosophy of Art* (1939). Readers familiar with these works will not quarrel with the claim that they offer us a comparative philosophy of the most fruitful kind.

Much of Schuon's vast corpus focuses primarily on the Sufi tradition and on classical and Christian thinkers. Nonetheless, one is likely, at any turn, to come across illuminating references to Eastern metaphysicians and theologians, Shankara and Ramanuja being two to whom Schuon often refers. However, four of his works entail more detailed comparisons of Eastern and Western doctrines: *The Transcendent Unity of Religions* (1954), *Language of the Self* (1959), *In the Tracks of Buddhism* (1967), and *Logic and Transcendence* (1975). The last-mentioned work is also where Schuon confronts the profane philosophies of the modern period most directly.

Many perennialist works also fall under the umbrella of comparative mysticism, the distinction between "philosophy" and "mysticism" being somewhat fluid in the traditional worlds of the Orient. In the academic domain we might say that comparative mysticism oscillates between philosophy and comparative religion. Impressive work has been done in this arena by several scholars and thinkers. Rudolf Otto's *Mysticism East and West* (1926), D.T. Suzuki's *Mysticism Christian and Buddhist* (1957), Toshihiko Izutsu's *A Comparative Study of the Key Philosophical Concepts in Sufism and Taoism* (1967), and Thomas Merton's *Zen and the Birds of Appetite* (1968) are amongst the more commanding works.

CHAPTER 3

Shankara's Doctrine of *Maya*

Maya is most strange. Her nature is inexplicable.

Shankara[1]

Brahman is real; the world is an illusory appearance; the so-called soul is *Brahman* itself, and no other.

Shankara[2]

The doctrine of *maya* occupies a pivotal position in Shankara's metaphysics. Before focusing on this doctrine it will perhaps be helpful to make clear Shankara's purposes in elaborating the Advaita Vedanta. Some of the misconceptions which have afflicted English commentaries on Shankara will thus be banished before they can cause any further mischief. Firstly, Shankara should not be understood as a "philosopher" in the modern Western sense. Ananda Coomaraswamy has rightly insisted that,

> The Vedanta is not a philosophy in the current sense of the word, but only as it is used in the phrase *Philosophia Perennis*. . . . Modern philosophies are closed systems, employing the method of dialectics, and taking for granted that opposites are mutually exclusive. In modern philosophy things are either so or not so; in eternal philosophy this depends upon our point of view. Metaphysics is not a system but a consistent doctrine; it is not merely concerned with conditioned and quantitative experience but with universal possibility. It therefore considers possibilities that may be neither possibilities of manifestation nor in any sense formal, as well as ensembles of possibilities that can be realized in a given world.[3]

---

1 Shankara, *The Crest-Jewel of Discrimination*, trans. Swami Prabhavananda & C. Isherwood (New York: New American Library, 1970), p. 49. (The transliteration and italicizing of Sanskrit terms has been standardized throughout.)

2 Shankara quoted in T.M.P. Mahadevan, *Ramana Maharshi: The Sage of Arunacala* (London: Unwin & Allen, 1978), p. 120.

3 A.K. Coomaraswamy, "The Vedanta and Western Tradition" in *Coomaraswamy, Vol.*

This alerts us to the kind of confusion which bedevils any attempt to accommodate Advaita Vedanta within the assumptions and the vocabulary of a purely rational and dialectical philosophic outlook; this remains true whether one is engaged in exposition or apparent "refutation." The same misconceptions will ambush any study resting on the assumption that metaphysics is but a branch of philosophy.

> [W]hat essentially distinguishes the metaphysical from the philosophical proposition is that the former is symbolical and descriptive, in the sense that it makes use of rational modes as symbols to describe or translate knowledge possessing a greater degree of certainty than any knowledge of a sensible order, whereas philosophy . . . is never anything more than what it expresses. When philosophy uses reason to resolve a doubt, this proves precisely that its starting point is a doubt that it is striving to overcome, whereas . . . the starting point of a metaphysical formulation is always essentially something intellectually evident or certain, which is to be communicated, to those able to receive it, by symbolical or dialectical means designed to awaken in them the latent knowledge that they bear unconsciously and, it may even be said, eternally within them.[4]

Metaphysics, then, both grows out of and points to the plenary and unitive experience of Reality. It attempts to fashion out of the ambiguities and limitations of language, and with the aid of symbolism, dialectics, analogy, and whatever lies at hand, principles and propositions which testify to that Reality. Metaphysics is, in brief, "the doctrine of the uncreated."[5]

Shankara was not the "author" of a new "philosophy" but a metaphysician and spiritual teacher. His purpose was to demonstrate the unity and consistency of the Upanishadic teachings on *Brahman*, and to explain certain apparent contradictions "by a correlation of different formulations with the point of view implied in them."[6] Like his gurus Gaudapada and Govinda, Shankara was engaged in an explication

2: *Selected Papers, Metaphysics* (Princeton: Princeton University Press, 1977), p. 6.

4 F. Schuon, *The Transcendent Unity of Religions* (New York: Harper & Row, 1975), pp. xxix-xxx.

5 T. Burckhardt, *Alchemy: Science of the Cosmos, Science of the Soul* (Harmondsworth: Penguin, 1971), p. 36.

6 A.K. Coomaraswamy, "Vedanta and Western Tradition," p. 4. See also p. 22.

of Vedanta and the development of a framework, both doctrinal and practical, for the quest of liberation.

However, Shankara's teachings should in no sense be considered irrational or anti-rational; he was, indeed, a masterful logician and a most formidable opponent in debate. The point is simply that his metaphysic, while it mobilizes reason where appropriate, cannot be strait-jacketed in any purely rationalistic framework. Reason was not the idol it has become for some but rather a tool, an instrument, not the ultimate avenue to, or test of, Reality. Shankara himself warned that:

> the pure truth of *Atman*, which is buried under *maya*, can be reached by meditation, contemplation, and other spiritual disciplines such as a knower of *Brahman* may prescribe—but never by subtle argument.[7]

Mircea Eliade has suggested that:

> Four basic and interdependent concepts, four 'kinetic ideas' bring us directly to the core of Indian spirituality. They are *karma, maya, nirvana,* and *yoga.* A coherent history of Indian thought could be written starting from any one of these basic concepts; the other three would inevitably have to be discussed.[8]

This claim not only emphasizes the cardinal importance of the doctrine of *maya* but also forewarns us of the hazards of considering it in isolation.

T.R.V. Murti has remarked that any absolutism, be it that of Madhyamika Buddhism, Vedanta or Bradleian philosophy, must posit a distinction between the ultimately Real and the empirically or relatively real. It thus establishes a doctrine of two truths and, consequently, a theory of illusion to explain the relationship.[9] Mahadevan has clearly

---

7 Shankara, *Crest-Jewel of Discrimination*, p. 43.

8 M. Eliade, *Yoga: Immortality and Freedom* (Princeton: Princeton University Press, 1969), p. 3. It should perhaps be noted that by *nirvana* Eliade is here signaling whatever bears on the Absolute, be it called *nirvana, Brahman,* or whatever. Similarly, the term *yoga* is to be understood in its full amplitude both as "spiritual means" and "union," rather than as referring only to a particular *darshana*.

9 T.R.V. Murti, *The Central Philosophy of Buddhism* (London: Allen & Unwin, 1974), p. 104 and pp. 320ff. See also R. Brooks, "Some Uses and Implications of Advaita Vedan-

articulated the problem which Advaita Vedanta had to resolve:

> Truth, knowledge, infinitude is *Brahman*. Mutable, non-intelligent,
> finite, and perishing is the world. *Brahman* is pure, attributeless, im-
> partite, and immutable. The world is a manifold of changing phe-
> nomena, fleeting events, and finite things. . . . The problem for the
> Advaitin is to solve how from the pure *Brahman* the impure world
> of men and things came into existence. It is on this rock that most of
> the monistic systems break.[10]

Shankara's resolution of this problem hinges on the doctrine of *maya*.

The Samkhya-Yoga *darshana* had postulated the existence of two
distinct and ultimate entities, *purusha* (loosely, "spirit") and *prakriti*
(loosely, "nature" or "matter," not excluding subtle matter). The nature
of reality had been explained in terms of a cooperative relationship
between these two entities, *prakriti* being for man "a veritable fairy
godmother."[11] For Shankara and the Advaitins this formulation was
untenable: no such relationship could exist between two entities so
disparate. Not only did they believe that the Samkhya view could not
be supported logically but it also compromised the sole reality of *Brahman* which Shankara identified as the central teaching of the *Upanishads*. The alternatives to the Samkhya view were either a full-blown
materialism which could immediately be thrown out of court under
the auspices of Upanishadic *shruti*, or the belief that material existents
are in some sense less than real—illusions utterly dependent on the
reality of *Brahman* for their existence but their apparent independence
and multiple existences grounded in some pervasive error. Such was
the Advaitin view and it was along these lines that the puzzling relationship of the phenomenal world to *Brahman* was to be explained, the
doctrine of *maya* being the key to the whole argument.

Let us consider the suggestive etymology of the term *maya* which
has been translated, or at least signaled, by a kaleidoscopic array of
terms. These can be sampled in two clusters: (a) "illusion," "conceal-

---

ta's Doctrine of *Maya*" in *The Problem of Two Truths in Buddhism and Vedanta*, ed. M.
Sprung (Dodrecht: D. Reidel, 1973), p. 98.

10 T.M.P. Mahadevan, *The Philosophy of Advaita* (Madras: Ganesh & Co, 1957), p. 227.

11 For a discussion of the Samkhya position see M. Hiriyana, *The Essentials of Indian
Philosophy* (London: Unwin, 1978), pp. 107-120.

ment," "the web of seeming," "appearance," "glamour," "relativity,"
"classification," "contingency," "objectivization," "distinctivization,"
"exteriorization"; (b) "cosmic power," "divine art," "universal unfolding," "cosmic magic," "the power of Ishvara," and "the principle of self-
expression." Clearly, behind these terms there is a principle of considerable subtlety. However, in these translations, we can see two strands
of meaning—more or less negative in the first group, positive in the
latter. The Sanskrit terms *avarana* ("concealment") and *vikshepa* ("projection") are closely associated with the notion of *maya* and designate
two aspects, or guises, of it. These twin faces of *maya* are reflected in
Hindu temple iconography and are woven through the etymology of
the word.

The word *maya* is linked to the root "matr": "to measure, form,
build, or plan." Several Greco-Latin words are also connected with this
root: meter, matrix, matter, and material.[12] On a more immediate, liter-
al level the word refers simply to "that which" (*ya*) "is not" (*ma*).[13] In its
more positive meanings we find *maya* is related to the Assyrian *maya*
(magic) and to *Maya*-Devi (mother of Shakyamuni Buddha), Maia
(mother of Hermes) and Maria (mother of Jesus).[14] Here we can detect
the obvious association with the feminine and Shaktic pole of manifestation. These etymological considerations provide clues to the various
meanings which will emerge more clearly in subsequent discussion.

As Mahadevan has said, following Shankara, "To logic *maya* is a
puzzle. Wonder is its garment; inscrutable is its nature."[15] This does not
mean that nothing whatsoever can be said about *maya* in logical terms
but rather that the ratiocinative process must necessarily arrive, sooner
or later, at certain impasses which cannot, by their nature, be overcome
logically. Shankara did elaborate a detailed and acute dialectical ex-
amination of *maya*; in itself this could not unlock the nature of *maya*,
but through it the mind could be cleared of certain misconceptions.
The condensed exposition following attempts to rehearse Shankara's
argument in outline and in its most salient points.

Maya is a power or potency of *Brahman*, coeval with *Brahman*,

12 A. Watts, *The Way of Zen* (Harmondsworth: Penguin, 1972), p. 59.

13 T.M.P. Mahadevan, *Outlines of Hinduism* (Bombay: Chetana, 1956), p. 149.

14 W. Perry (ed.), *A Treasury of Traditional Wisdom* (London: Allen & Unwin, 1971), p. 83.

15 T.M.P. Mahadevan, *Philosophy of Advaita*, pp. 232-233.

completely dependent on and inseparable from *Brahman*, neither independent nor real in itself. It is not different from *Brahman* on pain of contradicting Scriptural declarations of non-difference, but it is also not non-different from *Brahman* as there cannot be identity between the Real and the unreal. Nor can *maya* be both different and non-different as such contradictions cannot reside in one and the same thing. The relationship between *maya* and *Brahman* is thus *tadatmya*, neither identity nor difference nor both. A similar dialectic exposes *maya's* status considered in terms of the Real. *Maya* is not real because it has no existence apart from *Brahman*, because it disappears at the dawn of knowledge, because it does not constitute a limit on *Brahman*. However, it is not altogether unreal because it does project the world of appearances. It is not both real and unreal because of contradiction.

Maya is not possessed of parts. If it were partite it would have a beginning and consequently the Lord and the *jivas* which are reflections thereof would have a beginning. Furthermore, *maya* with a beginning would necessitate another *maya* as its cause and there would thus be a contingence of infinite regress. However, *maya* cannot be partless because of the contingency of its not being the primal cause. It is the cause only of partite phenomena, and cannot be both partite and impartite because of contradiction.

Maya, has a phenomenal and relative character and is an appearance only (*vivarta*). It is of the nature of superimposition (*adhyasa*) and is removable by right knowledge. Its locus is *Brahman* but *Brahman* is in no way affected by *maya*. *Maya* is beginningless (*anadi*), for time arises only within it; it is unthinkable (*acintya*), for all thought is subject to it; it is indescribable (*anirvacaniya*), for all language results from it.[16] Because its nature is outside the determination of normal human categories it is indeterminable (*anirvaniya*) and indefinable. *Maya*, indeed, is most strange!

Before moving into an exploration of Shankara's views on the relationship of the world to *Brahman* and the role of *maya* in "mediating" this relationship, a small digression: it is sometimes suggested, often obliquely rather than directly, that the classical Indian view of reality is somewhat idiosyncratic. We have seen in the Vedanta the refusal to

---

16 See E. Deutsch, *Advaita Vedanta: A Philosophical Reconstruction* (Honolulu: University of Hawaii Press, 1969), p. 29, and "Introduction" to *Crest-Jewel of Discrimination*, pp. 16ff.

equate the "real" with the existent. Such a position sits uncomfortably with modern Western notions derived from our recent intellectual history. However, in the long view it is the modern notion of reality (as the existent) which looks eccentric, even within the Western tradition. A view more in accord with the Vedanta is everywhere to be found in traditional wisdoms. Here we shall restrict ourselves to two illustrative examples. St. Augustine:

> I beheld these others beneath Thee, and saw that they neither altogether are, nor altogether are not. An existence they have because they are from Thee; and yet no existence, because they are not what Thou art. *For only that really is that remains unchangeably. . . .*[17]

Here we not only see a view quite in agreement with the Indian insistence on eternality and immutability but a line of thinking which, like Shankara's, accommodates certain paradoxical possibilities— things which "neither altogether are, nor altogether are not." From Hermes Trismegistus:

> That which is dissoluble is destructible; only that which is indissoluble is everlasting. . . . Nothing that is corporeal is real; only that which is incorporeal is devoid of illusion.[18]

This anticipates some of the themes of Shankara's doctrine of *maya*.

*

As we have seen already the nub of the problem confronting Advaita was the relationship of the empirical world of multiple phenomena to *Brahman*.[19] It was to this question that much of Shankara's work was addressed and it is here that the doctrine of *maya* comes into full play. The Upanishadic view had suggested that the world, in all its multiplic-

---

17 Augustine, *Confessions*, 9.vii (Harmondsworth: Penguin, 1969) (italics mine).

18 From *Stobaei*, quoted in W. Perry, *A Treasury of Traditional Wisdom*, p. 101.

19 Ultimately it is obviously improper to speak of any "relationship" between *Brahman* and the world as it is anchored in a dualist conception which Advaita seeks to overcome. However such a notion is expedient if this caution is kept in mind. Further, we will be less wide of the mark if we speak of the relationship of the world to *Brahman*, but not the obverse.

ity, emanates from, subsists in, and ultimately merges in *Brahman*. In the *Mundaka Upanishad*, by way of example, we find this:

> As a spider spreads and withdraws (its thread). . .
> so out of the Immutable does the phenomenal universe arise.

And this:

> As a thousand sparks from a blazing fire
> Leap forth each like the other,
> So friend, from the Imperishable, modes of being
> Variously spring forth and return again thereto.

This "projection" of *Brahman* is not to be understood as something other than *Brahman*. As the same Upanishad tells us,

> Immortal in very truth is *Brahman*
> East, west, north and south
> below, above *Brahman* projects Itself
> *Brahman* is the whole universe.[20]

This is by no means the pantheistic notion wherein the cosmos and the Absolute are identified, but is to be understood in the spirit of the old Rabbinic dictum: "God is the dwelling place of the universe; but the universe is not the dwelling place of God."[21] The *Shvetashvatara Upanishad* describes the Lord (Ishvara) as the *mayin*, the wonder-working powerful Being out of whom the world arises.[22] The word *maya* is used in this sense in the *Rig Veda*.

Shankara's purpose was to make explicit and to explain more fully the Upanishadic view that the universe is really only in the nature of an appearance, devoid of any ultimate ontological reality. Following the *Upanishads* Badarayana had insisted on the sole reality of *Brahman*, "The alone, supreme, eternal" which "through the glamour of Ignorance, like a magician, appears manifold. . . ."[23] Shankara's metaphysic

---

20 *Mundaka Upanishad* 1.i.vii & 2.ii.xii.

21 Quoted in *Radhakrishnan: Selected Writings on Philosophy, Religion and Culture*, ed. R.A. McDermott (New York: E.P. Dutton, 1970), p. 146.

22 *Shvetashvatara Upanishad*, 4.x.

23 Per P. Duessen, *The System of the Vedanta* (New York: Dover, 1973), p. 187.

elucidates the nature of this manifold. The key principle is *maya* and the crucial process *adhyasa* (superimposition). We have already established that

> [T]he term *maya* combines the meanings of "productive power" and "universal illusion"; it is the inexhaustible play of manifestations, deployments, combinations, and reverberations, a play with which *Atma* clothes itself even as the ocean clothes itself with a mantle of foam, which is ever renewed and never the same.[24]

"*Maya*" can be used to signify both the principle which effects the illusory world, the power which superimposes the manifold and sensuous on the supersensuous *Brahman*, and the effects of this power, i.e., the world. In the ensuing discussion the sense in which it is being used will be clear from the context.

The relationship of the world to *Brahman*, according to Shankara, is paradoxical. The world is illusory, an appearance only. Now, several obvious questions present themselves: if there is only one Reality (*Brahman*) how can its non-duality be sustained in the face of the multiple world? What is the nature of the illusory world of *maya*? In what sense can we speak of the world and *Brahman* as being both different and non-different? Is not *Brahman* (the cause) affected by *maya* (the effect)? What is Shankara's stance in regard to Ishvara and his relationship to *maya*?

The first question has already been partially answered. The phenomenal world, simply, is not real—it is not eternal and immutable, and it is sublated by the experience of *Brahman*. We recall the words of the *Bhagavad Gita*: "of the non-real there is no coming to be: of the real there is no ceasing to be."[25] The world is not real. It has no ontological or ultimate status. Nevertheless, while the world is not real (*sat*), nor, says Shankara, is it altogether unreal (*asat*). It is apparently real (*vyavaharika*). It is perceived and it exhibits spatial, temporal, and causal order. "There could be no non-existence" (of external entities) says Shankara, because "external realities are perceived."[26] It is the existence

---

24 F. Schuon, *Logic and Transcendence: A New Translation with Selected Letters* (Bloomington, IN: World Wisdom, 2009), p. 75n.

25 *Bhagavad Gita* 2:16.

26 *The Brahma-Sutra Bhasya of Sankaracarya*, trans. Swami Gambirananda (Calcutta: Advaita Ashrama, 1965), pp. 418ff.

and the apparent reality of the world which is in need of explanation.

It has often been remarked that *maya* can be viewed from several standpoints: from that of mundane experience, the phenomenal world of *maya* is real; from that of the inquiring mind *maya* and all her effects are a riddle, a puzzle, a Sphinx; from the viewpoint of the realized being, *maya* simply is not. The problematic relationship between *maya* and *Brahman* is only apparent from the empirical, worldly, and *maya*-created point of view. It is only because of ignorance (*avidya*) that we are unable to see the non-duality of *Brahman*. Non-duality exists *a priori*: the separation of the world from *Brahman* is an illusory "fissure" which from its own standpoint, within the limits imposed by the very nature of *maya*, is enigmatic. Right Knowledge reveals the non-duality of *Brahman* quite uncompromised and unqualified by the phenomenal realm.[27]

Clearly this still leaves many questions unanswered: If this world is illusory, how is the illusion to be explained? What is the nature of the illusion? Shankara distinguishes three kinds of illusion: a phenomenal or "objective" illusion such as our waking perception of the empirical world (*vyavaharika*); a private, subjective illusion such as a dream; and a third kind of illusion, altogether unreal, non-existent, and absurd, of which the hare's horn is the most oft-cited example.[28]

The illusion of the world is of the first kind: the world is not simply a hallucination or a chimera, nor is it an absurd non-entity. *Maya*, and thus the world, is not real but it is existent. It is certainly not non-existent. Why does this illusory world have an apparently objective homogeneity? Because the world is not an illusion of each particular individual, in which case each individual would "dream" a different world, but an illusion of the human collectivity. The empirical and objective "solidity" of the world proves not its reality but the collective nature of the illusion.[29] Mircea Eliade has written of the association of *maya* with

27 See F. Schuon, *Logic and Transcendence*, p. 185. Shankara's argument is supported by the theory of *vivartavada* which demonstrates that the world of *maya* is only an apparent manifestation of *Brahman*. For commentary see E. Deutsch, *Advaita Vedanta*, pp. 27-2. It should be noted that *Brahman*, properly speaking, is non-dual rather than one as the category of number is not applicable.

28 See "Introduction" to *Crest-Jewel of Discrimination*, p. 15.

29 F. Schuon, *Gnosis: Divine Wisdom, A New Translation with Selected Letters* (Bloomington, IN: World Wisdom, 2006), p. 54, and *Spiritual Perspectives and Human Facts: A New Translation with Selected Letters* (Bloomington, IN: World Wisdom, 2007), p.

temporality. His commentary is worth quoting at some length:

> [T]he veil of *maya* is an image-formula expressing the ontological
> unreality both of the world and of all human experience: we em-
> phasize ontological, for neither the world nor human experience
> participates in absolute Being. The physical world and our human
> experience also are constituted by the universal becoming, by the
> temporal: they are therefore illusory, created and destroyed as they
> are by Time. But this does not mean they have no existence or are
> creations of my imagination. The world is not a mirage. . . . The
> physical world and my vital and psychic experience exist, but they
> exist only in Time. . . . Consequently, judged by the scale of absolute
> Being, the world and every experience dependent upon temporality
> are illusory. . . . Many centuries before Heidegger, Indian thought
> had identified, in temporality, the "fated" dimension of all existence.
> . . . In other words, the discovery of historicity, as the specific mode
> of being of man in the world, corresponds to what the Indians have
> long called our situation in *maya*. . . . In reality our true "self" . . . has
> nothing to do with the multiple situations of our history.[30]

Whence comes this illusion and how is it maintained? The brief
answer is that it derives from *maya* as *avidya* (ignorance, or nescience)
and is generated and sustained by *adhyasa* (superimposition). Some
commentators have distinguished *avidya* from *maya*, associating
avidya not only with the negative aspect of *maya* and thus with the *jiva*
but not with Ishvara. Shankara himself used the two terms more or less
interchangeably. The question has generated a philosophical squabble
but Mahadevan has persuasively argued that the distinction cannot
be maintained with any philosophic integrity. He exposes the faulty
constructions of some of the post-Shankaran commentators who have
been bent on separating *avidya* from *maya*. Nevertheless Mahadevan
does concede that the distinction does have some empirical utility:

> When *prakriti* generates projection or when it conforms to the desire
> of the agent as is the case with Ishvara it is called *maya* in empiri-
> cal usage. When it obscures or when it is independent of the agent's
> will it is known as nescience (*avidya*). Apart from this adjunct-con-

179-180.

30 M. Eliade, *Myths, Dreams and Mysteries* (London: Collins, 1972), pp. 239-240.

ditioned distinction, there is no difference between *maya* and ne-science.[31]

It is in this sense that some speak of *maya* as being cosmic in significance, *avidya* subjective. Until the dawn of knowledge all are subject to ensnarement in the web of appearances. This is the source of the illusion. The "mechanism," as it were, through which the illusion is generated and sustained is *adhyasa*, the super-imposing of limitations and multiplicities upon *Brahman*. Because of *avidya* and through *adhyasa* we mistakenly take phenomenal distinctions to be real. This, according to Gaudapada, is like seeing footprints of birds in the sky.[32]

Padmapada, one of Shankara's disciples, explained that superimposition means that manifestation of the nature of something in another which is not of that nature." So it is when one says, "I am deaf" where a property of the organ of hearing is imposed on the self.[33] An example Shankara himself used was "the sky is blue."[34] In like manner we couple the unreal with the Real and vice versa.[35] As a recent commentator has observed,

> The main or primary application of *adhyasa* is made with respect to the self. It is the superimposition on the Self (*Atman*, *Brahman*) of what does not properly belong to the Self (finitude, change) and the superimposition on the non-self of what does properly belong to the Self (infinitude, eternality) that constitute *avidya*.[36]

Thus *maya* makes possible the "impossible"—the appearance of the infinite and unconditioned as if finite and contingent.

We can now see how and why *maya* makes the world-nature inscrutable to the discursive mind. *Maya* is an "ontic-noetic state where-

---

31 T.M.P. Mahadevan, *Philosophy of Advaita*, p. 231. See also P.T. Raju, *Idealistic Thought of India* (Boston: Harvard University Press, 1953), p. 115.

32 Gaudapada, *Mandukya-Karika* III.48, IV.28, quoted in T.M.P. Mahadevan, *Ramana Maharshi*, p. 120.

33 E. Deutsch, *Advaita Vedanta*, p. 34.

34 *Crest-Jewel of Discrimination*, p. 62.

35 *Crest-Jewel of Discrimination*, p. 62.

36 E. Deutsch, *Advaita Vedanta*, p. 34

in limitations (*upadhis*) are imposed on Reality."[37] All attachments, aversions, dreams, fears, and thoughts, all memories, cognitions, and mental modifications of whatever kind are grounded in *maya*. "The mind which is a product of *maya* cannot in full measure understand the nature of its parent."[38] It is only intuition (in the full and characteristically Indian sense—*jnana*) that can apprehend the *Brahman*-nature. In this context it is worth remembering that in a metaphysic such as Shankara's "logical proof is no more than a thoroughly provisional crystallization of intuition."[39] In this order *maya* is not, in fact, inexplicable but only not self-explanatory.[40]

The second question we posed in reference to the world-*Brahman* relationship: how we are to understand the "difference" and "non-difference"? We have already seen how in strictly logical terms this relationship can only be enunciated negatively, i.e. *maya* and *Brahman* are neither different, nor non-different, nor both. Nevertheless we can speak provisionally, metaphorically as it were, of "difference" and "non-difference." The difference of *maya* and *Brahman* is clear enough. It is the non-difference which is more puzzling. In metaphysical terms the following principial demonstration articulates the relationship precisely:

> That the Real and the unreal are "not different" does not in any way imply either the unreality of the Self or the reality of the world; the Real is not "nondifferent" with respect to the unreal, but the unreal is "non-different" with respect to the Real—not insofar as it is unreality, but insofar as it is a "lesser Reality," which is nonetheless "extrinsically unreal" in relation to absolute Reality.[41]

Whilst ultimately unreal, "cosmic existence partakes of the character of the real and the unreal."[42] The relationship of the relative to the

37 E. Deutsch, *Advaita Vedanta*, pp. 28 & 30.

38 T.M.P. Mahadevan, *Philosophy of Advaita*, p. 250 & p. 248. See also J.G. Arapura, "*Maya* and the Discourse about *Brahman*" in *The Problem of Two Truths*, p. 111, and S. Radhakrishnan, *Selected Writings*, p. 140.

39 F. Schuon, *Spiritual Perspectives*, p. 3.

40 M. Hiriyana, *The Essentials of Indian Philosophy*, p. 161.

41 F. Schuon, *Spiritual Perspectives*, p.103.

42 S. Radhakrishnan, *Selected Writings*, p. 143.

Absolute is elaborated in one fashion or another in all traditional metaphysics and is to be found in the esoteric and sapiential dimension of most religious traditions, albeit couched in the vocabulary appropriate to the tradition in question. It can, for instance, be formulated no less precisely in the terminology of the theistic Occidental traditions, i.e. in terms not of *Brahman* and *maya* but in terms of God and man. This is provided that we remember that,

> In the three Semitic monotheisms, the name "God" necessarily embraces all that belongs to the Principle [the Absolute] with no restriction whatever, although the exoterisms obviously consider the ontological aspect alone.[43]

In other words, "God" refers, in this context, to the trans-ontological and Beyond-Being "dimension" of Reality and not to personalized theological notions of God which correspond not to *nirguna-Brahman* but to *saguna-Brahman* which encompasses Ishvara. One such formulation explicates the relationship this way:

> That we are conformed to God—"made in His image"—this is certain; otherwise we would not exist.
> That we are contrary to God, this is also certain; otherwise we should not be different from God.
> Apart from analogy with God, we would be nothing.
> Apart from opposition to God, we would be God.
>
> The separation between man and God is at one and the same time absolute and relative. . . . The separation is absolute because God alone is real, and no continuity is possible between nothingness and Reality, but the separation is relative—or rather "nonabsolute"—because nothing is outside God.
> In a sense it might be said that this separation is absolute from man to God and relative from God to man.[44]

This kind of enunciation is closest in spirit to the Sufic tradition but similar statements of the Absolute-Relative can be found in other Oc-

43 F. Schuon, *Light on the Ancient Worlds: A New Translation with Selected Letters* (Bloomington, IN: World Wisdom, 2006), p. 75n.

44 F. Schuon, *Spiritual Perspectives*, p. 171.

cidental wisdoms, not excluding the Christian and Judaic.

Our next question: is not *Brahman* in some sense affected, contaminated, as it were, by *maya*? Are not the effects implicit in the cause? By no means, says Shankara. We shall not here rehearse the theories of apparent manifestation (*vivartavada*) or transformation (*parinamavada*) but simply recall the famous analogy with which Shankara resolved this problem.

> As the magician is not affected by this illusion (*maya*) which he himself has created, because it is without reality (*avatsu*), so also *Paramatman* is not affected by the illusion of *Samsara*. . . . Consequently it is false to hold that the cause is polluted by the qualities, materiality, etc. of the effect, if they return into that essence.[45]

The illusion is caused by the power of the magician and the ignorance of the audience: for the magician there is *no illusion whatsoever*. So with *Brahman*, *maya* is illusion until the dawn of knowledge; thence *maya* is not. *Brahman*, says Shankara, cannot be affected by *maya* just as the desert sands cannot be muddied by the waters of a mirage.[46]

Maya is sometimes referred to as "the power of Ishvara" which brings us to the question of the place of Ishvara in the Advaitin scheme and his connections with *maya*. Ishvara's nature is of *saguna-Brahman* which might roughly be signified as "qualified *Brahman*,"[47] the qualifications having only an *ad hoc* validity and existing only from a strictly *maya*-based point of view. In a sense Ishvara can be represented as the cosmic parallel to the *jiva* with the qualification that Ishvara remains untouched by *avidya*. Further, "Ishvara is the reflection of *Brahman* in *maya*, and the *jiva* is the same reflection of *Brahman* in *avidya*, which is only "part" of *maya*."[48] *Brahman* thus appears as Ishvara when considered from the relatively ignorant viewpoint of the *jiva*. As Vivekananda so aptly put it, "Personal God [Ishvara] is the reading of the Impersonal by the human mind."[49] *Brahman* is in all senses prior

45 Shankara quoted in P. Duessen, *System of the Vedanta*, p. 275. See also p. 278.

46 *Crest-Jewel of Discrimination*, p. 49.

47 M. Hiriyana, *Essentials of Indian Philosophy*, pp. 164-165. See also F. Schuon, "The Mystery of the Veil," *Studies in Comparative Religion*, 11:2, Spring 1977, p. 71.

48 P.T. Raju, *Idealistic Thought of India*, pp. 116ff.

49 "Introduction" to *Crest-Jewel of Discrimination*, p. 23.

to Ishvara. Metaphysically speaking "*Maya* non-manifested . . . is Being: Ishvara."[50] Here we find a principle analogous to Meister Eckhart's distinction between God (the ontological, Being "dimension" of the Absolute; Ishvara) and the God-head (the Absolute, Beyond-Being, unqualified; *Brahman*).[51]

Considered in religious rather than metaphysical terms Ishvara becomes the creator of the universe, the great magician who conjures up the spectacle of the realm, out of whom the world arises. Being untouched by *avidya* and divine in nature, Ishvara also becomes an exemplar and a focus of bhaktic worship. Whilst ruthlessly non-dualistic in his metaphysics Shankara himself addressed prayers to the deities. He was sympathetically disposed towards bhaktic forms of worship, denying only that ultimate realization could be reached by such practices. Certainly he did not see *bhakti* only as a concession to the weakness of the popular mind—as some neo-Vedantins would have it. Ishvara not only provides a focus for *bhakti* but also helps to bring the world into a more immediately intelligible relationship with *Brahman*.

Up to this point we have, for the most part, been considering the negative aspects of *maya*—illusion, concealment, *avidya*. Mention of Ishvara provides a bridge to the other side of *maya*, the aspect of projection and of "divine art," and to the related notion of *lila*. *Maya* is indeed "cosmic illusion" but is

> also "divine play." It is the great theophany, the "unveiling" of God "in Himself and by Himself," as the Sufis would say. *Maya* is like a magic fabric woven from a warp that veils and a weft that unveils; a quasi-incomprehensible intermediary between the finite and the Infinite—at least from our point of view as creatures—it has all the shimmering ambiguity appropriate to its half-cosmic, half-divine nature.[52]

As this passage suggests, the Sufic doctrine of the veil is, in some respects, analogous to the doctrine of *maya* as articulated in Advaita Vedanta. *Maya* has also been called the principle of "self-expression"

---

50 F. Schuon, *Light on the Ancient World*, p. 81n.

51 For an accessible discussion of this distinction see H. Smith, *Forgotten Truth: The Primordial Tradition* (New York: Harper & Row, 1976), pp. 54-59.

52 F. Schuon, *Light on the Ancient World*, p. 75.

(i.e., Ishvara). In this context:

> Creation is expression. It is not a making of something out of nothing. It is not making so much as becoming. It is the self-projection of the Supreme. Everything exists in the secret abode of the Supreme. The primary reality contains within itself the source of its own motion and change.[53]

This perspective on *maya* also embraces the idea of *lila* to which we will return presently. But first a digression is in order to meet possible objections to the notion that *maya* simultaneously has both a negative and a positive character.

How is it, it may be asked, that *maya* both conceals and projects? This is the kind of question likely to vex an either/or line of ratiocinative thought. The objection is best met by analogy. We turn here to Frithjof Schuon, who illuminates many traditional doctrines in terms intelligible across the linguistic and symbolic barriers of the various traditional wisdoms:

> It is very easy to label as "vague" and "contradictory" something one cannot understand because of a failure of "intellectual vision." In general, rationalist thinkers refuse to accept a truth that presents contradictory aspects and is situated, seemingly beyond grasping, between two extrinsic and negative enunciations. But there are some realities that can be expressed in no other way. The ray that proceeds from a light is itself light inasmuch as it illuminates, but it is not the light from which it proceeded; therefore it is neither this light nor something other than this light; in fact it is nothing but light, though growing ever weaker in proportion to its distance from its source. A faint glow is light for the darkness it illuminates but darkness for the light whence it emanates. Similarly *Maya* is at once light and darkness: as "divine art" it is light inasmuch as it reveals the secrets of *Atma*; it is darkness inasmuch as it hides *Atma*. As darkness it is "ignorance," *avidya*.[54]

The idea of *lila* can also be explored in another, larger context. A perennial line of questioning which inevitably arises in any consid-

---

53 S. Radhakrishnan, *Selected Writings*, p. 141.

54 F. Schuon, *Spiritual Perspectives*, pp. 104-105.

eration of the religious doctrines of creation and manifestation runs along these lines: why does manifestation occur in the first place? Why, in crude terms, does the world exist? Here we shall not concern ourselves with questions of beginning and end, of temporality and eschatology, which, in Vedanta, are always subordinate to the inquiry into "the relation of ground and consequent." Rather, the question here is this: is there any "explanation" for the appearance, as it were, of *maya*? Here we will touch lightly on three responses to this question: the conventional Vedantin attitude; the notion of *lila*; and a metaphysical "explanation" not itself drawn from Shankara's metaphysic but in no way incompatible with it.

Radhakrishnan has articulated the typical Vedantin response to these kinds of questions when he writes:

> If we ask why the Supreme has this . . . character, why it is what it is [and thus the "why" of *maya*] we can only accept it as a given reality. It is the ultimate irrationality in the sense that no logical derivation of the given is possible. It is apprehended by us in spiritual consciousness and accounts for the nature of experience in all its aspects. It is the only philosophical explanation that is possible or necessary.[55]

In other words certain questions about *maya* cannot be resolved outside the plenary experience. Elsewhere Radhakrishnan reminds us that, "If we raise the question as to how [or why] the finite rises from out of the bosom of the infinite, Shankara says that it is an incomprehensible mystery. . . ."[56] As Murti has observed, the doctrine of *maya* is not, in itself, an explanation of this mystery.[57]

As we have seen already, any attempt to explain the "creation" or "origin" of the world is bound to fail not only because the mind is trapped in *maya* but also because the very notion of creation is an error. As Gaudapada stressed, "this is the supreme truth: nothing whatever is born" (or "created").[58] It is only when we have torn the veil of

55 S. Radhakrishnan, *Selected Writings*, p. 141.

56 S. Radhakrishnan, *The Hindu View of Life* (London: Unwin, 1974), pp. 48-49.

57 T.R.V. Murti, "The Individual in Indian Religious Thought" in *The Indian Mind: Essentials of Indian Philosophy and Culture*, ed. C. Moore (Honolulu: University of Hawaii Press, 1967), p. 337.

58 Gaudapada quoted in T.M.P. Mahadevan, *Ramana Maharshi*, p. 120.

maya, as it were, that we can see that this kind of question is ultimately meaningless.[59]

All this notwithstanding, the notion of *lila*, is in some sense a kind of metaphorical explanation. In the *Brahma-Sutra Bhasya* Shankara says:

> The activity of the Lord . . . may be supposed to be more sport [*lila*] proceeding from his own nature, without reference to any purpose.[60]

This recalls Krishna's words in the *Bhagavad Gita*.

> There is naught in the three worlds that I have need to do, nor anything I have not gotten that I might get, yet I participate in action.[61]

This idea of the playfulness of the Creator Lord is found in the *Rig Veda*, the *Upanishads*, and the *Gita* though the word *lila* as such is not always used.[62] The notion conveys that Ishvara's creation answers to no compelling necessity or constraint but arises out of an inherent exuberance or joy. It is spontaneous, purposeless, without responsibility, or moral consequence—in short, like play.

Ramakrishna was fond of recounting the following story which contains something of this idea of the playfulness of Ishvara. (The anecdote is perfumed with the scents of Hindu spirituality.)

> Once there came a *saddhu* here [Ramakrishna would relate] who had a beautiful glow on his face. He just sat and smiled. Twice a day, once in the morning and once in the evening, he'd come out of his room and look around. He'd look at the trees, the bushes, the sky, and Ganges and he'd raise his arms and dance, beside himself with joy. Or he'd roll on the ground, laughing and exclaiming "Bravo! What fun! How wonderful it is, this *maya*. What an illusion God has conjured up!" This was his way of doing worship.[63]

59 P.T. Raju, *Idealistic Thought*, pp. 113-114.

60 Shankara, *Brahma-Sutra Bhasya* II.i.33 in E. Deutsch, *Advaita Vedanta*, p. 38. For the context see Swami Gambhirananda's translation, p. 361.

61 *Bhagavad Gita* 3:22-25. See A.K. Coomaraswamy, "*Lila*" in *Selected Papers: Metaphysics*, p. 150.

62 A.K. Coomaraswamy, "*Lila*," pp. 151ff. See also "Play and Seriousness" in the same volume, pp. 156-158.

63 C. Isherwood, *Ramakrishna and His Disciples* (Calcutta: Advaita Ashrama, 1974),

It may be noted in passing that the idea of God's playfulness is not peculiar to the Hindu tradition. This formulation from Meister Eckhart, for instance, is in no way at odds with Shankara's: "There has always been this play going on in the Father-nature . . . sport and players are the same."[64] Or this, from Boehme: "The creation is the same sport out of himself."[65]

The third response is the metaphysical "resolution" of the problem of manifestation. To translate the following formulation back into specifically Hindu terms we need only substitute *Brahman* for "the Absolute" and "Essence," and *maya* for "illusion."

> As for the question of the "origin" of illusion, it is amongst those questions that can be resolved—or rather there is nothing in it to resolve—though this resolution cannot be adjusted to suit all logical needs; there are demonstrations which, whether they are understood or not, are sufficient in themselves and indeed constitute pillars of metaphysical doctrine. . . . [T]he infinitude of Reality implies the possibility of its own negation and . . . since this negation is not possible within the Absolute itself, it is necessary that this "possibility of the impossible" should be realized in an "inward dimension" that is "neither real nor unreal," a dimension that is real on its own level while being unreal in respect of the Essence; thus we are everywhere in touch with the Absolute, from which we cannot emerge but which at the same time is infinitely distant, no thought ever circumscribing it.[66]

While Shankara maintains the traditional reticence on this question it is clear that such a demonstration is precisely attuned to his metaphysics—this is anything but accidental. The harmony of all sapiential doctrines, of metaphysics expounded within the protective cadre of a properly constituted religious tradition, derives not from any subjective or psychological source. Rather, it springs from the direct apprehension of Reality which is the ultimate purpose of the

---

p. 103.

64 A.K. Coomaraswamy, "*Lila*," p. 148.

65 A.K. Coomaraswamy, "*Lila*," p. 148.

66 F. Schuon, *Gnosis: Divine Wisdom*, p. 58 As Schuon has also written, "Divine *Maya*, Relativity, is the necessary consequence of the very Infinitude of the Principle. . ." (*Logic and Transcendence*, p. 75).

gnostic or jnanic dimension within each religion.[67] Such metaphysics must be sharply differentiated from the self-contradictory notion of metaphysics as a branch of profane philosophy, i.e. a so-called metaphysics deriving from purely subjective and mental resources, cut off from the spiritual disciplines and bereft of the supports transmitted by a religious tradition.

In Shankara's teachings the doctrine of *maya* is integral not only to a profound metaphysic but to the spiritual therapies which were its inevitable accompaniment. Neither Shankara nor any other Hindu metaphysician had the slightest interest in the doctrine as an intellectual curiosity but only as part of a way towards Right Knowledge, towards liberation. Certainly the doctrine of *maya*, properly understood, never led anyone into "pessimism" or "nihilism" such as is postulated by some critics of Hinduism. The denial of the ultimate reality of the world was inextricably linked with the affirmation that enlightenment and liberation were possible, possible indeed within this life. To separate the doctrine of *maya* from the belief in *jivanmukti* can only lead to the sort of lop-sided view that falls prey to the prejudices mentioned above. On this issue we can do no better than recall the words of Eliade when he wrote:

> [P]erhaps more than any other civilization, that of India loves and reverences Life, and enjoys it at every level. For *maya* is not [a] gratuitous cosmic illusion. . . . [T]o become conscious of the cosmic illusion does not mean, in India, the discovery that all is Nothingness, but simply that no experience in the world of History has any ontological validity and therefore, that our human condition ought not to be regarded as an end in itself. . . .[68]

The doctrine of *maya* helps us to develop an attitude in which the world can be rightly regarded. If we are mindful of the fugitive and illusory nature of the world then the realm of *maya* itself can help us in

---

67 Contemporary and modernistic commentators, tyrannized by ratiocinative modes of thought, often betray their own ignorance in their attempts to criticize Shankara's doctrines. Thus, for example, Renou when he asserts that the idea of *maya* "disguises the mutual irreducibility of the One and the Many" (L. Renou, *Religions of Ancient India* [New York: Schocken, 1968], p. 56). This signals a failure to understand that from the enlightened point of view, the "Many" is not.

68 M. Eliade, *Myths, Dreams and Mysteries*, pp. 242-243.

our quest—were it otherwise the Hindus would not have elaborated complex cosmological and other sciences.[69] The essential purpose of the doctrine is to free us from the snares of material existence, to deliver us from the countless solicitations of the world which only tighten the bonds of ignorance and chain us to the samsaric wheel.

This kind of teaching we find on all sides where spiritual welfare is the focus of attention. A few eloquent examples derived from other traditions will recall the universality of this theme in religious teachings:

> The phenomena of life may be likened unto a dream, a phantom, a bubble, a shadow, a glistening dew, or lightning flash, and thus they ought to be contemplated. (*Prajna-Paramita*)[70]

> The world is finite, and truly that other is infinite: image and form are a barrier to that Reality. (*Rumi*)[71]

> A life devoted to the interests and enjoyments of this world, spent and wasted in the slavery of earthly desires, may be truly called a dream, as having all the shortness, vanity, and delusion of a dream. . . . (*William Law*)[72]

It is Shankara's purpose to awaken us from this dream, to awaken us to the true Self and to Reality through Right Knowledge. The point of doctrines like that of *maya* is to lead us beyond the level where the question is asked (the level of mental modifications) into the realm where we can experience the answer. Once the plenary, unitive experience of realization has dispelled our ignorance *maya* no longer is. As the *Shvetashvatara Upanishad* tells us:

> By becoming what one is
> The whole world of appearance will once again
> Be lost to sight at last.[73]

---

69 See S.H. Nasr, *Man and Nature: The Spiritual Crisis of Modern Man* (London: Allen & Unwin, 1976), pp. 188-189.

70 Quoted in W. Perry, *A Treasury of Traditional Wisdom*, p. 96.

71 Quoted in W. Perry, *A Treasury of Traditional Wisdom*, p. 112.

72 Quoted in W. Perry, *A Treasury of Traditional Wisdom*, p. 95.

73 *Shvetashvatara Upanishad* 1.x.

Herein lies the purpose, the justification, the end of all Shankara's doctrines. The metaphysics Shankara elaborated is not only the crown-jewel of India's religious thought but a spiritual therapy addressed to our innermost nature and to our most profound needs.

CHAPTER 4

"The Last Blade of Grass":
The Bodhisattva Ideal in the Mahayana

Doers of what is hard are the Bodhisattvas, the great beings who
have set out to win supreme enlightenment. They do not wish to attain their own private *nirvana*. On the contrary. They have surveyed
the highly painful world of being, and yet, desirous to win supreme
enlightenment, they do not tremble at birth and death. They have set
out for the benefit of the world, for the ease of the world, out of pity
for the world. They have resolved: "We will become a shelter for the
world, a refuge for the world, the world's place of rest, the final relief
of the world, islands of the world, lights of the world, leaders of the
world, the world's means of salvation."

Prajnaparamita Sutra

The unfolding of the Mahayana marked a decisive phase in the history of the Buddhist tradition. Against earlier forms of Buddhism the
Mahayana represented a metaphysical shift from a radical pluralism
to an absolutism anchored in the doctrine of *shunyata*; epistemologi-
cally, through Nagarjuna's Madhyamika, the Mahayana moved from a
psychologically-oriented empiricism to a mode of dialectical criticism;
ethically the center of gravity shifted from the *arhat* ideal of private
salvation to that of the Bodhisattva, one attuned to the universal deliverance of all beings "down to the last blade of grass." It has often been
remarked that the two pre-eminent contributions of the Mahayana to
the spiritual treasury of Buddhism are the metaphysic of *shunyata* and
the Bodhisattva ideal. To these might be added the doctrine of the *Trikaya*, the Three Bodies of the Buddha who now appears as a cosmic
and metacosmic figure.

After some prefatory remarks about the emergence of the Bodhisattva ideal this essay explores its significance within the spiritual
economy of the Mahayana, and its relationship to the pivotal Mahayanist doctrines centering on *karuna* (compassion), *prajna* (wisdom),
and *shunyata* (voidness). It also takes up some subsidiary questions relating to the Bodhisattva's "status" *viz.* the Buddha, the issue of "self-power" and "other-power," and the popular appeal of the Bodhisattva ideal.

Although our knowledge of early Buddhism remains somewhat sketchy there is some evidence to suggest that by about the second century AD the pre-Mahayanist tradition was affected by a kind of dogmatic constriction and possibly by certain pharisaic currents within the *sangha*. From the (later) Mahayanist perspective there had developed an exaggerated reliance on the Abhidharma (the systematic explication of the doctrines) and the Vinaya (the disciplinary rules of the monastic community), and an undue emphasis on the ideal of private salvation. Dr. Har Dayal has herein located the source of the Bodhisattva ideal:

> They the monks became too self-centered and contemplative.... The Bodhisattva doctrine was promulgated by some Buddhist leaders as a protest against this lack of true spiritual fervor and altruism among the monks of that period.[1]

This suggests rather too narrow a view of the impulses behind the ideal. Leaving aside various historical exigencies, it can be said that the blossoming of the Bodhisattva conception, in one form or another, was inevitable. Frithjof Schuon has elaborated the "spiritual logic," so to speak, which made it so:

> As far as the Mahayanic ideal of the Bodhisattva is concerned . . . account must be taken of the following fundamental situation: Buddhism unfolds itself in a sense between the empirical notions of suffering and cessation of suffering; now the notion of compassion springs from this very fact, it is an inevitable or necessary link in what might be called the spiritual mythology of the Buddhism. To say suffering and cessation of suffering is to say compassion, given that man is not alone on earth.[2]

We are not here concerned with either the early Theravadin-Mahayanist disputes generated by the emergence of the Bodhisattva ideal except to say that some polemical excesses perhaps answered to certain necessities insofar as they were "defensive reflexes" to preserve

---

1 H. Dayal, *The Bodhisattva Doctrine in Buddhist Sanskrit Literature* (first published 1932) (New Delhi: Motilal Barnisidass, 1999), pp. 2-3.

2 F. Schuon, *Treasures of Buddhism* (Bangalore: Select Books, 1998), p. 113. See also D.T. Suzuki, *Essays in Zen Buddhism: Third Series* (London: Rider, 1970), p. 78.

or affirm the integrity of the spiritual outlook in question. Be that as it may, one is still exposed in the scholarly literature to certain over-simplifications which discolor any overview of the Buddhist tradition. Edward Conze, for instance, is guilty of the charge when he makes the following, quite astonishing claim

> The rationalist orthodoxy of Ceylon has a vision of Buddhism which is as truncated and impoverished as the fideism of Shinran, and it is no accident that they are both geographically located at the outer periphery of the Buddhist world.[3]

Such asseverations betoken a failure to grasp the principle that under the canopy of any great religious tradition there will inevitably emerge a variety of spiritual perspectives answering to different needs. Nor is it difficult to find many words wasted on the "selfishness" of the *arhat* ideal in the Theravada—another polemical abuse. Nothing need be added to Schuon's salutary remarks that

> [I]f there is in the Mahayana an element which calls for some cau-tion from a metaphysical point of view, it is not the path of the Bo-dhisattva but, what is quite different, the ideal of the Bodhisattva insofar as it is polemically opposed to the "non-altruistic" spiritual-ity of the pure contemplative, as if, firstly, all true spirituality did not necessarily include charity, and secondly, as if the consideration of some contingency or other could enter into competition with pure and total Knowledge.[4]

Finally, by way of introduction, it should be noted that the Bodhi-sattva conception is not exclusively Mahayanist. For all Buddhists the Buddha himself was a Bodhisattva before his final enlightenment. The Theravadin perspective generally restricts itself to this understanding of the term although the Sarvastivadins had elaborated a fairly full-bodied ideal before the time of the Mahayana.[5] The decisive contri-bution of the Mahayana was to "unfold to its furthest limits all that

3 E. Conze, *Thirty Years of Buddhist Studies: Selected Essays* (Oxford: Bruno Cassirer, 1967), p. 40.

4 F. Schuon, *Treasures of Buddhism*, p. 125.

5 See E. Conze, *Buddhism: Its Essence and Development* (New York: Harper & Row, 1959), pp. 125-126.

was to be found in the ideal,"[6] to give it its richest and most resonant expression.

The Bodhisattva Ideal and the Path to its Attainment

There is no shortage of either traditional accounts or scholarly explications of the Bodhisattva ideal and of the path to be followed by its adherents. Let us state the matter briefly. The Bodhisattva is one who voluntarily renounces the right to enter *nirvana*, who, under certain inextinguishable vows, undergoes countless rebirths in the samsaric realm in order to devote his/her energies, in a spirit of boundless compassion, to the deliverance of all beings down to "the last blade of grass." The Bodhisattva is committed to the practice of the six *paramitas* (perfections), particularly the all-encompassing ideal of *prajna* (wisdom). The Bodhisattva advanced on the path becomes an exemplar of sacrificial heroism and moral idealism as well as an aspirant to complete enlightenment.

What of the path? Firstly there is the awakening of the thought of enlightenment which matures into a decisive resolve to attain enlightenment for the benefit of all beings. After making the Great Resolves, entailing many vows, the Bodhisattva (for such he/she now is, although still on the early part of the path) perfects the six *paramitas* and progresses through ten *bhumis* (levels or stages). A crucial transformation takes place at the seventh *bhumi* by which stage the Bodhisattva has fully penetrated the nature of *shunyata* and has thus perfected the *paramita* of wisdom. The Bodhisattva is now "eligible" for entry into *nirvana* which has been perpetually renounced. However, the Bodhisattva now takes on the nature and functions of a celestial or transcendent figure and assumes a dharmic body—the *monomay-akaya*, a mind-made body of wonder-working powers whereby he/she can manifest anywhere, anytime. The Bodhisattva is now beyond the terrestrial limitations of time and space, and is free from all karmic determinations having entered a realm of pure, effortless, compassionate activity, of spiritual action undefiled by any of the contaminations of ignorance (dualistic notions, for instance). The Bodhisattva's compassionate wisdom (or, more strictly, wisdom-in-its-compassionate-aspect) is now a super-abundance and universal in its applications. On completion of the tenth and final *bhumi* the Bodhisattva becomes

6 D.T. Suzuki, *Essays in Zen Buddhism*, p. 79.

Tathagata, fully Perfect Being.[7]

The importance of the initial vows cannot be over-estimated. They take many different forms but are always variations on a theme, as it were. Here is one formulation which sounds the keynote of all the vows:

> I take upon myself . . . the deeds of all beings, even of those in the hells. . . . I take their suffering upon me. . . . I bear it, I do not draw back from it, I do not tremble at it, I do not lose heart. . . . I must bear the burden of all beings, for I have vowed to save all things living, to bring them safe through the forest of birth, age, disease, death, and rebirth. I think not of my own salvation, but strive to bestow on all beings the royalty of supreme wisdom. So I take upon myself all the sorrows of all beings. . . . Truly I will not abandon them. For I have resolved to gain supreme wisdom for the sake of all that lives, to save the world.[8]

The similarity to the sacrificial ideal incarnated in Christ is striking. We can also discern a parallel with Christian doctrine in the idea of the transference of suffering and of merit. This was a radical doctrinal innovation and was integral to the Mahayanist conception of both the Buddha and the Bodhisattva. Nevertheless, one must be wary of attempts to explain the Bodhisattva ideal in terms of "borrowings" from Christianity. The differences are no less striking. We note, for instance, the emphasis in the Buddhist vow on the attainment of wisdom which assumes a secondary place in the Christian perspective, addressed as it is primarily to man's affective and volitional nature.

The vows set before the Bodhisattva the goal for all time, and direct all spiritual development. Furthermore, and this point is fundamental in the Mahayana,

---

7 This adumbrated version of the ideal and the path is derived from several sources; it is an unexceptional account which follows the traditional sources. For a detailed discussion of the significance of the *Tathagata,* not canvassed in this article, see T.R.V. Murti, *The Central Philosophy of Buddhism: A Study of Madhyamika System* (London: Allen & Unwin, 1980). For a detailed account of the ten *bhumis* see N. Dutt, *Mahayana Buddhism* (Calcutta: Firma KLM, 1976), Chapters 4 & 5.

8 Taken from A.L. Basham, *The Wonder that was India: A Survey of the Indian Sub-Continent Before the Coming of the Muslims* (London: Collins Fontana, 1967), pp. 277-278. For an extended version of the Bodhisattva's vows see Santideva, *A Guide to the Bodhisattva Way of Life (Bodhisattvacharya-vatara),* trans. S. Batchelor (Dharamsala: Library of Tibetan Works & Archives, 1979), pp. 29-34.

Man becomes what he wills. . . . Spiritual realization is a growth from within, self-creative and self-determining. It is not too much to say that the nature of the resolve determines the nature of the final attainment.[9]

Lama Anagarika Govinda articulates the same principle when he writes

If . . . we take the view that consciousness is not a product of the world but that the world is a product of consciousness . . . it becomes obvious that we live in exactly the type of world we have created . . . and that the remedy cannot be an "escape" from the world but only a change of "mind." Such a change, however, can only take place if we know the innermost nature of this mind and its power.[10]

It is, of course, a change of "mind," a transformation of consciousness, that the Bodhisattva envisages in the original vows. The vows are reaffirmed during the ninth *bhumi* by which time they are no longer statements of intent but pure spiritual acts with incalculable effects.[11]

The six *paramitas* to be actualized in the Bodhisattva are charity (*dana*), morality (*sila*), forbearance (*kshanti*), vigor (*virya*), concentration (*samadhi*), and wisdom (*prajna*). In some schools these six *paramitas* are linked with the first six *bhumis*, the correspondence first being postulated by Chandrakirti in the *Madhyamakavatara*.[12] However, the practice of the six *paramitas* is simultaneous, all of them being informed by the all-embracing ideals of *karuna* and *prajna*. Indeed, the first five *paramitas* cannot be separated from *prajna* of which they are secondary aspects, each destined to contribute in their own way to the attainment of liberating knowledge.

---

9 T.R.V. Murti, *Central Philosophy of Buddhism*, pp. 266-267.

10 A. Govinda, *Foundations of Tibetan Mysticism: According to the Esoteric Teachings of the Great Mantra,* Om Mani Padme Hum (London: Rider, 1969), p. 274. This passage might suggest the Yogacarin view of "mind-only" but as Lama Govinda makes clear in the same work, this is not the intention of the passage above. For a similar statement but one protected by the appropriate qualifications see A. Govinda, *The Way of the White Clouds: A Buddhist Pilgrim in Tibet* (London: Rider, 1974), p. 123.

11 See E. Conze, *Thirty Years of Buddhist Studies*, pp. 42-43.

12 See T.R.V. Murti, *Central Philosophy of Buddhism*, p. 269.

During the early *bhumi*s the Bodhisattva's energies must be dedicated in the first place to the realization of *shunyata* without which the perfection of *prajna* is not possible. Recall the incident in the *Life of Milarepa* when the sage is asked by his disciples whether they should engage in an active life of good deeds. His reply:

> If there is not attachment to selfish aims, you can. But that is difficult. Those who are full of worldly desires can do nothing to help others. They do not even profit themselves. It is as if a man, carried away by a torrent, pretended to save others. Nobody can do anything for sentient beings without first attaining transcendent insight into Reality. Like the blind leading the blind, one would risk being carried away by desires. Because space is limitless and sentient beings innumerable, you will always have a chance to help others when you become capable of doing so. Until then, cultivate the aspiration toward Complete Enlightenment by loving others more than yourselves while practicing the Dharma.[13]

In considering the later stages of the Bodhisattva's spiritual trajectory we enter realms where any verbal articulation of the realities in question is problematic. Any formulation must be in the nature of a suggestive metaphor, a signpost. Much of the Mahayanist literature concerning this subject, especially in the Himalayan regions, resorts to a densely symbolic mythology and its accompanying iconography.[14]

The attainment of insight into *shunyata* makes possible the compassionate mission of the Bodhisattva, unhindered by dualistic misconceptions. Once in the seventh *bhumi*, with the assumption of the *monomayakaya*, the Bodhisattva can appear in manifold guises, each one appropriate to the spiritual necessities of the case. Thus the Bodhisattva can appear in forms fierce and gruesome as well as benign and attractive—as we see in the resplendent and sometimes startling iconography of the Vajrayana. Before reaching the seventh level the Bodhisattva remains in the phenomenal realm and his compassionate acts partake of "strain and strenuosity," but now the Bodhisattva leaves behind all terrestrial and karmic constraints and enters the realm of

---

13 L. Lhalungpa (trans.), *The Life of Milarepa* (New York: E.P. Dutton, 1977), p.171.

14 For an illuminating discussion of the often-misunderstood nature, in a traditional context, of both "symbol" and "myth," see essays on these subjects in K. Raine, *Defending Ancient Springs* (Cambridge: Golgonooza, 1985).

spontaneous, effortless, and pure spiritual action. The *Dasha-bhumika* explains the transition to effortlessness thus:

> It is like a man in a dream who finds himself drowning in a river; he musters all his courage and is determined at all costs to get out of it. And because of these efforts and desperate contrivances he is awakened from the dream and when thus awakened he at once perceives that no further doings are needed now. So with the Bodhisattva. . . .[15]

This does not mean that the Bodhisattva settles into quietistic inertia but rather that his/her being has been transformed into compassionate wisdom radiating through the universe. It might be compared to the Christian conception of God's love which is universal, non-discriminating, indifferent, making the sun to rise on the evil as well as the good, and sending rain on both the just and the unjust.[16] Murti speaks of the Bodhisattva being "actuated by motiveless altruism . . . his freedom is full and complete by itself; but he condescends to raise others to his level. This is a free phenomenalizing act of grace and compassion."[17]

If we return to Schuon's claim that the Bodhisattva ideal is implicit in the Buddhist vision which turns on the two poles of suffering and deliverance, we can now see more clearly what is meant by this claim. Schuon elaborates the claim in writing that the Bodhisattva

> incarnates the element of compassion—the ontological link as it were between pain and Felicity—just as the Buddha incarnates Felicity and just as ordinary beings incarnate suffering: he must be present in the cosmos as long as there is both a *samsara* and a *Nirvana*, this presence being expressed by the statement that the Bodhisattva wishes to save "all beings."[18]

The Bodhisattva Ideal and the Metaphysic of *Shunyata*

The Bodhisattva enterprise is oriented towards enlightenment, as the etymology of the term itself makes clear:

---

15 Quoted in D.T. Suzuki, *Essays in Zen Buddhism*, p. 225. See also H. Shurmann, *Buddhism: An Outline of Its Teaching and Schools* (London: Rider, 1973), pp. 112-113.

16 *Matthew* 5:45.

17 T.R.V. Murti, *Central Philosophy of Buddhism*, p. 263.

18 F. Schuon, *Treasures of Buddhism*, p. 113.

Prajna informs and inspires the entire spiritual discipline; every virtue and each act of concentration is dedicated to the gaining of insight into the real. The stress has shifted *viz.* earlier Buddhist practices from the moral to the metaphysical axis . . . all the other *paramitas* are meant to purify the mind and make it fit to receive the intuition of the absolute. It is *prajna* that can make of each of them a *paramita*—a perfection.[19]

We have already noted, in the cautions of Milarepa, the emphasis on *prajna*. Without the guidance of insight, would-be compassion is often no more than sentiment, all too easily conscripted by what Chögyam Trungpa has called "the bureaucracy of the ego" and turned, unwittingly, to destructive and futile ends.

In the Mahayanist perspective *karuna* (compassion) is inseparable from *prajna*—insight into *shunyata* which, for the moment, we can translate in conventional fashion as "emptiness" or "voidness." The relationship is stated by Milarepa in this characteristic formulation:

If ye realize Voidness, Compassion will arise within your hearts;
If ye lose all differentiation between yourself and others,
fit to serve others ye will be. . . .[20]

Karuna arises out of *prajna*. Compassion, at least in its full amplitude, cannot precede *prajna*; it is a function of *prajna*. On this point the Mahayanists are unyielding. As Herbert Guenther has pointed out, *karuna* means not only compassion but also action.[21] This anticipates the point at issue here: *karuna* is the action attending an awareness of *shunyata*. However, even this formulation implies a dualism not to be found in the reality itself. Compassion, it might be said, is the dynamic aspect of knowledge or awareness and as such, is a criterion of its authenticity. To recast this in moral terms more characteristic of the Occidental religious traditions we can say that virtue is integral to wisdom. As Schuon has remarked, "a wisdom without virtue is in fact

---

19 T.R.V. Murti, *Central Philosophy of Buddhism*, p. 267.

20 This translation is from W. Evans-Wentz (ed.), *Tibet's Great Yogi Milarepa: A Biography from the Tibetan*, trans. Kazi Dawa-Samdup (London: Oxford University Press, 1951), p. 273.

21 H.V. Guenther & C. Trungpa, *The Dawn of Tantra* (Berkeley: Shambhala, 1975), p. 31.

imposture and hypocrisy."[22] At this juncture an interesting comparison with Christianity arises. Buddhism insists that *karuna* without *prajna* is a contradiction in terms, a chimera, the blind leading the blind. Christianity, with its more bhaktic orientation, alerts us, in the first place, to the illusoriness of a wisdom bereft of *caritas*—a "sounding brass" or a "tinkling cymbal."[23] Ultimately, of course, the principle at stake is the same, but the different accents are illuminating.

In the Mahayana *karuna* and *prajna* come to be seen not only as inseparable but as identical: reference to one or the other signifies the same reality when viewed from a particular angle. The fully-fledged Bodhisattva is simultaneously fully enlightened and boundlessly compassionate. The compassionate aspect of the Bodhisattvas is stressed not because they are in any sense deficient in wisdom but because their cosmic function is to highlight and to radiate this dimension of wisdom-awareness. Ultimately *karuna* is identified not only with *prajna* but with *shunyata* itself. This is so because the duality of knower and known must be transcended. Further, because the universe itself is of the nature of *shunyata*, *karuna* also comes to be identified with the universe itself. Heinrich Zimmer put it this way:

> Within the hearts of all creatures compassion is present as the sign of their potential Bodhisattvahood; for all things are *shunyata*, the void—and the pure reflex of the void . . . is compassion. Compassion, indeed, is the force that holds things in manifestation—just as it withholds the Bodhisattva from *nirvana*. The whole universe, therefore, is *karuna*, compassion, which is also known as *shunyata*, the void.[24]

The same principle is approached from a different angle in this formulation:

> [T]he sapiential Mahayana intends to maintain its solidarity with the heroic ideal of the Bodhisattva, but by bringing it back to a strictly metaphysical perspective: it specifies that compassion is a dimension

22 F. Schuon, *Roots of the Human Condition* (Bloomington, IN: World Wisdom Books, 1991), p. 86.

23 *1 Corinthians* 12:1.

24 H. Zimmer, *Philosophies of India*, ed. J. Campbell (London: Routledge & Kegan Paul, 1951), p. 553.

of Knowledge, then it adds that the neighbor is non-real . . . there is no one whom our charity could concern, nor is there a charity which could be "ours."[25]

Now this, to say the least, is somewhat perplexing to the ratiocinative mind. There is no gainsaying the fact that, at least on the level of mundane experience and "common sense," we are here faced with several conundrums. What is the meaning of the Bodhisattva's mission in the face of *shunyata*? If all is "emptiness" is this much ado about nothing? Is the Bodhisattva's enterprise somewhat akin to the monkey trying to take hold of the moon in the water? What are we to make of such characteristic claims as "Where an attitude in which *shunyata* and *karuna* are indivisible is developed, there is the message of the Buddha, the *Dharma*, and the *Sangha*?"[26] And then too, we must ask, in what sense should we understand the Bodhisattva's refusal to enter *nirvana* until all beings are saved? How be it that an enlightened being is not thereby "in" *nirvana*? And what of the well-known formulation that "*Samsara* is *nirvana*," and vice versa, or, similarly, that "Form is void, Void is form?"

Such questions can only adequately be answered through an understanding of the term *upaya*, usually translated as "skilful means" but perhaps more adequately rendered as "provisional means which have a spiritually therapeutic effect" or, to use Schuon's more poetic term, "saving mirages." Buddhism is directed in the first place to our most urgent spiritual needs, the soteriological purpose everywhere informing and shaping the means of which the tradition avails itself. In other words, Buddhism, like all religious traditions, resorts to certain mythological and doctrinal "accommodations" which

> while objectively inadequate, are nonetheless logically appropriate for the religious axiom they serve and are justified by their effectiveness *pro domo* as well as by their indirect and symbolic truth.[27]

---

25 F. Schuon, *Treasures of Buddhism*, p. 110.

26 Quoted in H.V. Guenther & C. Trungpa, *The Dawn of Tantra*, p. 32.

27 F. Schuon, *Form and Substance in the Religions* (Bloomington, IN: World Wisdom, 2002), p. 4. See also F. Schuon, *Understanding Islam* (Bloomington, IN: World Wisdom Books, 1998), pp. 174ff.

Of course, Buddhism is not peculiar in dealing with "partial truths" in respect of its formal elements but the Madhyamika-based traditions have been conspicuously alert to the dangers of identifying Truth or Reality with any dogmatic or conceptual forms which can never be more than markers guiding the aspirant. Nagarjuna's whole dialectic (nearly two millennia before our own much vaunted post-modernists!) is directed towards demonstrating the inadequacy and self-contradiction of all mental and conceptual formulations. Indeed, the Mahayanists speak of Reality itself only in apparently negative terms reminiscent of the Upanisadic *neti neti*. Nevertheless, certain truths can be brought within the purview of the average mentality through "therapeutic errors." It is therefore important to make the necessary discriminations in considering myths and doctrines which might be situated on different levels and which may answer to varying spiritual needs and temperaments.

Clearly any adequate understanding of the Bodhisattva ideal rests on an understanding of *shunyata*. Unhappily the conventional English translations— "emptiness," "voidness"—often carry negative implications and associations which can only blur our understanding of *shunyata*. We cannot here recapitulate the Nagarjunian dialectic nor explore the ramifications of the doctrine of *shunyata*. However, it is useful to note Guenther's remark that "openness" is at least as helpful a pointer as "emptiness." In similar vein, Lama Govinda stresses that an understanding of *shunyata* heightens our awareness of the "transparency" of phenomena. *Shunyata*, he writes,

> is not a negative property but a state of freedom from impediments and limitations, a state of spontaneous receptivity. . . . [S]*hunyata* is the emptiness of all conceptual designations and at the same time the recognition of a higher, incommensurable, and indefinable reality which can only be experienced in the state of perfect enlightenment.[28]

The penetration of *shunyata* allows the Bodhisattva to experience the phenomenal realm as it actually is and not under the illusory aspects it assumes when experienced in a state of ignorance. Understanding *shunyata*, the Bodhisattva does not repudiate the world of

---

28 A. Govinda, *Creative Meditation and Multi-Dimensional Consciousness* (Wheaton, IL: Quest Books, 1976), p. 11. On the "transparency" of *shunyata* see also p. 51.

suffering beings as an utter non-reality; to do so would be to succumb to what the Mahayanists call *uccheddadarsanam*—i.e., a kind of nihilism. As D.T. Suzuki has pointed out,

> That the world is like a mirage, that it is thus empty, does not mean that it is unreal in the sense that it has no reality whatsoever. But it means that its real nature cannot be understood by a mind that cannot rise above the dualism of "to be" (*sat*) and "not to be" (*asat*).[29]

The Bodhisattva's *karuna* issues from the overcoming of this dualism. As one translation of the *Lankavatara Sutra* has it,

> The world transcends (the dualism of) birth and death, it is like the flower in the air; the wise are free from (the ideas of being and non-being); yet a great compassionate heart is awakened in them.[30]

The mission of the Bodhisattva, far from being "invalidated" by *shunyata*, actually derives from it. T.R.V. Murti has explicated this in commanding fashion, especially in the light of the *shunyata-prajna-karuna*-universe equation already discussed:

> *Shunyata* is *prajna*, intellectual intuition, and is identical with the Absolute. *Karuna* is the active principle of compassion that gives concrete expression to *shunyata* in phenomena. If the first is Transcendent and looks to the Absolute, the second is fully immanent and looks down towards phenomena. The first is the . . . universal reality of which no determinations can be predicated; it is beyond the duality of good and evil, love and hatred, virtue and vice; the second is goodness, love and pure act. . . . [T]he Bodhisattva . . . is thus an amphibious being with one foot in the Absolute and the other in phenomena.[31]

Prajna perceives the emptiness, openness, and indivisibility of the Absolute while *karuna* sees the diversity of the phenomenal realm. But these aspects of awareness are inseparable: the Bodhisattva is the living embodiment, the "personification" of this truth.

29 D.T. Suzuki, *Essays in Zen Buddhism*, p. 215.

30 Sung translation, quoted by D.T. Suzuki, *Essays in Zen Buddhism*, p. 215.

31 T.R.V. Murti, *Central Philosophy of Buddhism*, p. 264.

The Bodhisattva appreciates the lack of any self-existent reality in the phenomenal world and understands the impermanent and fugitive nature of all things within the world of time and space. Simultaneously the Bodhisattva takes account of the relative reality of manifested beings and thus sets out to eradicate evil on the samsaric plane and to help deliver all beings from the Round of Existence. In other words, the Bodhisattva experiences whatever measure of reality belongs to the phenomenal world while being immune to dualistic misconceptions and their karmic effects. "The Bodhisattva weeps with suffering beings and at the same time realizes that there is one who never weeps, being above sufferings, tribulations, and contaminations."[32] Because of his identification with all beings the Bodhisattva suffers; because of his wisdom he experiences the blissful awareness of the full plenitude of the Void.[33]

What of the Bodhisattva's "location" in *Samsara/nirvana*? In the Mahayanist literature we can find different formulations of the Bodhisattva's "whereabouts": he remains in *Samsara*; he is "on the brink" of *nirvana*; he is in *nirvana* because *nirvana* is *Samsara*. Here we are in a realm not amenable to factual exactitude and will only succeed in tightening the "mental knots" if we approach these expressions in the either/or mode of rationalist, analytical, and empiricist philosophy; rather, we need to understand the truths enshrined in these different formulations.

The first expression, as well as signaling various truths which we have already discussed, suggests that enlightenment is possible within the samsaric realm:

> The condition of the gnostic Bodhisattva would be neither conceivable nor tolerable if it were not a matter of contemplating the Absolute at once in the heart and in the world. . . .[34]

The second symbolizes the truth that time and eternity, phenomena and the Void, do not exist as independent opposites but are aspects

32 D.T. Suzuki, *Essays in Zen Buddhism*, pp. 229 & 216.

33 See M. Pallis, *The Way and the Mountain* (London: Peter Owen, 1960), p. 182. See also Pallis' remarks in a footnote on the parallels with the doctrine of the Two Natures of Christ.

34 F. Schuon, *Treasures of Buddhism*, p.119.

of the one reality, all of the nature of *shunyata*. The Bodhisattva is a link or axis that joins the apparently separate realms of the phenomenal, the celestial, and the metacosmic. (In this context the Bodhisattva conception is closely related to the doctrine of the *Trikaya*.) Thirdly, from the enlightened "point of view" the opposition between *Samsara* and *nirvana* is seen to be illusory, all dualities having been transcended in the light of the supreme unitive knowledge. Thus there can be no question of the Bodhisattva being either "here" or "there."

When the *Prajnaparamita Sutra* and other scriptures tell us that "Form is void and Void is form" this must be understood in the sense of what *is* before we project our conceptualizations and designations onto it. The formulation cannot be fully understood independently of the intuition of *shunyata*. Once the liberative knowledge has been attained then, and then only, will the duality of *Samsara* and *nirvana* disappear. Thus the *Lankavatara Sutra* speaks in one and the same breath of the Bodhisattva both being and not being "in" *nirvana*:

> The Bodhisattvas, O Mahatmi, who rejoice in the bliss of the *samadhi* of cessation are well furnished with the original vows and the pitying heart, and realizing the import of the inextinguishable vows, do not enter *nirvana*. They are already in *nirvana* because their views are not at all beclouded by discrimination.[35]

Many of these considerations are synthesized in a magisterial passage by Frithjof Schuon:

> If the Bodhisattva is supposed to "refuse entry into *Nirvana* so long as a single blade of grass remains undelivered," this means two things: firstly—and this is the cosmic viewpoint—that the function of the Bodhisattva coincides with what in Western language may be termed the permanent "angelic presence" in the world, a presence which disappears only with the world itself at the final reintegration, the "Apocatastasis"; secondly—and this is the metaphysical viewpoint—it means that the Bodhisattva, realizing the "emptiness" of things, thereby also realizes the "emptiness" of the *samsara* as such and at the same time its nirvanic quality . . . expressed in the sentence "Form is void and Void is form." The *samsara*, which seems at first

35 *The Lankavatara Sutra: A Mahayana Text*, trans. D.T. Suzuki (London: Routledge & Kegan Paul, 1973), p. 184.

to be inexhaustible, so that the Bodhisattva's vow appears to have something excessive or even demented about it, becomes "instantly" reduced—in the non-temporal instaneity of *prajna*—to "universal Enlightenment" (*Sambodhi*); on this plane, every antinomy is transcended and as it were consumed. "Delivering the last blade of grass" amounts, in this sense, to seeing it in its nirvanic essence or to seeing the unreality of its non-deliverance.[36]

The Bodhisattva and the Buddha(s)

In keeping with its cosmic perspective, the Mahayana, unlike the Theravadin tradition, sees the Buddha as the embodiment of a spiritual principle, one who "acted out" his life for the benefit of all sentient beings still lost in the "forest of birth, disease, old age, death, and rebirth," his own enlightenment, in the words of the *Saddharmapundarika Sutra*, having been attained "inconceivable thousands of millions of world ages" ago.[37]

The Theravadins had recognized three ultimate spiritual possibilities: Self-Buddhas (*Paccekabuddha*), the perfected saint (*arhat*), and the Complete Perfect Buddha (*Sammasambuddha*). The *arhat* ideal occupied the pivotal position, it being the possibility open to the ordinary human being who was prepared to tread the path mapped by Shakyamuni. This ideal rested on an austere monastic asceticism. The Mahayana, on the other hand, established the Perfect Buddha as an ideal whose realization was open to all and equated it with the aspirations of the Bodhisattva. It also elaborated a conception of a host of transcendent Buddhas and celestial Buddha-Lands—Pure Lands or Paradises, of which Amitabha's Western Paradise has been, historically, the most important. The celestial Buddhas and Paradises, as well as the Bodhisattvic figures such as Avalokiteshvara, Manjushri, Vajrapani, and Tara, have played a particularly important part in the iconography of the Tibeto-Himalayan branches of the Mahayana.

The most significant Mahayanist distinction between the Buddha and the Bodhisattva is not determined by "degrees" of enlightenment but by function. That of the Bodhisattva is a dynamic and salvatory one implying a perpetual "descent" into *Samsara* (thus recalling the Hindu

36 F. Schuon, *Treasures of Buddhism*, p. 139.

37 *Saddharmapundarika Sutra* ("Lotus of the Good Law" *Sutra*), cited in H. Shurmann, *Buddhism: An Outline of Its Teaching and Schools*, p. 99.

conception of the *avatar*). From one point of view it might be said that "the Buddha represents the contemplative aspect and the Bodhisattva the dynamic aspect of *nirvana*," or that "the former is turned towards the Absolute and the latter towards contingency."[38] As the Bodhisattva and the Buddha are of the same nature there is no rigid distinction between them but a subtle relationship which appears in changing guises under different lights. It is said in the *Lankavatara Sutra*, for instance, that the Bodhisattvas are incapable of reaching their final goal without the "other-power" (*adhishthana*) of the Buddha, without his all-pervading power.[39] However, it is also sometimes said in the Mahayanist texts that it is by virtue of the compassion of the Bodhisattva that the Buddhas come into the world. In the *Saddharmapundarika Sutra*, for instance, we find this: "From the Buddhas arises only the disciples and the *Pratyekabuddhas* but from the Bodhisattva the perfect Buddha himself is born."[40]

Self-Power, Other-Power, and the Bodhisattva

The question of self-power and other-power has fuelled a good deal of reckless polemic within nearly all of the major religious traditions. Buddhism is no exception. Edward Conze has remarked that the ineffable reality of salvation can be viewed from three distinct vantage points: (a) as the product of self-striving under the guidance of an infallible teacher, (b) as the work of an external and personified agent accepted in faith, and (c) as the doing of the Absolute itself. From a metaphysical point of view doubtless the third represents the least restricted outlook. However, the relative merits of these perspectives are not at issue here; rather we must consider this question in the context of our primary concern, the Mahayanist understanding of the Bodhisattva.

The Theravadins, by and large hold to the first of these views. Take this from an eminent contemporary Theravadin:

[M]an has the power to liberate himself from all bondage through his own personal effort and intelligence. . . . If the Buddha is to be

38 F. Schuon, *Treasures of Buddhism*, p. 133.

39 See D.T. Suzuki, *Essays in Zen Buddhism*, pp. 202-205.

40 See *Tattvasamgraha*, in H. Zimmer, *Philosophies of India*, p. 552. For discussion of some recent scholarly debate about the relationship of the Bodhisattvas and Buddhas see P. Williams, *Mahayana Buddhism: The Doctrinal Foundations* (London: Routledge, 1989), pp. 204-214.

called a "savior" at all, it is only in the sense that he discovered and showed the path to Liberation, *Nirvana*. But we must tread the path ourselves. . . . [A]ccording to the Buddha, man's emancipation depends on his own realization of the Truth, and not on the benevolent grace of a god or any external power. . . .[41]

In the Mahayana we find a less monolithic attitude. The Zen schools, in the main, also emphasize self-power (*jiriki*) rather than other-power (*tariki*) while the Jodo and Shin branches of Buddhism place overwhelming importance on both faith and grace.[42] Taken overall the Mahayana encompasses all the points of view posited above. The precise way in which the saving power of the Buddha(s) and Bodhisattvas is envisaged varies according to the prevailing spiritual climate and the proclivities of the peoples in question. However, the Bodhisattva conception can provide a meeting-place for the truths which underlie the different attitudes under discussion. Lama Govinda, by way of example, pays due respect to both the "other-power" of the Bodhisattva and the "self-power" of the aspirant which, so to speak, "collaborate:"

> The help of a Bodhisattva is not something that comes from outside or is pressed upon those who are helped, but is the awakening of a force which dwells in the innermost nature of every being, a force which, awakened by the spiritual influence or example of a Bodhisattva, enables us to meet fearlessly every situation. . . .[43]

Before leaving this question we might profitably remind ourselves of a general point made by Frithjof Schuon:

> All great spiritual experiences agree in this: there is no common measure between the means put into operation and the result. "With men this is impossible, but with God all things are possible," says the Gospel. In fact, what separates man from divine Reality is the slightest of barriers: God is infinitely close to man, but man is infinitely far from God. This barrier, for man, is a mountain: man stands in front

41 W. Rahula, *What the Buddha Taught* (London: Gordon Fraser, 1978), pp. 1-2.

42 For a salutary corrective to overheated polemics on this subject see M. Pallis, *A Buddhist Spectrum: Contributions to Buddhist-Christian Dialogue* (London: Allen & Unwin, 1980), pp. 52-71.

43 A. Govinda, *Foundations of Tibetan Mysticism*, p. 233.

of a mountain which he must remove with his own hands. He digs away the earth, but in vain, the mountain remains; man however goes on digging, in the name of God. And the mountain vanishes. It was never there.[44]

Despite its theistic vocabulary this has a certain Buddhist resonance and recalls the man drowning in the river. The multivalent spirituality of the Mahayana certainly takes full account of the spiritual possibilities latent in the principle.

No doubt Buddhism as a whole is founded upon "self-power" but since "other-power" is a spiritually efficacious possibility it was bound to appear somewhere within the orbit of the tradition. In the Tibeto-Himalayan area, where the Bodhisattva ideal is pre-eminent, we find a happy and judicious blend of the two elements. In the everyday life of the common people there was unquestionably a great deal of emphasis on the miraculous effects flowing from a faithful devotion to the Buddha and the Bodhisattvas. As Conze has observed, the Madhyamika dialectic and the doctrine of *shunyata* has exercised a potent appeal for Buddhists of a "jnanic" disposition. However, the popular appeal of the Mahayana is, in good measure, to be explained by the "spiritual magnetism" of the Bodhisattva ideal which could "stir the hearts of all" and provide "the basis for immediate action."[45] Furthermore, the Bodhisattva ideal helped introduce into Buddhism a more explicitly religious element, particularly through bhaktic practices, as well as a cosmic perspective without which Buddhism might easily have degenerated into what Murti calls "an exalted moral naturalism."[46] In the popular teachings much is made of the unlimited merits and "boundless treasury of virtues" (*gunasambhava*) of the Bodhisattvas. It is worth noting that the three principal virtues—Merit, Compassion, Wisdom—correspond analogically with the paths of *karma-yoga*, *bhakti-yoga*, and *jnana-yoga* in the Hindu tradition.[47] The Bodhisattva ideal also provided fertile ground for the flowering of Buddhist mythology and ico-

---

44 F. Schuon, *Stations of Wisdom* (London: John Murray, 1961), p. 157.

45 E. Conze, *Thirty Years of Buddhist Studies*, p. 54.

46 T.R.V. Murti, *Central Philosophy of Buddhism*, p. 263. On the place of the Bodhisattvas in devotional practices see P. Williams, *Mahayana Buddhism*, pp. 215-276.

47 F. Schuon, *Treasures of Buddhism*, p. 117. See also H. Zimmer, *Philosophies of India*, p. 535.

nography, particularly in the Vajrayana and in the Far East where the cult of Kuan-Yin remains pervasive to this day.[48]

Conclusion

The Bodhisattva ideal has been of incalculable importance in the Mahayana, although it has not everywhere received the same emphasis. It gathered together in a vivid, living ideal the principles of *prajna* and *karuna* and tied them firmly to the metaphysic of *shunyata*. The conception found its most luxuriant expression in the Vajrayana where it played an integrative role for many different aspects of Buddhist teaching and practice. On the popular level the Bodhisattva provided an exemplar of the spiritual life and a devotional focus. Cosmologically, the Bodhisattva was an axial figure running through terrestrial, celestial, and transcendental realms. Metaphysically considered the Bodhisattva conception, rooted in the doctrine of *shunyata*, provided a resolution of dualistic conceptions of *Samsara* and *nirvana* and provided a bridge between the Absolute and the relative. In its reconciliation of all these elements in the Bodhisattva Mahayana Buddhism finds one of its most characteristic and elevated expressions. Let us leave the final word with Saraha, reputedly the teacher of the Mahayana's greatest metaphysician, Nagarjuna:

> He who clings to the Void
> And neglects Compassion
> Does not reach the highest stage.
> But he who practices only Compassion
> Does not gain release from the toils of existence.
> He, however, who is strong in the practice of both,
> Remains neither in *Samsara* nor in *Nirvana*.[49]

---

48 See J. Blofeld, *Bodhisattva of Compassion: The Mystical Tradition of Kuan Yin* (Boston: Shambhala, 1977).

49 From Saraha, *Treasury of Songs*, quoted in W. Perry (ed.), *A Treasury of Traditional Wisdom* (London: Allen & Unwin, 1971), p. 607

CHAPTER 5

"Grass Upon the Hills":
Traditional and Modern Attitudes to Biography

Put on the mantle of nothingness,
and drink of the cup of annihilation,
then cover your breast with the belt of belittlement
and put on your head the cloak of non-existence.

Attar[1]

In a traditional civilization, it is almost inconceivable that a man
should lay claim to the possession of an idea.

René Guénon[2]

All that is true, by whomsoever spoken, is from the Holy Ghost.

St. Ambrose[3]

In Porphyry's *Life of Plotinus* we are told that the sage resisted all attempts to unravel his personal history:

[H]e could never be induced to tell of his ancestry, his parentage, or
his birthplace. He showed too, an unconquerable reluctance to sit to
a painter or a sculptor, and when Amelius persisted in urging him
to allow of a portrait being made he asked him, "Is it not enough to
carry about this image in which nature has enclosed us? Do you really think I must consent to leave, as a desirable spectacle to posterity, an image of the image?"[4]

---

1 Farid Ud-Din Attar, *The Conference of the Birds*, ed. & trans. C.S. Nott (Boulder: Shambhala, 1971), pp. 124-125. I have substituted the words "mantle" and "cloak" for Nott's "khirk" and "burnous."

2 R. Guénon, *The Crisis of the Modern World* (London: Luzac, 1975), pp. 52-53.

3 St. Ambrose quoted in Letter to *The New English Weekly*, January 1946, in A.K. Coomaraswamy, *Selected Letters of Ananda K. Coomaraswamy*, ed. R.P. Coomaraswamy & A. Moore Jr. (New Delhi: Oxford University Press, 1988), p. 108.

4 Porphyry's "On the Life of Plotinus" in Plotinus, *The Enneads*, trans. S. MacKenna (London: Faber, 1960), p. 1.

The episode is instructive. We see in this anecdote not only an attitude everywhere to be found amongst the wise and the pious but also, at least implicitly, the principle which informs it: the outer person, the egoic self with all its attendant contingencies, is of no lasting significance; it is only the Inner Self which matters and which is not a mere "image." An aversion to any preoccupation with purely personal and temporal considerations is, of course, a characteristic mark of the mystic. It is sometimes thought that a predilection for anonymity and self-effacement is "Eastern" or "oriental." The simple fact is that such an attitude is common amongst those of high spiritual attainment wherever they be found. But

> to an age which believes in personality and personalism, the impersonality of the mystics is baffling; and to an age which is trying to quicken its insight into history the indifference of mystics to events in time is disconcerting.[5]

Between the spiritual posture exemplified by Plotinus and the modern European mania for biographical anecdotage lies a veritable abyss. This is not the place for a detailed inquiry into the development of that voracious appetite for all manner of biographical literature. However, a few general remarks will serve as a backdrop against which to sketch out the traditional attitude.

One of the most potent factors affecting the history of the modern world has been a humanistic individualism, the seeds of which were germinated in the Renaissance. The erosion of traditional Christian values by the Renaissance, the Scientific Revolution, the so-called Enlightenment, and the materialist ideologies of the nineteenth century has been matched by a corresponding growth of a secularist worldview which has helped to promote what can properly be called a pseudo-cult of individualism. Several other developments have also stimulated an interest in mundane biography. Historicism in its various guises (Marxism, for instance) has sharpened our awareness of "events in time" and emphasized the influence of our social environment. More recently psychologism—so called because its practitioners are more often than not dealing in a kind of ideology—has focused attention on the apparently unique experience of each individual person.

---

5 A reviewer in *The Harvard Divinity School Bulletin* XXXIX, 1942, p. 107.

European thought since the Renaissance has also been increasingly dominated by a despotic scientism, one bereft of any metaphysical basis and operating outside the framework of religious tradition.
The impact of this scientism, conspiring with the ideologies of industrial capitalism, has done nothing to check the rise of secular humanism and individualism—quite the contrary. The implications of these
changes in the European ethos have been profound and far-reaching.
They have everything to do with the modern fascination with biography.

Part and parcel of this intellectual and cultural change is the triumph of empiricism and of a wholesale philosophical relativism. All
phenomena are reduced to a level where they can be investigated empirically and are situated on the plane of the "natural" or the "cultural."
This trend is writ large over the pages of Europe's recent history, evi-
denced by such characteristically modern systems of thought as philosophical rationalism, positivism, dialectical materialism, existentialism, and the like. We can see a somewhat paradoxical expression of it
in Enlightenment theories of "natural religion." A recurrent set of assumptions about "reality," "human nature," and "knowledge," embedded in this ideational network, has infiltrated almost every academic
discipline and shaped our modern modes of inquiry. Scientistic reductionism pervades comparative religion as much as any of the other disciplines that have been herded together as "social sciences": the term
itself exposes the kinds of assumptions under discussion. The interest in biography is intertwined with these changes in the European
mentality and is linked with the habit of mind which might be called
the "relativizing impulse." In the biographical field this appears as the
tendency to see whatever a person thinks or believes as no more than
a function of social background and personal experience. Whilst this
has often been a healthy corrective to culture-bound and ethnocentric
views of "reality" and "normality," it has also seduced many minds into
an all-embracing relativism. In castigating this outlook Schuon has
written that it "will not ask whether it is true that two and two make
four but from what social background the man has come who declares
such to be the case. . . ."[6] In other words, questions about a more or less
accidental background take precedence over questions of truth and

---

6 F. Schuon, *Logic and Transcendence: A New Translation with Selected Letters* (Bloomington, IN: World Wisdom, 2009), p. 6.

falsity. Once the objective nature of truth is compromised and everything is seen through the spectacles of relativism, then, of course, such a tendency becomes inevitable.

Psychologism is one of the components of this relativism which has now penetrated the European mentality to such an extent that it is more or less "invisible," so much is it taken for granted. The interest in biography has been consolidated by a psychologistic outlook which is less interested in *what* a person believes than in *why* they believe it. One of the symptoms of a rampant psychologism is what has been called the "psycho-genetic fallacy," namely, the belief that to explain the psychological motivation for an idea is to explain the idea itself. Some thinkers make the even graver error of supposing that if an idea or belief correlates with some "subconscious wish" then, *ipso facto*, this invalidates the idea as such. However, as Erich Fromm points out, "Freud himself states that the fact that an idea satisfies a wish does not mean necessarily that the idea is false. . . . The criteria of validity does [sic] not lie in the psychological analysis of motivation. . . ."[7] No one will deny that there is an intimate nexus between a person's spatio-temporal situation and his or her beliefs, attitudes, values, ideas, and so on. Most of us are creatures of our environment, mentally as well as in other ways. The issue at stake here is this: is this *all* we are? The traditional attitude to biography suggests a resoundingly negative response to this kind of question. However, before turning to earlier understandings we should remind ourselves of another trend in modern European thought.

There are those people who, it seems, "invent" or "discover" "new" ideas—Newton, Darwin, Freud, or Einstein, to name a few from the "pantheon" of modern science. Similarly in the world of the arts: Michelangelo, or Beethoven, or Tolstoy, we are told, was a creative "genius," a special kind of individual. What so impresses us about such figures is that they seem to have fashioned, out of their own subjective resources, some new idea, some original art form, some fresh and startling perception of the world. Our adulation of such figures is fuelled by a passion for what is, often improperly, called "originality" ("novelty" would usually be more apt). There is no gainsaying the fact that the subjective resources, of, say, a Michelangelo were prodigious. It is the emphasis on subjectivity which is interesting and revealing.

---

7 E. Fromm, *Psychoanalysis and Religion* (London: Victor Gollancz, 1951), p. 20fn.

As Coomaraswamy remarked, "Individualists and humanists as we are, we attach an inordinate value to personal opinion and personal experience, and feel an insatiable interest in the personal experience of others."[8] Thus we tend to identify an idea or an art-form with the personality which apparently first gave it expression. This tendency issues from a humanistic individualism and has come to color the way in which we understand "ideas." It is certainly no accident that the very notion of "genius" (certainly in the sense in which it is now understood) is largely a product of Renaissance humanism. Again, there are links with the interest in biography.

The cultural pedigree of this web of ideas and values which we have signaled in short-hand by terms like "individualism," "humanism," and "scientism" need not concern us here. At present the point is simply this: the interest in biography has grown in a distinctive climate of ideas. There is, on the other hand, an attitude to biography quite at odds with some of these trends—the attitude evinced by Plotinus. Before turning to some of the principles which sponsor a distaste for biography, a personal reminiscence might not be out of place.

Some years ago a friend had the privilege of looking after a Tibetan lama and of introducing him to a culture which, to him, was strange indeed. One of the phenomena which most astonished the lama was the European interest in biography. He was amazed to learn that quite ordinary people should write about their own lives and those of others, and that there should be a sizeable market for such personal histories. For him the only biography which could be of any possible value or interest was the life of a saint or sage, an exemplary life rather than one made up of the "paraphernalia of irrelevant living."[9] Coming from what was until recently one of the last bastions of an authentic traditional culture, the lama was expressing a point of view which nowhere would have seemed idiosyncratic until modern times.

*

When pressed to write his autobiography Ananda Coomaraswamy, the great art historian and perennial philosopher, replied:

8 A.K. Coomaraswamy, *Christian and Oriental Philosophy of Art* (New York: Dover, 1956), pp. 61-62.

9 The phrase is borrowed from Patrick White's novel *The Twyborn Affair* (London: Jonathan Cape, 1979), p. 386.

I must explain that I am not at all interested in biographical matter relating to myself and that I consider the modern practice of publishing details about the lives and personalities of well-known men is nothing but a vulgar catering to illegitimate curiosity. . . . All this is not a matter of "modesty" but of principle.[10]

It was the same principle which left Coomaraswamy indifferent to the question of copyright in his own works.[11] Plotinus has already introduced us to the principle at hand: the plane of the individual human ego, of the conditioned, subjective personality and of its doings in the world, is the plane of *maya*, of ephemerality and flux, of impermanence. Insofar as a person is no more than a "product" of this environment, they are as nothing in the face of Reality. Likewise, any ideas, or for that matter any art, which grows out of purely subjective and conditioned resources are of no lasting moment. The highest and most urgent purpose of life is to free oneself from the limiting contingencies of one's spatio-temporal situation and from the fetters of the ego, to liberate one's Self from one's self, so to speak, or as Coomaraswamy put it, to become no one.

In one form or another this lies close to the heart of all the great religious teachings. As R.D. Laing observed:

In fact all religious . . . philosophies have agreed that such egoic experience is a preliminary illusion, a veil, a film of *maya*—a dream to Heraclitus, and to Lao-Tzu, the fundamental illusion of all Buddhism, a state of sleep, of death, of socially accepted madness, a womb state to which one has to die, from which one has to be born.[12]

Such is precisely the point of Christ's teaching about the corn of wheat,[13]

10 A.K. Coomaraswamy, Letter to S.D.R. Singam, May 1946, in *Selected Letters*, p. 25.

11 See comments by Doña Luisa Coomaraswamy quoted in W. Perry, "The Man and the Witness" in *Ananda Coomaraswamy: Remembering and Remembering Again and Again*, ed. S.D.R. Singam (Kuala Lumpur: privately published, 1974), p. 6; see also N. Krsnamurti, "Ananda Coomaraswamy" in the same volume, p. 172, and W. Perry, "Coomaraswamy: The Man, Myth and History," *Studies in Comparative Religion*, 11:3, 1977, p. 160.

12 R.D. Laing *The Politics of Experience* (Harmondsworth: Penguin, 1967), p. 113.

13 *John* 12:24-25.

of the Prophet's "Die before ye die,"[14] and of an inexhaustible wealth of spiritual maxims of like intent from all over the world. Black Elk, the revered Sioux holy-man, espoused the same principle when he said, in the inimitable idiom of the Plains Indians,

> [W]hat is one man that he should make much of his winters, even when they bend him like a heavy snow? So many other men have lived and shall live that story, to be grass upon the hills.[15]

The lack of historically accurate biographies of the great saints and sages, especially in the East, has sometimes been regretted by scholars. Often we hear talk about "a lack of a sense of history." This is to see the issue only in negative terms. Frithjof Schuon has commented on this question with reference to two of the great Eastern traditions:

> What characterizes Buddhism—as also Hinduism *a fortiori*—is precisely that it likes to express . . . its consciousness of the "mythological" character of all formal data; and that is why it hardly bothers to give its symbols any semblance of historicity, indeed quite the contrary: it is intent on awakening a presentiment of the great rending of the veil and on suggesting in advance that facts themselves are but "emptiness."[16]

We cannot plumb the depths of the philosophical and metaphysical issues involved here but the contrast with the modern European obsession with history is marked enough.[17] From a traditionalist point of view this obsession with history and the vogue of private biography are nothing other than symptoms of disproportion in the modern outlook, especially when these are pursued, as they usually are, in the context of profane scholarship. They signify a preoccupation with the worldly and

14 Quoted in M. Lings, *A Sufi Saint of the Twentieth Century: Shaikh Ahmad al-'Alawi: His Spiritual Heritage and Legacy* (Berkeley: University of California Press, 1971), p. 160.

15 J.G. Neihardt (ed.), *Black Elk Speaks: Being the Life Story of a Holy Man of the Oglala Sioux* (London: Abacus, 1974), p. 13.

16 F. Schuon, *Treasures of Buddhism* (Bangalore: Select Books, 1998), p. 205.

17 For some discussion of the traditional Indian attitude to biography see Swami Tapasyananda's Introduction to Madhava-Vidyaranya's *Sankara Digvijaya: The Traditional Life of Sri Sankaracharya* (Madras: Ramakrishna Math, 1978).

ephemeral, and an indifference to ultimate ends. (The emphasis on a sacred history, as in the Judaic tradition, is another matter altogether.)

Closely associated with this stance is another principle of crucial importance. It concerns the nature of "ideas," of "truth," and of our relationship to truth. The great French metaphysician, René Guénon, stated the principle in striking and unequivocal terms:

> [I]f an idea is true it belongs equally to all those capable of under-standing it; if it is false there is no reason to be proud of having thought it. A true idea cannot be "new," since truth is not a product of the human mind; the truth exists independently of ourselves, and it is for us simply to comprehend it; outside of this knowledge there can be nothing but error. . . .[18]

Here Guénon is speaking, of course, of the principial domain and not of the realm of material exactitudes. In one of his early books Frithjof Schuon remarked that, "it will be useless to look for anything 'pro-foundly human' in this book . . . for the simple reason that nothing human is profound."[19] He was re-stating the same principle.

The notion of the independence and non-personal nature of truth is nothing new, being repeatedly affirmed within the religious tradi-tions. Something of the traditionalist attitude to truth is anticipated in a passage such as this, from an early Buddhist Scripture:

> Whether Buddhas arise, O monks, or whether Buddhas do not arise, it remains a fact and the fixed and necessary constitution of being, that all its constituents are transitory. This fact a Buddha discovers and masters, and when he has discovered and mastered it, he an-nounces, teaches, publishes, proclaims, discloses, minutely explains, and makes it clear.[20]

We might compare this with the following passage from Cooma-raswamy:

18 R. Guénon, *Crisis of the Modern World*, p. 53.

19 F. Schuon, *The Transcendent Unity of Religions* (London: Faber, 1953), p. 15. This passage was omitted from later editions.

20 From *Anguttara Nikaya* III.134. Can one imagine the Buddha claiming that this ideas was "his"? The notion is absurd.

There can be no property in ideas. The individual does not make them but *finds them*; let him see to it that he really takes possession of them, and work will be original in the same sense that the recurrent seasons, sunset and sunrise are ever anew although in name the same.[21]

This is the only kind of "originality" in which the traditionalists are interested.

The traditionalist disposition is also governed by certain moral and spiritual values, humility not the least of them. We might profitably pause to ponder the implications of a more or less random sample of maxims which affirm another one of the principles informing the traditionalist tendency to self-effacement.

A man may receive nothing except it be given him from heaven. (*St. John*)[22]

[N]o creature, howsoever rational and intellectual, is lighted of itself, but is lighted by the participation of eternal Truth. (*St. Augustine*)[23]

Outward existence can perform no act of itself; its acts are those of its Lord immanent in it. (*Ibn Arabi*)[24]

[N]o good thing can be done by man alone. . . . (*Black Elk*)[25]

Nothing could be further from the spirit of a humanistic individualism. We are free to take such teachings seriously or not, but in their light one begins to understand the moral dimension of the practice of anonymity in the eyes of the world. What Coomaraswamy called "the

---

21 Quoted in N. Krsnamurti, "Ananda Coomaraswamy," p. 172. On his own role Coomaraswamy wrote, "I regard the truth . . . as a matter of certainty, not of opinion. I am never expressing an opinion or any personal view, but an orthodox one" (letter to George Sarton, November 1934, in *Selected Letters*, p. 31).

22 *John* 3:27.

23 Augustine quoted in W. Perry (ed.), *A Treasury of Traditional Wisdom* (London: Allen & Unwin, 1971), p. 276.

24 Ibn Arabi quoted in W. Perry (ed.), *A Treasury of Traditional Wisdom*, p. 341.

25 J.G. Neihardt (ed.), *Black Elk Speaks*, p. 13.

invisibility proper to the complete philosopher"[26] is anchored in the virtue of humility, one which Schuon describes as "as a state of emptiness in which our thoughts and actions appear foreign to us."[27]

Today the traditionalist posture—the distaste for personal biography, the affirmation of the non-personal nature of truth, the immunity to self-publicizing, the refusal to identity ideas as one's "own"—is less than common. Nevertheless there remain those who resist all attempts to identify the ideas to which they give expression with themselves as individual persons, refusing to participate in a kind of "capitalism" of ideas where these are seen as the "creation" and "property" of this or that thinker. (The copyright laws are, after all, not so different from those regulating patents!) Sarvepalli Radhakrishnan, explaining to his editor his reluctance to make public details of his private life, wrote, "there is a sense in which our writings, though born out of ourselves, are worth more than what we are."[28] Thomas Merton disclaimed any "originality" in his work, writing of one of his books, "We sincerely hope that it does not contain a line that is new to Christian tradition."[29] These remarks share something with the traditionalist position.

Traditionalists like Guénon and Coomaraswamy were quite unconcerned with any aspiration towards a personal "creativity" or "originality" in the sense in which the words are now usually understood. Their purpose was the re-expression of the *sophia perennis*, the timeless wisdom which is everywhere and always the same but which, according to the exigencies of the age, can be expressed anew in such a way as to bring humankind back to the truths it enshrines and the spiritual path which its realization entails.

We can see, then, that this attitude to biography is only one thread in a whole fabric of ideas and values. It is interwoven with principles and values concerning the nature of the human situation, truth, knowledge, the role of ideas, and the traditionalists' view of their own function as writers. Any kind of "intellectual individualism," if one might so put it, is out of the question. Thus Coomaraswamy, for instance,

---

26 Coomaraswamy in S.D.R. Singam (ed.), *Ananda Coomaraswamy*, p. 223.

27 F. Schuon, *Spiritual Perspectives and Human Facts: A New Translation with Selected Letters* (Bloomington, IN: World Wisdom, 2007), p. 212.

28 Letter to P.A. Schilpp, reproduced in *The Philosophy of Sarvepalli Radhakrishnan*, ed. P.A. Schilpp (New York: Tudor, 1972), p. 4.

29 T. Merton, *New Seeds of Contemplation* (New York: New Directions), 1972, p. xiv.

abjures any suggestion that he is propounding his own ideas:

> I am not a reformer or propagandist. I don't "think for myself". . . .
> I am not putting forward any new or private doctrines or interpre-
> tations. . . . For me, there are certain axioms, principles, or values
> beyond question; my interest is not in thinking up new ones, but in
> the application of these that are.[30]

In other words, it is a matter of being a vehicle for the expression of
ideas which belong to everyone and therefore to no one.

---

30 A.K. Coomaraswamy, Letter to Herman Goetz, January 1947, in *Selected Letters*, p.
33. See also his remarks in "The Seventieth Birthday Address": "[T]he greatest thing I
have learned is never to think for myself . . . what I have sought is to understand what
has been said, while taking no account of the 'inferior philosophers'" (*Coomaraswamy
2: Selected Papers, Metaphysics*, ed. R. Lipsey [Princeton: Princeton University Press,
1977], p. 434).

CHAPTER 6

Joseph Epes Brown's
The Spiritual Legacy of the American Indian

Joseph Epes Brown's *The Spiritual Legacy of the American Indian* first appeared in 1982, some thirty years after *The Sacred Pipe: Black Elk's Account of the Seven Rites of the Oglala Sioux*, the two being Brown's most salient contributions to our understanding not only of the ritual life of the Oglala but of the spiritual heritage of the Plains Indians at large. These two volumes, along with John Neihardt's *Black Elk Speaks* (first published 1932), and Frithjof Schuon's *The Feathered Sun* (1990), provide the foundations for a properly-constituted understanding of these subjects, one surpassing anything to be found in the anthropological and scholarly literature. However, one must acknowledge the work of several comparative religionists who, less inhibited by the materialistic/functionalistic assumptions which tyrannize much anthropological research and more attuned to the realm of the sacred, have been able to give us much more adequate interpretations of the religious life of the American Indians; we may mention such figures as Åke Hultkrantz, Mircea Eliade, Walter H. Capps, and Arthur Versluis. In recent decades these sources have been augmented by a burgeoning literature which, insofar as possible, allows Indians to narrate their own lives and to explain the spiritual practices of their people; recall such works as Thomas Mails' *Fools Crow* (1979), Luther Standing Bear's *Land of the Spotted Eagle* (1980), and Michael Fitzgerald's *Yellowtail: Crow Medicine Man and Sun Dance Chief* (1991).

What, it might be asked, are the ideal credentials for someone writing about "the spiritual legacy of the American Indians"? Well, here at least are some of them: a penetrating intellectual discernment in doctrinal and spiritual matters, informed by an understanding of the *philosophia perennis* which underlies all integral traditions; the capacity to decipher the symbolic vocabulary in which the myths, doctrines, arts, and religious practices of primal traditions are necessarily expressed; a first-hand, existential immersion in the traditional spiritual life of the peoples in question, accompanied by a properly qualified master or adept able to explain authoritatively the meaning of the phenomena at hand; a moral integrity and probity of character which ensures that the inquiry is not contaminated by subjective prejudices and ambitions; a detachment from such sentimentalities and delusions of modernism as cultural evolutionism, progressivism, and historicism, to name three closely related follies. If it further be asked how many writers on American Indian religions fulfill these criteria, then one can only answer, precious few! Joseph Epes Brown (1920-2000) was one such. Indeed, as Seyyed Hossein Nasr has written,

> America has not produced another scholar of the Native American traditions who combined in himself, as did Joseph Brown, profound spiritual and intellectual insight, and traditional understanding, the deepest empathy for those traditions, nobility of character and generosity. . . .[1]

Professor Nasr's reference to "nobility of character" should not go unremarked: the Plains Indians themselves and the various forms in which they expressed their spiritual genius exhibited a nobility and a grandeur—often evinced through the symbolism of the eagle, the solar bird *par excellence*—which can only be fully appreciated by those with something of these same qualities in their own souls.

Now we have to hand the commemorative edition of *The Spiritual Legacy of the American Indian*. All the essays we found in the first edition are reproduced here. Several of these—"The Spiritual Legacy," "The Roots of Renewal," "Sun Dance: Sacrifice, Renewal, Identity"— have become classics and have re-appeared in various anthologies and compilations. But how good it is to have these gems strung again on a single cord, to be discovered, we may pray, by a whole new generation of readers, Indian and non-Indian alike. These pieces comprise an invaluable introduction to the spiritual economy of the American Plains Indians in general. Dr. Brown works on a large canvas and is particularly deft in sketching out for the general reader the *principles* which must inform any real *understanding*—something radically different from the mere accumulation of *information*. His explication of myths, rites, and symbols is profound without ever becoming too burdened

---

1 Nasr quoted in the "Biography of Joseph E. Brown" in J.E. Brown, *The Spiritual Legacy of the American Indians: Commemorative Edition with Letters while Living with Black Elk*, eds. E. Brown, M. Brown Weatherly & M.O. Fitzgerald (Bloomington, IN: World Wisdom, 2007), p. 130.

with detail or retreating into abstract and rarified metaphysical realms where many readers would be unable to follow. He also throws into sharp relief the sacramental value which, for the Indians, permeated the whole of the natural order, and thereby signals the ways in which the modern world might yet find a way out of the ecological catastrophes which we have brought upon ourselves, upon "all our relatives," and indeed, on Mother Earth herself on whose bounty depends our very existence. It is a bitter irony that it should have taken the ever escalating environmental calamity to awaken an interest in the ways of the Indians, a calamity rooted in the scission between Heaven and Earth.

Those familiar with the first edition of *The Spiritual Legacy* will be excited by several intensely interesting additions: a lucid and informative preface by the three editors (Dr. Brown's wife, daughter, and former student and friend, Michael Fitzgerald), drawing attention to the significance of some of the new material to be found in the new edition; an Introduction by the late Professor Åke Hultkrantz, the renowned scholar under whom the author studied in Stockholm, giving a conspectus of Brown's work and situating it in the framework of the *philosophia perennis*; a most welcome biography of Brown; a comprehensive bibliography; a series of previously unpublished photographs of some of the most imposing of the spiritual leaders amongst the Indians. All of this would give us reason enough to acquire the commemorative edition but, most important of all, we also find a substantial selection from letters written by Joseph Brown during his sojourn with Black Elk in the late 1940s—that providential encounter from which flowed *The Sacred Pipe* which, as I have already intimated, is one of a very small handful of books which truly is indispensable for an understanding of the traditions of the Plains Indian. These letters dramatically illuminate hitherto unknown aspects of the lives of both the author and of the Oglala sage. They also provide rare insights into the life and teachings of other spiritual leaders encountered during Brown's years amongst the Indians, and give some account of his visits to the Hopi, Navajo, and Pueblo peoples.

A good deal of controversy has accumulated around the figure of Black Elk in recent years, particularly concerning the volatile question of the relationship between his commitment to the ancestral ways and his conversion to Catholicism. Much ink has been spilt on this subject, often obscuring rather than clarifying the spiritual and intellectual issues at stake. The excerpts from Dr. Brown's letters, published here for the first time, provide a rich vein of material which no one engaged in the debate about Black Elk will henceforth be able to ignore. Of special interest are the tantalizing references in these letters to the medicine man's relationship with his adopted son, Father Gall, a Trappist monk of the Abbaye Notre Dame de Scourmont in Belgium, and the brother of Frithjof Schuon.

This commemorative volume stands as an eloquent and beautiful tribute—to the primordial tradition which is its subject, to Black Elk whose testimony and example was a veritable font of wisdom for the author, and to Joseph Brown himself, in whom the Indians found a true friend and a scholar adequately equipped to expound that spiritual wisdom which is indeed the Indians' most precious legacy.

11. The Wastelands of Modernity

To say that man is the measure of all things is meaning-less unless one starts from the idea that God is the meas-ure of man. . . ; nothing is fully human that is not deter-mined by the Divine, and therefore centered on it. Once man makes of himself a measure, while refusing to be measured in turn . . . all human landmarks disappear. . . .

FRITHJOF SCHUON

CHAPTER 7

The False Prophets of Modernity:
Darwin, Marx, Freud, and Nietzsche

> While nineteenth century materialism closed the mind of man to what is above him, twentieth century psychology opened it to what is below him.
>
> *René Guénon*[1]

> That which is lacking in the present world is a profound knowledge of the nature of things; the fundamental truths are always there, but they do not impose themselves because they cannot impose themselves on those unwilling to listen.
>
> *Frithjof Schuon*[2]

> The loss of God is death, is desolation, hunger, separation. All the tragedy of man is in one word, "godlessness."
>
> *Metropolitan Anthony of Sourzah*[3]

Permit me to begin with a personal reminiscence. Nearly thirty years ago, a decade after completing my undergraduate degree, I decided to return to university to pursue postgraduate studies. I wanted to write a thesis on the work of Frithjof Schuon, which had first struck me, lightning-like, through the anthology *The Sword of Gnosis*. I was interviewed by the Chair of the Religious Studies Department at the university in question and was told, bluntly, that my plan to write a dissertation on the work of Schuon was unacceptable: such a subject did not fall within the Department's frame of what constituted "serious scholarship." I was advised to construct a new research proposal. I will not

---

1 R. Guénon, *L'Erreur Spirite* (1923), quoted in A.K. Coomaraswamy, *Hinduism and Buddhism* (Delhi: Munshiram Manoharlal, 1996), p. 61.

2 F. Schuon, "No Activity Without Truth" in *The Sword of Gnosis* (Baltimore: Penguin, 1974), p. 28; a different translation of this article can be found in H. Oldmeadow (ed.), *The Betrayal of Tradition* (Bloomington, IN: World Wisdom, 2004), pp. 3-14.

3 Metropolitan Anthony of Sourozh, *God and Man* (London: Hodder & Stoughton, 1974), p. 68.

here rehearse the somewhat Kafkaesque story of how, through various stratagems, I finally persuaded the reluctant professor that I should be allowed to proceed with my original plan. Two years later I submitted my dissertation. I was asked to identify two possible examiners; well, I thought, I'd better grasp the nettle, and so nominated the two most distinguished academics in the field. My thesis was duly dispatched and I spent an anxious couple of months waiting for their reports. Each examiner evidently took the view that mercy must sometimes prevail over justice; their reports were generous to a fault. The two examiners were Professors Seyyed Hossein Nasr and Huston Smith.

I recount this episode for two reasons. Firstly, it provides me with the opportunity to acknowledge a debt of gratitude to Professor Nasr and Professor Smith, and to say what a singular honor it is to share the same platform at this conference. Secondly, it reminds us of the melancholy fact that the Wisdom of the Ages is very rarely welcomed in academia. The contemporary Western intelligentsia, so-called, has been almost completely seduced by the anti-traditional forces of modernity, a theme which I want to elaborate in this brief address.

Recall this passage from St. Paul:

> Whatsoever things are true, whatsoever things are honest, whatsoever things are just, whatsoever things are pure, whatsoever things are lovely, whatsoever things are of good report; if there be any virtue, and if there be any praise, think on these things. (*Philippians* 4:8)

Many of the speakers at this conference will no doubt be following this sage advice. But it has fallen to my lot to speak about less congenial matters; sometimes this is necessary to clear away those ideas and habits of mind which obscure our view of "whatsoever things are true." If some of my remarks seem intemperate my rejoinder is the same as Frithjof Schuon's: "Some people may reproach us with lack of reticence, but we would ask what reticence is shown by philosophers who shamelessly slash at the wisdom of countless centuries?"[4]

The Crisis of Modernity

Let us start with a recognition that there is indeed a fundamental crisis in the modern world and that its root causes are spiritual. The crisis

---

4 F. Schuon, *Stations of Wisdom* (London: John Murray, 1961), p. 20n.

itself can hardly be disputed. Some of the symptoms: ecological catastrophe, a material sign of the rupture between Heaven and Earth;
a rampant materialism and consumerism, signifying a surrender to
the illusion that man can live by bread alone; the genocidal extirpation of traditional cultures by "modernization"; political barbarities on
an almost unimaginable scale; social discord, endemic violence, and
dislocations of unprecedented proportions; widespread alienation, en-
nui, and a sense of spiritual sterility amidst the frenetic confusion and
din of modern life; a religious landscape dominated by internecine
and inter-religious strife and by the emergence of xenophobic funda-
mentalisms in both East and West; the loss of any sense of the sacred,
even among those who remain committed to religious forms, many of
whom have retreated into a simplistic and credulous religious literalism or into a vacuous liberalism where "anything goes."

The *Vishnu Purana* is a Hindu text dating back nearly two millennia. From that work, here is a description of the degenerations which
can be expected in the latter days of the Kali Yuga:

> Riches and piety will diminish daily, until the world will be com-
> pletely corrupted. In those days it will be wealth that confers distinc-
> tion, passion will be the sole reason for union between the sexes, lies
> will be the only method of success in business, and women will be
> the objects merely of sensual gratification. The earth will be valued
> only for its mineral treasures, dishonesty will be the universal means
> of subsistence, a simple ablution will be regarded as sufficient puri-
> fication. . . . The observances of castes, laws, and institutions will no
> longer be in force in the Dark Age, and the ceremonies prescribed by
> the Vedas will be neglected. Women will obey only their whims and
> will be infatuated with pleasure . . . men of all kinds will presump-
> tuously regard themselves as equals of Brahmins. . . . The Vaishyas
> will abandon agriculture and commerce and will earn their living
> by servitude or by the exercise of mechanical professions. . . . The
> dominant caste will be that of the Shudras. . . .[5]

Is this not a painfully accurate picture of our present condition?

5 *Vishnu Purana*, quoted in W. Stoddart, *An Outline of Hinduism* (Washington, DC:
Foundation for Traditional Studies, 1993), pp. 75-76. These passages, in a different
translation, can be found in *The Vishnu Purana: A System of Hindu Mythology and
Tradition*, Vol. 2, trans. & ed. H.H. Wilson & N.S. Singh (Delhi: Nag Publishers, 1980),
pp. 662-3, 866-867.

Here is another diagnosis of the contemporary condition, written fifty years ago but even more apposite today. It comes from the English writer Dorothy Sayers:

> Futility; lack of a living faith; the drift into loose morality, greedy consumption, financial irresponsibility, and uncontrolled bad temper; a self-opinionated and obstinate individualism; violence, sterility, and lack of reverence for life and property. . . ; the exploitation of sex, the debasing of language . . . , the commercializing of religion, . . . mass hysteria and "spell-binding" of all kinds, venality and string-pulling in public affairs, . . . the fomenting of discord. . . ; the exploitation of the lowest and stupidest mass-emotions. . . .[6]

Little wonder, then, that when Mahatma Gandhi was asked what he thought about "Western Civilization," he replied, "I think it would be a good idea."

These "signs of the times"—and the inventory is by no means exhaustive—are plain enough to those with eyes to see. No amount of gilded rhetoric about "progress," the "miracles of modern science and technology," or the "triumphs of democracy" (to mention just three shibboleths of modernity) can hide the fact that our age is tyrannized by an outlook inimical to our most fundamental needs, our deepest yearnings, our most noble aspirations. More problematic is the question of how we arrived at this state of affairs and in which direction we might turn for some remedy. As Frithjof Schuon observes,

> That which is lacking in the present world is a profound knowledge of the nature of things; the fundamental truths are always there, but they do not impose themselves because they cannot impose themselves on those unwilling to listen.[7]

Those truths, so often derided in the modern world, can be found in Tradition—and by this term we mean something very different from the jaundiced senses it has accumulated in the modern mentality ("the blind observance of inherited customs," and the like).

For want of a better word we might call the dominant worldview of

6 D. Sayers, *Introductory Papers on Dante* (1954), quoted in E.F. Schumacher, *A Guide for the Perplexed* (London: Jonathan Cape, 1977), pp. 151-152.

7 F. Schuon, "No Activity Without Truth," p. 28.

the post-medieval West "modernism."[8] For present purposes the term comprises the prevalent assumptions, values, and attitudes of a worldview fashioned by the most pervasive intellectual and moral influences of recent European history, an outlook in conformity with the current *Zeitgeist*. One might classify the constituents of modernism under any number of different schema. Lord Northbourne typifies modernism as "anti-traditional, progressive, humanist, rationalist, materialist, experimental, individualist, egalitarian, free-thinking, and intensely sentimental."[9] Seyyed Hossein Nasr gathers these tendencies together under four general features of modern thought: anthropomorphism (and by extension, secularism); evolutionist progressivism; the absence of any sense of the sacred; an unrelieved ignorance of metaphysical principles.[10]

Modernism is a spiritual disease which continues to spread like a plague across the globe, destroying traditional cultures wherever they are still to be found. Although its historical origins are European, modernism is now tied to no specific area or civilization. Its symptoms can be detected in a wide assortment of inter-related "mind sets" and "-isms," sometimes involved in cooperative co-existence, sometimes engaged in apparent antagonism, but always united by the same underlying assumptions. Scientism, rationalism, relativism, materialism, positivism, empiricism, evolutionism, psychologism, individualism, humanism, existentialism—these are some of the guises in which modernism clothes itself. The pedigree of this family of ideas can be traced back through a series of intellectual and cultural upheavals in European history and to certain vulnerabilities in Christendom which left it exposed to the subversions of a profane science. The Renaissance, the Scientific Revolution, and the so-called Enlightenment were all incubators of ideas and values which first ravaged Europe and then spread throughout the world like so many bacilli. Behind the bizarre array of ideologies which have proliferated in the last few centuries we can discern a growing and persistent ignorance concerning

---

8 The term should not here be confused with its more restricted meaning, referring to certain experimental artistic and literary developments originating in late nineteenth century Europe.

9 Lord Northbourne, *Religion in the Modern World* (London: J.M. Dent, 1963), p. 13.

10 See S.H. Nasr, "Reflections on Islam and Modern Thought," *The Islamic Quarterly*, 23:3, 1979, pp. 119-131.

ultimate realities and an indifference, if not always an overt hostility, to the eternal verities conveyed by Tradition. Not without reason did William Blake characterize the modern worldview as "Single Vision," a horizontal understanding of reality which strips the "outer" world of its mystery, its grandeur, and its revelatory function, and denies our human vocation. As the visionary poet so acutely remarked, "Man is either the ark of God or a phantom of the earth and the water."[11]

The contrast of tradition and modernity is likely to be most illuminating when it is informed by the following considerations:

> When the modern world is contrasted with traditional civilizations, it is not simply a question of looking on each side for what is good and bad; since good and evil are everywhere, it is essentially a question of knowing on which side the lesser evil is to be found. If someone tells us that such and such a good exists outside tradition, we respond: no doubt, but it is necessary to choose the most important good, and this is necessarily represented by tradition; and if someone tells us that in tradition there exists such and such an evil, we respond: no doubt, but it is necessary to choose the lesser evil, and again it is tradition that contains it. It is illogical to prefer an evil that involves some benefits to a good that involves some evils.[12]

No one will deny that modernity has its compensations, though these are often of a quite different order from the loudly trumpeted "benefits" of science and technology—some of which are indubitable but many of which issue in consequences far worse than the ills which they are apparently repairing. Furthermore, many so-called "advances" must be seen as the poisoned fruits of a Faustian bargain which one day must come to its bitter finale. What indeed is a man profited if he gain the whole world but lose his own soul? On the other hand, one real advantage of living in these latter days is the ready access we have to the spiritual treasuries of the world's religious and mythological traditions, including esoteric teachings which have hitherto been veiled in secrecy.

11 Blake quoted in K. Raine, "The Underlying Order: Nature and the Imagination" in *Fragments of Infinity: Essays in Religion and Philosophy, A Festschrift in Honour of Professor Huston Smith*, ed. A. Sharma (Bridport: Prism, 1991), p. 208.

12 F. Schuon, *Light on the Ancient Worlds: A New Translation with Selected Letters* (Bloomington, IN: World Wisdom, 2006), p. 32

Let us turn our attention to just a few characteristic prejudices of modern thought and to those habits of mind which have robbed us of our birthright as the children of God. I will do so by referring briefly to four representatives of modern thought, each an accomplice in the development of the modern outlook. Clearly, in the short time available I cannot rehearse their theories in any detail. Moreover, I am less concerned with these figures as individual personalities than with those tendencies which they articulate and crystallize, and particularly with the way that they popularized certain key ideas and themes. As René Guénon has remarked, in the intellectual order modernity is rooted in a series of pseudo-mythologies which, in the end, amount to little more than negations, parodies, and inversions of traditional understandings. My four representative figures will be altogether familiar to you: Charles Darwin, Karl Marx, Sigmund Freud, and Friedrich Nietzsche. It is no accident that they all belong to the nineteenth century, the period in which the seeds of revolt against Tradition, sown in the late medieval period and the early Renaissance, produced their fullest, most seductive, and most noxious blooms, at least on the mental plane; the full consequences of that rebellion lay in wait in the twentieth century, surely the most blood-stained on record.

Charles Darwin (1809-1882)

Darwin's hypothesis, foreshadowed in the work of many other contemporary scientists and social theorists alike and germinated in the sinister population theories of Malthus, is one of the most elegant, seductive, and pernicious of all "pseudo-mythologies." In a beguiling admixture of fact, imaginative speculation, circular argumentation, and painstaking system-building Darwin seemed to produce an objective and scientific account of the development of species, to provide an account of how life-forms came to be as they are. At the heart of the Darwinian schema lies a preposterous inversion of traditional understandings. In the opening passage of St. John's Gospel, one of the most exalted mystical texts, we are told that "In the beginning was the Word, and the Word was with God, and the Word was God. . . . And the Word became flesh. . . ." (*John* 1:1,14). Darwin proposes precisely the opposite, that "In the beginning was the Flesh (that is, matter), which became Word (consciousness, or Spirit). . . ." Out of inert matter, through some quite unexplained process, emerged microscopic life forms and over a very, very long period of time, through endless transformations and mutations and in accord with principles which Darwin claimed to have discovered, these became *homo sapiens*. In brief, the microscopic organisms from the prehistoric algal slime—organisms whose origins Darwin is utterly unable to explain—turn into Man. Or to put it even more tersely, the primeval amoeba turns into a St. Francis, an Ibn Arabi, a Lao Tze! Darwin's whole thesis hinges on the proposition that one species can transform itself into another. Whatever partial insights Darwin's work might yield this central theme is an absurdity which flies in the face of all traditional wisdom. To call man a "trousered ape" betrays a profound misunderstanding of the human condition; as E.F. Schumacher observed, one might as well call a dog "a barking plant or a running cabbage."[13]

Darwinism was a "grand narrative" perfectly suited to all the prejudices of the age—an account of the beginnings and the development of life which erased the Creator, now replaced by a clutch of more or less inexorable "laws" which were amenable to objective explanation, an account, moreover, which looked to an inevitable advance. Darwin's transformationist hypothesis not only came to dominate scientific thinking but was soon appropriated, in the form of Social Darwinism, to buttress all manner of malignant ideas about race, empire, "Progress," and the development of civilizations. The pseudo-mythology of evolutionism lent itself to social ideologies in which the brutal imperatives of competition, self-interest, "survival," and racial "hygiene" were all valorized as "natural."[14] Consider, if you can, the implications of a passage such as the following, from Darwin's own *The Descent of Man*:

> At some future period, not very distant as measured by centuries, the civilized races of man will almost certainly exterminate and replace the savage races throughout the world. At the same time the anthropomorphic apes . . . will no doubt be exterminated. The break between man and his nearest allies will then be wider, for it will intervene between man in a more civilized state, as we may hope, even than the Caucasian, and some ape as low a baboon, instead of as now between the negro or Australian and the gorilla.[15]

13 E.F. Schumacher, *A Guide for the Perplexed*, p. 31.

14 On the social effects of Darwinist ideas see Marilynne Robinson's essay, "Darwinism" in *The Death of Adam: Essays on Modern Thought* (New York: Picador, 2005), pp. 28-75.

15 Quoted in M. Robinson, "Darwinism," p. 35

Darwinism has become a kind of pseudo-religion, a fact which explains the zealotry with which many scientists remain willfully blind to the mounting scientific evidence against the Darwinian scheme, especially in its absurd claim that one species can transform into another. There are many angles from which Darwinism might be exposed as fraudulent—scientific, logical, religious, and metaphysical. We cannot here rehearse any kind of critique but it is perhaps worth noting that in many respects it is a pity that the fight against Darwinism has been carried out by fundamentalist creationists who are quite unable to meet Darwin on his own ground. Nonetheless, it should also be noted that however naive and sometimes obscufatory such critics often are, their fundamental intuition is valid.

Darwin and his epigones offer us a spectacular instance of the truth of René Guénon's observation that

> when profane science leaves the domain of the mere observation of facts, and tries to get something out of an indefinite accumulation of separate details which is its sole immediate result, it retains as one of its chief characteristics the more or less laborious construction of purely hypothetical theories. These theories can necessarily never be more than hypothetical, for facts in themselves are always susceptible of diverse explanations and so never have been and never will be able to guarantee the truth of any theory . . . and besides, such theories are not really inspired by the results of experience to nearly the same extent as by certain preconceived ideas and by some of the predominant tendencies of modern thought.[16]

The principle which needs always to be foregrounded in any discussion of modern science is to be found in the Vedantic insistence that the world of *maya* (i.e., the time-space world which science investigates) is not inexplicable; it is only not self-explanatory. Shankara says that any attempt to understand the material world without knowledge of the Real is akin to an attempt to explain night and day without reference to the sun. In any case, a profane science can only ever tell us about auxiliary and mechanical causes; it can never get to the root of things, just as it must remain mute whenever we confront questions about *meaning* and *value*. As to modern science's endless accumula-

16 R. Guénon, *The Reign of Quantity & The Signs of the Times* (Ghent, NY: Sophia Perennis et Universalis, 1995), p. 149.

tion of empirical data we need only recall Gai Eaton's remark that this is a matter of knowing more and more about less and less, and that "our ignorance of the few things that matter is as prodigious as our knowledge of trivialities."[17]

Karl Marx (1818-1883)

A year or two back a British newspaper conducted a poll in which readers were asked to nominate the most influential thinker of the last thousand years. The runaway winner was Karl Marx, the German philosopher, social theorist, Father of Communism (both as a body of theory and as a revolutionary political movement), the grave-digger of capitalism and religion alike. He might also be described as the author of what Carlyle so properly called the "Dismal Science" of economics. Marx needs no further introduction here; nor is there any point in providing an overview of his theory of dialectical materialism and its endlessly elaborated analyses of the forces of production and distribution in his ponderous *magnum opus*, a landmark in the emergence of that family of disciplines which herd together under the canopy of "the social sciences." No, here I can do no more than allude to a few ideas which have become the stock-in-trade of the modern outlook. Let us begin with some well-known words from Friedrich Engels' funeral oration:

> Just as Darwin discovered the law of development of organic nature, so Marx discovered the law of development of human history: the simple fact, hitherto concealed by an overgrowth of ideology, that mankind must first of all eat, drink, have shelter, and clothing, before it can pursue politics, science, art, religion, etc.; that therefore the production of the immediate material means, and consequently the degree of economic development attained by a given people or during a given epoch, form the foundation upon which the state institutions, the legal conceptions, art, and even the ideas on religion, of the people concerned have been evolved, and in the light of which they must, therefore be explained, instead of vice versa, as had hitherto been the case.[18]

17 Cited as an epigraph in *Tomorrow: The Journal of Parapsychology, Cosmology and Traditional Studies*, 12:3, 1964, p. 191.

18 F. Engels, "Speech at the Graveside of Karl Marx," in *Karl Marx and Frederick Engels: Selected Works* (Moscow: Progress Publishers, 1968), p. 435.

It was altogether appropriate that Engels should link the thought of Marx and Darwin. Indeed, Marx himself remarked, "Darwin's book [*On the Origin of Species* (1859)] is very important and serves me as a basis in natural science for the class struggle in history."[19] Both could be said to be children of the so-called Enlightenment: both imagined themselves to be engaged in a more less scientific enterprise; each popularized a form of evolutionist thought, in the biological and social domains respectively; both detonated a depth-charge under the foundations of religious belief.

Return for a moment to the passage from Engels. Notice the reduction of man to an economic and social animal, a being whose nature is entirely conditioned, indeed determined by material circumstances over which he has little control. Man's spiritual dimension is thereby stripped away as no more than the residue of a now-obsolete religious conception which hitherto has alienated man from his true nature as a social being, fashioned by the material forces of history. We are all familiar with Marx's characterization of religion as "the opium of the people," a drug which deflects their attention from their real circumstances with its illusory promises of an afterlife and which anaesthetizes their political will. Here is a famous passage from Marx's somewhat fragmentary but lethal writings on religion:

> Man, who looked for a superman in the fantastic reality of heaven and found nothing there but the reflection of himself, will no longer be disposed to find but the semblance of himself, the non-human (*Unmensch*) where he seeks and must seek his true reality. . . . Man makes religion, religion does not make man. In other words, religion is the self-consciousness and self-feeling of man who has either not yet found himself or has already lost himself again. . . . The struggle against religion is therefore . . . the struggle against the other world, of which religion is the spiritual aroma. . . . Religion is the sigh of the oppressed creature, the heart of a heartless world, just as it is the spirit of a spiritless situation. It is the opium of the people. The abolition of religion as the illusory happiness of the people is required for their real happiness. . . . The criticism of religion disillusions man and makes him think and act and shape his reality like a man who has been disillusioned and has come to reason, so that he will revolve round himself and therefore

---

19 Letter to Lasalle, January 16, 1861, quoted in F. Wheen, *Karl Marx: A Life* (London: Fourth Estate, 1999), p. 364.

round his true sun. Religion is only the illusory sun which revolves round man as long as he does not revolve round himself.[20]

Following Feuerbach and Marx, Engels asserted that "All religion, however, is nothing but the fantastic reflection in men's minds of those external forces which control their daily life, a reflection in which the terrestrial forces assume the form of supernatural forces."[21] This now-threadbare idea has become the very calling card of the modern intellectual.

Hand-in-hand with this repudiation of religion and all that it entails, is a secular humanism. In his doctoral thesis Marx had written,

> Philosophy makes no secret of it. Prometheus' confession "in a word, I detest all Gods," is its own confession, its own slogan against all Gods in heaven and earth who do not recognize man's self-consciousness as the highest divinity.[22]

Linked with this humanism, which finds antecedents in the thought of Enlightenment thinkers such as Rousseau, there is Marx's Utopianism, a strain of thought which anticipates a world in which all the social iniquities and inequalities, all the class oppressions of the past, are devoured in revolutionary violence, ushering in an era in which a man might "hunt in the morning, fish in the afternoon, rear cattle in the evening" and philosophize at night.[23] At this point in history I hardly need observe that Marx's romantic and apocalyptic Utopianism fuelled abuses so many and so monstrous that we can hardly grasp their magnitude—a case of making a hell on earth, as the Russian novelist Dostoevsky so chillingly predicted in his own dark masterpiece, *Notes from Underground* (1864). The hallmarks of Marx's thought, in brief: a corrosive and atheistic materialism, a Promethean humanism, and a sentimental and potentially murderous Utopianism, and all this dressed up in quasi-scientific garb.

---

20 *A Contribution to the Critique of Hegel's Philosophy of Right* (1844) in *K. Marx and F. Engels on Religion* (Moscow: Progress Publishers, 1957), pp. 37-38

21 *Anti-Dühring* (1878), in *K. Marx and F. Engels on Religion*, p. 131.

22 Preface to Marx's doctoral thesis, quoted in D. McLellan, *Karl Marx* (Glasgow: Fontana/Collins, 1975), p. 26.

23 From *The German Ideology* (1846), quoted in F. Wheen, *Karl Marx*, p. 96.

Sigmund Freud (1856-1939)

Sigmund Freud, the undisputed progenitor of modern psychology and psychiatry, remarked in a letter, "The moment a man questions the meaning and value of life he is sick, since objectively neither has any existence."[24] From a traditional point of view, one need hardly do more than adduce this extraordinary claim to throw Freud's theorizing out of court altogether. As we know, Freud himself harbored an animus towards religion which, in his own terms, could only be described as pathological. No one needs reminding that the relations between modern psychology and traditional religions have not always been friendly. Freud struck the key note in his insistence that, to state the matter as briefly as possible, religious beliefs were a thinly camouflaged prolongation of childhood traumas and pathologies. He identified "three powers which may dispute the basic position of science": art, philosophy, and religion, of which, he said, "religion alone is to be taken seriously as an enemy." Philosophy, he suggested, is basically harmless because, despite its ambitious pretensions, it "has no direct influence on the great mass of mankind: it is of interest to only a small number even of top-layer intellectuals and is scarcely intelligible to anyone else." Art "is almost always harmless and beneficent; it does not seek to be anything but an illusion."[25] This leaves religion as "an immense power" and an imposing obstacle to the scientific enlightenment of mankind, the project in which Freud understood himself to be engaged.

> The last contribution to the criticism of the religious *Weltanschauung* [he wrote], was effected by psychoanalysis, by showing how religion originated from the helplessness of children and by tracing its contents to the survival into maturity of the wishes and needs of childhood.[26]

Freud identified three fatal blows against what he called man's "narcissism," by which he meant the belief that man was made in the image of God: Copernican cosmology, Darwinian biology, and psy-

---

24 Letter to Maria Bonaparte, from *Letters of Sigmund Freud*, quoted in P. Rieff, *The Triumph of the Therapeutic: Uses of Faith After Freud* (Harmondsworth: Penguin, 1973), p. 29.

25 S. Freud, *New Introductory Lectures on Psychoanalysis* (London: Hogarth Press, 1974), pp. 160-161.

26 S. Freud, *New Introductory Lectures on Psychoanalysis*, p. 167.

choanalytical psychology.[27] We do not here have time to anatomize what Schuon has called the "psychological imposture" and its usurpation of religious functions which lie well beyond its competence, but the drift of much of Freud's thought can be signaled by a small sample of quotations, the sinister implications of which will be readily apparent to you. From *New Introductory Lectures on Psychoanalysis*:

[The *Weltanschauung* of science] asserts that there are no sources of knowledge of the universe other than the intellectual working-over of carefully scrutinized observations . . . and alongside of it no knowledge derived from revelation, intuition, or divination.[28]

Many of his observations on religion are now all too well-known. Here are a few:

[Religion is] a counterpart to the neurosis which individual civilized men have to go through in their passage from childhood to maturity.[29]

I should like to insist . . . that the beginnings of religion, morals, society, and art converge in the Oedipus complex.[30]

[Religious ideas] are illusions, fulfillments of the oldest, strongest, and most urgent wishes of mankind.[31]

And this, on the nature of the id, which Freud referred to as "the core of our being":

It is the dark, inaccessible part of our personality. . . . We call it a chaos, a cauldron of seething excitations. . . . It is filled with energy reaching it from the instincts, but it has no organization, produces

---

27 S. Freud, *Collected Papers*, Vol. 1, cited in W. Perry, "The Revolt Against Moses: A New Look at Psychoanalysis" in *Challenges to a Secular Society* (Oakton, VA: Foundation for Traditional Studies, 1996), pp. 17-38.

28 S. Freud, *New Introductory Lectures on Psychoanalysis*, p. 159.

29 S. Freud, *New Introductory Lectures on Psychoanalysis*, p. 168.

30 S. Freud, *Totem and Taboo* (London: Routledge & Kegan Paul, 1950), p. 156.

31 *The Future of an Illusion* (1927), in *The Complete Psychological Works of Sigmund Freud*, Vol. 21, ed. J. Strachey (London: Hogarth Press, 1964), p. 30.

no collective will, but only a striving to bring about the satisfaction of the instinctual needs subject to the observance of the pleasure principle. . . . The id of course knows no judgments of value. . . . The quantitative factor, which is intimately linked to the pleasure principle, dominates all its processes. Instinctual cathexes seeking discharge—that, in our view, is all there is in the id.[32]

Freud's theories about the "psychogenesis" of religion and his grotesque speculations about the early history of mankind, bear an unmistakably evolutionist cast. Here is a representative passage:

While the different religions wrangle with one another as to which of them is in possession of the truth, our view is that the truth of religion may be left altogether on one side. Religion is an attempt to master the sensory world, in which we are situated by means of the wishful world, which we have developed within us as a result of biological and psychological necessities. But it cannot achieve this. Its doctrines bear the imprint of the times in which they arose, the ignorant times of the childhood of humanity.[33]

As Guénon and others have noted, Freud's agenda might well be summed up in one of his own favorite lines from Virgil, and one which he inscribed on the title page of his first major work: "If I cannot bend the gods, I will stir up hell."[34] Guénon drew attention to some of the infernal influences unleashed by Freudian psychoanalysis, putting the matter most succinctly when he observed that "While nineteenth century materialism closed the mind of man to what is above him, twentieth century psychology opened it to what is below him."[35] A theme taken up by Schuon:

---

32 S. Freud, *New Introductory Lectures on Psychoanalysis*, pp. 74-75.

33 S. Freud, *New Introductory Lectures on Psychoanalysis*, p. 168.

34 From Virgil, inscribed in *Die Traumdeutung* (1899), noted in R. Guénon, *The Reign of Quantity & The Signs of the Times* (Ghent, NY: Sophia Perennis et Universalis, 1995), p. 355. For some commentary on Freud's ideas about religion see W. Smith, *Cosmos and Transcendence: Breaking Through the Barrier of Scientist Belief* (San Rafael, CA: Sophia Perennis, 2008), p. 109, and A. McGrath, *The Twilight of Atheism: The Rise and Fall of Disbelief in the Modern World* (London: Rider, 2004), pp. 66-77.

35 From *L'Erreur Spirite* (1923), quoted in A.K. Coomaraswamy, *Hinduism and Buddhism*, p. 61. Guénon's most devastating critique of psychologism is to be found in Chapters 24-25 of *The Reign of Quantity*.

What we term "psychological imposture" is the tendency to reduce everything to psychological factors and to call into question not only what is intellectual or spiritual—the first being related to truth and the second to life in and by truth—but also the human spirit as such, and thereby its capacity of adequation and, still more evidently, its inward illimitation and transcendence. The same belittling and truly subversive tendency rages in all the domains that "scientism" claims to embrace, but its most acute expression is beyond all doubt to be found in psychoanalysis. Psychoanalysis is at once an end-point and a cause, as is always the case with profane ideologies, like materialism and evolutionism, of which it is really a logical and fatal ramification and a natural ally.[36]

To put the matter slightly differently we might say that materialism, evolutionism, and psychologism are not in fact three distinct theories but rather variants of that singular and eccentric world view which Guénon exposed in *The Reign of Quantity* (1945).

Friedrich Nietzsche (1844-1900)

While Darwin, Marx and Freud have long been recognized as three massively influential thinkers in whose work several characteristically modern ideas are given their most dramatic and potent expressions, it is now perhaps time to add the name of Friedrich Nietzsche to the roster of the false prophets of modernity. Nietzsche is a particularly problematic case, partly because his work is full of coruscating insights of an almost entirely destructive kind. Here I can do no more than take brief note of his peculiar role in the development of modern thought. Nietzsche is best-known for his pronouncement of the "death of God" by which he meant that the foundations of a religious worldview had now collapsed and that no self-respecting intellectual could any longer subscribe to a belief in God. Here he is thundering against all traditional and religious conceptions:

> The "Law," the "will of God," the "sacred book," "inspiration"—all merely words for the conditions under which the priest comes to power, by which he maintains his power—these concepts are to be found at the basis of all priestly organizations, all priestly or priestly-

36 F. Schuon, "The Psychological Imposture" in *Survey of Metaphysics and Esoterism* (Bloomington, IN: World Wisdom Books, 1986), p. 195.

philosophical power-structures. The "holy lie"—common to Confucius, the Law-Book of Manu, Mohammad, the Christian Church—it
is not lacking in Plato. "The truth exists": this means, wherever it is
heard, the priest is lying. . . .[37]

Nietzsche also lodged a time-bomb under the whole idea of objective Truth; his philosophical legacy has yielded its most acidic fruits,
a century after his death, in the wholesale relativism of postmodernist theorizing as found in the work of such figures as Jacques Derrida
and Michel Foucault, to mention only two of the self-styled Parisian
oracles, those "monks of negation" whose work has exercised such
a corrosive effect on the Academy over the last three decades. Many
of you will be familiar with other leitmotiv in Nietzsche's work—his
lacerating attacks on Christianity, and particularly its spiritual egalitarianism; the extolling of the *Ubermensch*, the "Over-man," freed
from the restraints of stifling bourgeois morality, exercising the "will
to power" in an heroic "self-overcoming"; his consignment of traditional philosophy, metaphysics, and ethics to the dust-bin of human
history. As Schuon has remarked of Nietzsche, a certain nobility of
soul is evident in the work of this troubled genius, particularly in its
poetic expressions, marked by "the passionate exteriorization of an inward fire, but in a manner that is both deviated and demented"[38]—the
deviation evident in Nietzsche's peculiar amalgam of Machiavelli, German romanticism, and a pitiless Darwinism. What was lacking in this
"volcanic genius" was any real intellectual discernment which might
have channeled his profound reaction against the mediocrity of the age
in more profitable directions.

Nietzsche is indeed a particularly strange case: whilst celebrating
the "death of God" he simultaneously understood some of its most
appalling consequences. Consider, for instance, this famous passage
from *The Gay Science*:

Have you not heard of that madman who lit a lantern in the bright
morning hours, ran to the market-place and cried incessantly: "I am
looking for God! I am looking for God!"—As many of those did not

---

37 From *The Anti-Christ* (1888), in *The Vision of Nietzsche*, ed. P. Novak (Rockport:
Element, 1996), p. 52.

38 F. Schuon, *To Have a Center* (Bloomington, IN: World Wisdom Books, 1990), p. 15.

believe in God were standing there he excited considerable laughter. . . . The madman sprang into their midst and pierced them with his glances. "Where has God gone?" he cried. "I shall tell you. We have killed him—you and I. We are all his murderers. But how have we done this? How were we able to drink up the sea? Who gave us the sponge to wipe away the entire horizon? What did we do when we unchained this earth from its sun? Whither is it moving now? Whither are we moving now? Away from all suns? Are we not perpetually falling? Backward, sideward, forward, in all directions? Is there any up and down left? Are we not straying as through an infinite nothing? Do we not feel the breath of empty space? Has it not become colder? Is more and more night not coming on all the time? Must not lanterns be lit in the morning? Do we not hear anything yet of the noise of the gravediggers who are burying God? . . ."[39]

As one representative of the Orthodox Church, Metropolitan Anthony of Sourzah, put it: "The loss of God is death, is desolation, hunger, separation. All the tragedy of man is in one word, 'godlessness.'"[40] Nietzsche understood this all too well—but he couldn't help himself, seduced by his own delirious dream of the Dionysian *Ubermensch*.

Some Common Characteristics

Let me now quickly draw attention to some features shared by these four thinkers. These might serve as signposts to some of the most pervasive aspects of modern intellectual life:

• *A Spurious "Originality"*: Each of these thinkers imagines that he has discovered a hitherto unknown secret, a key with which to unlock the mysteries of the human condition. For Darwin it is the evolutionist schema fuelled by adaptations to the environment, mutations, and the "survival of the fittest"; for Marx, the dialectic of the material forces of history; for Freud the sexual drive with all its accompanying repressions, projections, complexes, and neuroses; for Nietzsche, the "will to power." There is an apparent novelty in the writings of each of these figures—hence their elevation to the pantheon of modern thought which treasures nothing so much as a mis-named "originality." In reality, such apparently new insights as are to be found in the works of these think-

---

39 From *The Gay Science* (1882), in *A Nietzsche Reader*, ed. R.J. Hollingdale (Harmondsworth: Penguin, 1977), pp. 202-203.

40 Metropolitan Anthony of Sourozh, *God and Man*, p. 68.

ers often turn out to be a distortion of ideas which have been in circulation for centuries, even millennia. By way of an example one might adduce Freud's unacknowledged debts to Kabbalah.[41] The theorizations of these false prophets often amount to little more than the negation, parodying, or inversion of traditional doctrines half-understood, wrenched out of their spiritual framework and "flattened out."

• *Evolutionism, Progressivism*: Secondly, all four of these "prophets of modernity" succumbed to evolutionist and progressivist ideologies which engendered a contempt for the past and for our ancestors, and indeed, for the very notion of tradition. Of course, the barbarities of the twentieth century, starting on the fields of Flanders, disenchanted some of the more intelligent apostles of Progress but it is truly remarkable to witness the tenacious grip this sentimental idea still has amongst the Western intelligentsia. Evolutionism and progressivism has also intruded into the domain of religion itself, evident in the thought of people such as Teilhard de Chardin, Vivekananda, and Aurobindo, to name only three. Not surprisingly, the consequences have been disastrous.

• *The Idolatry of Reason:* The modern mentality is rationalistic, materialistic, empiricist, historicist, and humanistic—in the narrow sense of the word—and these characteristics too are all too evident in the work of our representative figures, three of whom were regular worshippers at the Temple of Reason (Nietzsche being the exception). The adulation of Reason and of an empirical and materialistic science could only arise in a world in which the *sacra scientia* of the traditional worlds had been lost. To cleave to these much-vaunted modes of modern thought is simply to announce that one is entirely bereft of any metaphysical discernment, entrapped in the world of *maya*, that tissue of fugitive relativities which makes up the time-space world. As Frithjof Schuon has tersely remarked, "The rationalism of a frog living at the bottom of a well is to deny the existence of mountains; perhaps this is 'logic,' but it has nothing to do with reality."[42]

• *The Rejection of Tradition:* To succumb to the idolatry of Reason is also, necessarily, to turn one's back on the ever-present sources of traditional intellectuality and spirituality, which is to say doctrine

---

41 See W. Perry, "The Revolt Against Moses," pp. 17-38.

42 F. Schuon, *Logic and Transcendence: A New Translation with Selected Letters* (Bloomington, IN: World Wisdom, 2009), p. 36.

and spiritual method—the epochal Revelations providentially direct-ed towards various human collectivities, the traditions issuing from these Revelations, the Scriptures and commentaries of the doctors and sages of each tradition, the witness of the saints and mystics. All this is thrown out in favor of the prejudices of the day, largely fashioned by those pseudo-mythologies current at any particular moment. In the case of our four representatives of modernism we might well refer to the pseudo-mythologies of evolutionism, materialism, psychologism, and relativism.

• *The Denial of God*: Each of these thinkers leaves God out of the frame. In the case of Marx, Freud, and Nietzsche, the disavowal is quite explicit whilst in Darwin it is a matter of ignoring the question, which amounts to much the same thing. These are godless thinkers who tes-tify to the truth of Dostoevsky's frightful premonition that "without God, everything is permitted"—again, an insight shared by Nietzsche. The transcendent dimension of both the cosmos and the microcos-mic human being is stripped away to leave us in an entirely horizontal world in which there is no longer any sense of our dignity, responsibil-ity, and freedom as beings made "in the image of God." In such a world there is no longer any sense of the sacred from which we might take our spiritual bearings. Our souls cry out for bread but we are given stones.

• *The Denial of Man*: Finally, let us ask ourselves to what manner of self-understanding these pseudo-mythologies force-march us? In each case we are offered a meager and charmless portrait of the human condition: man as biological organism, as a highly evolved ape whose essential function is to ensure the survival of the species, and whose behavior is governed by the iron dictates of biological necessity; man as economic animal, fashioned by his material environment and by the impersonal forces of history; the human being as a puppet of the dark forces of the Id; man as a herd-creature, mediocre, cowardly, foolish, and deluded, redeemed only by the *Ubermensch* who dares to exercise the will to power. In the face of each of these degraded and bleak ac-counts of the human being, one can only ask, what could be expected of such a creature?—to which the inescapable answer is, not much! Is it not one of the most galling ironies of modernity that these much vaunted ideologies which, we are told *ad nauseam*, have emancipated us from "the shackles of ignorance and superstition," have, in reality robbed us of all that is most precious in the human estate "hard to obtain," by denying the Divine Spark which we all carry within? This, truly speaking, is a monstrous crime against God and thereby against humanity. In the light of our general theme at this conference let me now turn to a few very brief remarks about Tradition against which we are bound to judge the modern world.

The World of Tradition

St. Augustine speaks of "wisdom uncreate, the same now that it ever was, the same to be forevermore."[43] This timeless wisdom has carried many names: *philosophia perennis, Lex Aeterna, Hagia Sophia, Din al-Haqq, Akalika Dhamma,* and *Sanatana Dharma* are among the better known. In itself this truth is formless and beyond all conceptualizations. Any attempt to define it is, to borrow a metaphor, like trying to catch the river in a net. This universal wisdom, in existence since the genesis of time and the spiritual patrimony of all humankind, can also be designated as the Primordial Tradition. Guénon refers to "the Tradition contained in the Sacred Books of all peoples, a Tradition which in reality is everywhere the same, in spite of all the diverse forms it assumes to adapt itself to each race and period."[44] In this sense tradition is synonymous with a perennial philosophy or wisdom which is eternal, universal and immutable. The Primordial Tradition or *sophia perennis* is of supra-human origin and is in no sense a product or evolute of human thought. It is the birth-right of humanity. All the great religious teachings, albeit in the differing vocabularies appropriate to the spiritual economy in question, affirm just such a principle. Recall Krishna's declaration, in the *Bhagavad Gita* (4:6) of the pre-existence of his message, proclaimed at the dawn of time. Likewise Christ, speaking in his cosmic function as incarnation of the Truth, states, "Verily, verily, I say unto you, before Abraham was, I am" (*John* 8:58). "Tradition," then, in its most pristine sense is this primordial truth and as such takes on the status of a first cause, a cosmic datum, a principial reality woven into the very fabric of the universe and ingrained in the human spirit.

"Tradition" also has a secondary meaning, directly pertinent to our theme. Etymologically it simply means "that which is transmit-

43 St. Augustine, *Confessions*, IX.10.xxiv, in R. Bridges (ed. & trans.), *The Spirit of Man: An Anthology in English and French from the Philosophers and Poets* (London: Longmans, Green, 1918), book 1, selection 32.

44 R. Guénon in *La Gnose* (1909), quoted in W. Perry (ed.), *A Treasury of Traditional Wisdom* (London: Allen & Unwin, 1971), p. 20.

ted." Here the term cannot be equated with a formless and immutable Truth but is, rather, that Truth as it finds formal expression, through the medium of a divine Revelation, in the myths, doctrines, rituals, symbols, and other manifestations of any religious culture. As Lord Northbourne has observed, "Tradition, in the rightful sense of the word, is the chain that joins civilization to Revelation."[45] In this context "tradition" becomes more or less synonymous with "religion," always with the proviso that it is integral, orthodox religions of which we speak. Let us also not forget that

> When people talk about "civilization" they generally attribute a qualitative meaning to the term; now civilization only represents a value provided it is supra-human in origin and implies for the "civilized" man a sense of the sacred. . . .[46]

Traditional societies are grounded in this understanding. Society itself represents nothing of permanent or absolute value but only insofar as it provides a context for the sense of the sacred and the spiritual life which it implies. At radical odds with Tradition, in all of its senses, stands the world of modernity and the Promethean hubris which underpins it.

What, essentially is the message of Tradition and the traditions for the modern world? Well, this is a very large question which might be answered in any number of ways. A Hindu swami summed up the essential message of his own tradition through four propositions:

1. God is;
2. God can be realized;
3. To realize God is the supreme goal of human existence;
4. God can be realized in many ways.[47]

Might it not be said, my friends, that this, in capsule form, is the message of all religious traditions?

45 Lord Northbourne, *Religion in the Modern World*, p. 34.

46 F. Schuon, *Understanding Islam* (Bloomington, IN: World Wisdom Books, 1998), p. 26.

47 Swami Prabhavananda, *The Spiritual Heritage of India: A Clear Summary of Indian Philosophy and Religion* (Madras: Sri Ramakrishna Math, 1981), pp. 354-355.

Staying Afloat in the Kali Yuga

At a time when the forces of anti-Tradition sometimes seem overwhelming and when we feel unable to keep our hands to the plough, let us recall Frithjof Schuon's reminder that no effort on behalf of the Truth is ever in vain.[48] We must dispel the false charges sometimes leveled at traditionalists that they are dusty obscurantists "out of touch" with the contemporary world, that they want to "wind back the clock," that they are romantic reactionaries escaping into an idealized past. Let us never forget that the essential message of tradition is timeless and thus ever new, ever fresh, and always germane to both our immediate condition and to our ultimate destiny. As Schuon remarks, a "nostalgia for the past" is, in itself, nothing; all that is meaningful is "a nostalgia for the sacred" which "cannot be situated elsewhere than in the liberating 'now' of God."[49] No doubt our crepuscular era is riddled with all manner of confusion but there are always saints and sages in our midst to whom we can turn for guidance. In recent times one might mention such figures as the Algerian Sufi master, Shaykh Ahmed al-Alawi, or Hindu sages such as Paramahamsa Ramakrishna, Ramana Maharshi and Anandamayi Ma, or Native American visionaries such as Black Elk and Yellowtail, or the Christian monk, Henri Le Saux who became Swami Abhishiktananda, not to mention the many wise lamas and masters of the Far Eastern world, including such figures as His Holiness the Dalai Lama and Thich Nhat Hanh. Then, too, there is the abiding work and example of the great perennialists of the modern era: René Guénon, Ananda Coomaraswamy, Titus Burckhardt, Frithjof Schuon, and Martin Lings, to mention only a few who have already gone to the further shore. Finally let me finish with some words from Guénon from whom we can draw some encouragement in these dark and confused times:

> Those who might be tempted to give way to despair should realize that nothing accomplished in this order can ever be lost, that confusion, error, and darkness can win the day only in appearance and in a purely ephemeral way, that all partial and transitory disequilibrium must perforce contribute toward the greater equilibrium of the

48 F. Schuon, "No Activity Without Truth," p. 39.

49 F. Schuon, "On the Margin of Liturgical Improvisations" in *The Sword of Gnosis*, p. 353.

whole, and that nothing can ultimately prevail against the power of truth; their motto should be the one formerly used by certain initiatic organizations of the West: *Vincit Omnia Veritas* [Truth conquers all].[50]

---

50 These are the concluding words of René Guénon's *The Crisis of the Modern World* (first published 1927) (Hillsdale, NY: Sophia Perennis, 2001), p. 117.

CHAPTER 8

Frankenstein's Children:
Science, Scientism, and Self-Destruction

Our ignorance of the few things that matter is as prodigious as our knowledge of trivialities.

Gai Eaton[1]

No one will deny that modern science and its technical applications have brought the contemporary world many benefits, even if these often turn out, in the longer term, to be somewhat ambiguous. Nonetheless, many people feel a profound unease about many of the applications, interventions, and changes which come in the wake of scientific discoveries. One need only mention such phenomena as genetic engineering, cloning, cryogenics, industrial diseases, "behavior modification," the proliferation of drug-resistant viruses, nuclear and biological warfare, and environmental catastrophes of various kinds, to trigger well-founded apprehensions about where science and technology might be taking us. Not without reason have some of the most disturbing and resonant literary works of the past two centuries been concerned with the unforeseen effects of a runaway science—think, for instance, of Mary Shelley's *Frankenstein*, or Stevenson's *Dr. Jekyll and Mr. Hyde*, or Aldous Huxley's dystopian vision in *Brave New World*. Increasingly, many thoughtful people are questioning the modern shibboleth of an inexorable "progress," fueled by "science" and implemented by technology.

A decisive shift took place in the European worldview in the seventeenth century, through what we now think of as the Scientific Revolution: Descartes, Bacon, Copernicus, Galileo, and Newton were amongst the seminal figures. The triumph of the scientific outlook was more or less complete by the twentieth century and provided the basis of the prevailing intellectual orthodoxies amongst the European intelligentsia. Modern science is not simply a disinterested and, as it were,

---

1 Cited as an epigraph in *Tomorrow: The Journal of Parapsychology, Cosmology and Traditional Studies*, 12:3, 1964, p. 191.

a detached and "objective" mode of inquiry into the material world; rather, it is an aggregate of disciplines anchored in a bed of very specific and culture-bound assumptions about the nature of reality and about the proper means whereby it might be explored, explained, and controlled. It is, in fact, impossible to separate the methodologies of modern science from their theoretical base which we can signal by the term "scientism." Perhaps the central plank in the scientistic platform is the assumption that modern science contains within itself the necessary and sufficient means for any inquiry into the material world, and that it can and should be an autonomous and self-validating pursuit, answerable to nothing outside itself. This was a new idea in the history of human thought, radically at odds with the traditional view that any inquiry into the natural world could only properly proceed within a larger framework provided by philosophy and religion.

Modern science, as it has developed since the Renaissance, is flanked on one side by philosophical empiricism which provides its intellectual rationale, and by technology and industry on the other, a field for its applications. It is rational, analytical, and empirical in its procedures, material and quantitative in its object, and utilitarian in application. By its very nature modern science is thus unable to apprehend or accommodate any realities of a supra-sensorial order. Science (a method of inquiry) becomes scientism (an ideology) when it refuses to acknowledge the limits of its own competence, denies the authority of any sources which lie outside its ambit, and lays claim, at least in principle, to a comprehensive validity as if it could explain no matter what, and as if it were not contradictory to lay claim to totality on an empirical basis. (Witness Stephen Hawking's preposterous pretensions to a "Theory of Everything"!)

Critiques of scientism are much in vogue these days both from within the scientific community and from without. The insecure philosophical foundations of modern science, its epistemological ambiguities, its inability to accommodate its own findings within the Cartesian-Newtonian frame, the consequences of a Faustian pursuit of knowledge and power, the diabolical applications of science in the military industry, the dehumanizing reductionisms of the behavioral sciences—all of these have come under trenchant attack in recent times. New "discoveries" by physicists and the paradoxes of Quantum Theory throw conventional assumptions about time, space, and matter into disarray; Heisenberg's Uncertainty Principle, Chaos Theory, and the "New Physics" cut the ground from under the "objectivity" on which science has so much prided itself; the mechanistic conceptions of a material science, the very language of science, are found to be useless in the face of bewildering phenomena to which Western science has hitherto been blind. Everywhere cracks are appearing in the edifice of modern science. Titus Burckhardt, writing from a traditional viewpoint, exposes some of the issues involved here in writing:

> [M]odern science displays a certain number of fissures that are not only due to the fact that the world of phenomena is indefinite and that therefore no science could come to the end of it; those fissures derive especially from a systematic ignorance of all the noncorporeal dimensions of reality. They manifest themselves right down to the foundations of modern science, and in domains as seemingly "exact" as that of physics; they become gaping cracks when one turns to the disciplines connected with the study of the forms of life, not to mention psychology, where an empiricism that is relatively valid in the physical order encroaches strangely upon a foreign field. These fissures, which do not affect only the theoretical realm, are far from harmless; they represent, on the contrary, in their technical consequences, so many seeds of catastrophe.[2]

Social commentators have become more alert to the dangers of a totalitarian materialism, an instrumentalist rationality and its attendant technology. We see that rationality has been allowed to become man's definition instead of his tool. We sense that the disfigurement of the environment mirrors our internal state, that the ecological catastrophe is rooted in a spiritual crisis which no amount of science and technology can, of itself, remedy. We know the truth of Victor Frankl's claim that:

> The true nihilism of today is reductionism. . . . Contemporary nihilism no longer brandishes the word nothingness; today nihilism is camouflaged as nothing-but-ness. Human phenomena are thus turned into mere epiphenomena.[3]

---

2 T. Burckhardt, "Cosmology and Modern Science" in *The Sword of Gnosis*, ed. J. Needleman (Baltimore: Penguin, 1972), p. 131.

3 Quoted in E.F. Schumacher, *A Guide for the Perplexed* (London: Jonathan Cape, 1977), p. 15.

Commentators like René Guénon, Theodore Roszak, E.F. Schumacher, and Wendell Berry awaken us to the provincialism of modern science and to the dangers of "Single Vision."

Though modern science has doubtless revealed much material information that was previously unknown it has also supplanted a knowledge which infinitely outreaches it. We see this in the complacencies and condescensions of those scientists who like to suppose that we have "outgrown" the "superstitions" of our ancestors. Here is a random example from a prestigious contemporary scientist:

> I myself, like many scientists, believe that the soul is imaginary and that what we call our mind is simply a way of talking about the function of our brains. . . . Once one has become adjusted to the ideas that we are here because we have evolved from simple chemical compounds by a process of natural selection, it is remarkable how many of the problems of the modern world take on a completely new light.[4]

Here indeed is the fruit of a rampant materialism, an "intelligence without wisdom." It is nowadays a commonplace that many of the ills of our time stem from the rift between "faith" and "science" but few people have suggested any convincing means of reconciling the two. Certainly the effusions and compromises of the liberal theologians and "demytholgizers" are of no help, marking little more than a thinly-disguised capitulation of religion to science. One might adduce the works of the English theologian, Don Cuppitt, as a case in point. Nor should we be seduced by those apparently conciliatory scientists who seem willing to allow some sort of place for religious understandings, all the while making it clear that science will concede nothing of substance; here we can find no better exemplar of the mentality in question than E.O. Wilson's immensely popular but muddle-headed work, *Consilience.*[5] However, in the light of traditional metaphysical understandings many of the apparent contradictions between "science" and "religion" simply evaporate. It is not necessary, to say the least, to

---

4 F. Crick, *Molecules and Men*, quoted in T. Roszak, *Where the Wasteland Ends: Politics and Transcendence in Postindustrial Society* (New York: Doubleday, 1972), p. 88.

5 E.O. Wilson, *Consilience: The Unity of Knowledge* (New York, Vintage, 1999). This work has been subjected to the most searching criticism by Wendell Berry in *Life is a Miracle: An Essay Against Modern Superstition* (Washington, DC: Counterpoint, 2000).

throw religious beliefs on the scrapheap because they are "disproven" by modern science; nor is it necessary to gainsay such facts as modern science does uncover—provided always that what science presents as facts are so indeed and not merely precarious hypotheses.

The key to traditional understandings lies in the nature of their symbolism—a mode of knowledge quite inaccessible to the scientific mentality. No one will deny that, from one point of view, the earth is not the center of the solar system; this is no reason for jettisoning the more important truth which was carried by the symbolism of the geocentric picture of the universe. Another example: it is preferable to believe that God created the world in six days and that heaven lies in the empyrean above the flat surface of the earth than it is to know precisely the distance from one nebula to another whilst forgetting the truth embodied in this symbolism, namely that all phenomena depend on a higher Reality which determines us and gives our human existence meaning and purpose. A materially inaccurate but symbolically rich view is always preferable to the regime of brute fact. In falling under the tyranny of a fragmentary, materialistic, and quantitative outlook modern science is irremediably limited by its epistemological base. Of spiritual realities, modern science knows and can know absolutely nothing. As Frithjof Schuon observes:

> There is scarcely a more desperately vain or naive illusion—far more naive than Aristotelian astronomy!—than to believe that modern science, in its vertiginous course towards the "infinitely small" and the "infinitely great," will end up by rejoining religious and metaphysical truths and doctrines.[6]

The ways in which the triumph of scientism has contributed to man's dehumanization have been written about a good deal in recent years. It matters not a jot how quick contemporary scientists now are to disown discredited "facts" which stood between man and any true self-awareness—the mechanistic theories of the seventeenth century, for instance—on the grounds that these were, after all, only provisional hypotheses which a more "humane" scientific vision can now abandon. The simple fact is that modern science cannot be "humanized" or "reformed" from within itself because it is built on premises which are both inadequate and inhuman.

6 F. Schuon *Dimensions of Islam* (London: Allen & Unwin, 1969), p. 156.

CHAPTER 9

Computers:
An Academic Cargo Cult?

In the name of "science" and of "human genius" man consents to become the creation of what he has created and to forget what he is, to the point of expecting the answer to this from machines. . . .

Frithjof Schuon[1]

Machines are in themselves inhuman and anti-spiritual.

Frithjof Schuon[2]

In the 1620s Francis Bacon, in search of a new scientific method, looked forward to the day when "the mind itself be from the very outset not left to take its own course, but be guided at every step, and the business be done as if by machinery."[3] Descartes was gripped by a similar passion for a mode of thought which would be stripped of all its most personal qualities. Leibniz dreamed of a machine which, programmed with a question, would flash the answer on a screen. In 1958 Newell and Simon, two of the prime movers in the development of so-called artificial intelligence, wrote of machines that "think, that learn and create." The ability of these machines would increase rapidly until, "in the visible future . . . the range of problems they can handle will be co-extensive with the range to which the human mind has been applied."[4] The dream of an infallible, universal scientific method finds an echo today in the pursuit of a theory of everything and a machine for everything. It seems to many that science has brought us to a new frontier of knowledge, and that the dream of "intelligent" machines is now a reality.

---

1 F. Schuon, *Language of the Self* (Bloomington, IN: World Wisdom Books, 1999), p. 15.

2 F. Schuon, *Castes and Races* (London: Perennial Books, 1982), pp. 19-20.

3 Bacon quoted in T. Roszak, *Where the Wasteland Ends: Politics and Transcendence in Postindustrial Societ* (New York: Doubleday, 1972), p. 163.

4 Newell and Simn quoted in J. Weizenbaum, *Computer Power and Human Reason: From Judgement to Calculation* (San Francisco: W.H. Freeman, 1976), p. 179.

We now live, we are told, in the Information Age, one in which new forms of technology will transform our lives, a transition period bringing upheavals no less momentous than those of the Industrial Revolution. Leonard Sussman, an American expert on international communications, is an unexceptional champion of these changes. In a recent article he tells us that

> Nearly every man and woman on earth will [soon] be able to communicate in a few moments with someone continents away. Everyone will have immediate access . . . to a vast volume of diverse information—a volume such as even the world's finest libraries or news services cannot provide today. The cultures of even the smallest, least familiar peoples will be preserved, and made accessible to everyone, everywhere. New communications will induce the human mind to think more clearly, to test new possibilities, to gain confidence and even exhilaration from the process of idea- discovery.[5]

The new technologies bring their own educational imperatives. "The core of the problem and the key to its solution [Sussman tells us] is the need to computerize information, make it accessible to the broad public, and put hundreds of millions to work in the post-industrial information era."[6] Communications technology, he asserts, "will soon alter all the natural and social sciences, all levels of education, all forms of cultural activity, all geopolitics. Everywhere."[7] He enthuses about the fact that every eight years computer science doubles the entire volume of information available to us. He is hugely excited by the educational possibilities:

> The new technologies are the conduit for generating vast information-power. Almost simultaneously, world-wide, they convey, store or retrieve current speech, text, data or pictures, and information from all of human history. They also facilitate problem-solving in all human disciplines... widen the horizons of individuals through far greater cultural and educational opportunities... encourage the user to develop greater electronic literacy and the power of logical thinking... By mastering intricacies of the computer, we train our biologic

5 L. Sussman, "The Information Revolution," *Encounter*, November 1989, p. 60.
6 L. Sussman, "The Information Revolution," p. 61.
7 L. Sussman, "The Information Revolution," p. 65.

brains to think. And perhaps one day we will program the computer to develop artificial intelligence.[8]

In much the same vein, John Naisbitt tells us in *Megatrends* that

we now mass-produce information the way we used to mass-produce cars. In the information society, we have systematized the production of knowledge and amplified our brain power. . . . [W]e now mass-produce knowledge and this knowledge is the driving force of our economy.[9]

One could catalogue such commonplaces more or less indefinitely. On all sides we are told of the wonders of the new technologies and of the almost miraculous feats of the latest "generation" of computers. As Theodore Roszak has remarked:

[I]n the presence of so ingenious a technology, it is easy to conclude that because we have the ability to transmit more electronic bits more rapidly to more people than ever before, we are making real cultural progress—and that the essence of that progress is information technology.[10]

Computers as Cargo Cult

In the Western cultural tradition we can discern a line of thought running from Bacon and Descartes to the present apostles of the so-called "information revolution." But there is another current in the Western tradition, one which resists the ever more imperial claims of the sciences and which is suspicious about the claims made for machines of one kind and another. The Faust myth in its various forms, Blake's prophetic poems, Mary Shelley's *Frankenstein*, various works of the English and German Romantics, Dickens's novel *Hard Times*, the work of the great French metaphysician, René Guénon, and more recently Kurt Vonnegut's anti-Utopia *Piano Player* are amongst the many landmarks in this counter-tradition. To some it will no doubt seem fanciful that

8 L. Sussman, "The Information Revolution," p. 61.

9 Naisbitt quoted in T. Roszak, *The Cult of Information: The Folklore of Computers and the True Art of Thinking* (London: Paladin, 1986), p. 35.

10 T. Roszak, *The Cult of Information*, p. 29.

such writers have anything to tell us about our current situation.[11] Others will mutter about Luddites and self-interested cranks, to which one can only answer that history has proved the Luddites right in their fundamental intuition that machinery would indeed destroy many traditional arts and crafts, and thus annihilate many honorable vocations in which countless generations found dignified work.

The title of this essay suggests that the enthusiasm for the computer in particular, and for other forms of technological whizz-bangery, really amounts to a kind of cargo cult. A cargo cult is a quasi-religious movement driven by a mistaken attribution of supernatural powers to some quite mundane entity and the belief that the paying of homage to it will bring a superabundance of material benefits. Something of the kind is going on in academia. Not only do we look to these technologies to solve problems which are quite beyond their capacities but our technophilia constitutes a much more serious problem than those which we hope can be so solved.

I am no expert on computers or on any other form of technology which might be turned to educational ends. I am not embarrassed by this fact. It is important that ordinary people involve themselves in this debate. It will certainly not do to leave it in the hands of the experts. As Roszak remarks in *The Cult of Information,*

> the discussion of computers and information is awash with commercially motivated exaggeration and the opportunistic mystifications of the computer science establishment. The hucksters . . . have polluted our understanding of information technology with loose metaphors, facile comparisons, and a good deal of out-and-out obfuscation. There are billions of dollars in profit and a windfall of social power to account for why they should wish to do this. Already there may be a large public that believes it not only cannot make judgments about computers, but has no right to do so because computers are superior to its own intelligence—a position of absolute deference which human beings have never assumed with respect to any technology of the past.[12]

I am not blind to the limited but important benefits these new technologies can confer. I composed this essay on a Macintosh: its ad-

11 See N.R. Evans, "Ideologies of Anti-Technology," *Quadrant*, July 1980.

12 T. Roszak, *The Cult of Information*, p. 61.

vantages over the typewriter are considerable. I also make frequent if cautious use of the internet. But I share Roszak's view that the educational claims made for computers are not only grotesquely inflated but dangerous. I hope to indicate some of the grounds for concern and to explore a few ideas which, in my view, we should strenuously resist.

Thinking Machines?

The first such idea is that the computer is analogous to the human mind, that it can properly be called "intelligent," that it can replicate the higher functions of the human mind. The anthropomorphizing of machines, betrayed by the attribution of such qualities as "intelligence," "memory," and "friendliness," is by no means insignificant. Not only does the jargon endow computers with qualities they do not possess but it is often used to affirm the superiority of the computer to the human mind which, Naisbitt tells us, "not only is limited in its storage and processing capacity, but it also has known bugs; it is easily misled, stubborn and even blind to the truth. . . ."[13] Conversely, all too often we are subliminally exposed to the data processing model of the mind.

Another contemporary line of thinking leads us to Robert Jastrow's vision of a not-far-distant future where

> At last the human brain, ensconced in a computer, has been liberated from the weakness of the mortal flesh. . . . It is in control of its own destiny. The machine is its body; it is the machine's mind. . . . It seems to me that this must be the mature form of intelligent life in the Universe. Housed in indestructible lattices of silicon, and no longer constrained in the span of its years by the life and death cycle of a biological organism, such a kind of life could live forever.[14]

Thus we not only anthropomorphize the machine, we mechanize ourselves. I wish I could dismiss this as a nightmarish vision from a science fiction novel.

No one denies that computers can *store* vast amounts of data, far more than can be accommodated in the mind of any individual. Computers are also able to *process* this data with astonishing rapidity. Here indeed is an invention which can perform computational tasks with

---

13 Naisbitt quoted in T. Roszak, *The Cult of Information*, p. 52.

14 Jastrow quoted in T. Roszak, *The Cult of Information*, p. 134.

extraordinary speed and efficiency. There is no denying that the computer is hugely useful for administrative and data-sorting tasks—in university administrations and in libraries, for instance. But to move from here to the notion that computers can be developed to perform some of the higher functions of the human mind is a very dangerous move indeed. It is then not such a big step to such absurd lucubrations as the following, written by Marvin Minsky in 1970:

> In from three to eight years, we will have a machine with the general intelligence of a human being. I mean a machine that will be able to read Shakespeare, grease a car, play office politics, tell a joke, have a fight. At that point, the machine will begin to educate itself with fantastic speed. In a few months, it will be at genius level, and a few months after that, its power will be incalculable.[15]

He added that such machines might well decide to keep humans as pets. Minsky's colleagues at MIT thought this scenario was a bit reckless: the general feeling was that such a machine might take up to fifteen years to develop.

The mind-computer analogy depends on another confusion: the notion there is some common measure between information and knowledge. Much discussion of the possibilities of the computer blurs the crucial distinctions between information and information-processing on one hand and, on the other, those many capacities of the human mind which no computer could possibly replicate—memory, imagination, intuition, the creation of ideas, the ability to interpret— all of which all play their part in the development of what can properly be called knowledge. Unhappily, the word "information"

> has received ambitious, global definitions that make it all good things to all people. Words that come to mean everything may finally come to mean nothing; yet their very emptiness may allow them to be filled with a mesmerizing glamour. The loose but exuberant talk we hear on all sides these days about the "information economy," "the information society," is coming to have exactly that function. These oft-repeated catchphrases and clichés are the mumbo jumbo of a widespread public cult.[16]

15 T. Roszak, *The Cult of Information*, p. 10.

16 T. Roszak, *The Cult of Information*, p. 10.

The computational mode is sequential, regulated, predictable, formal, quantitative. But human experience, imagination, thought, and creativity are not amenable to this model: to reduce the complexities of the mind, and the processes of knowing and understanding to a computational model is to surrender to a reductionist and mechanistic scientism.

Computers cannot deal with the very stuff of human thought. They can only offer us mechanical counterfeits. Contrary to much contemporary opinion, thought is generated and organized not by data or information but by ideas. What are ideas? They are images, metaphors, organizing patterns which connect and make meaningful disparate phenomena and areas of experience. They derive from our subjective experiences, from the creative interplay of imagination and memory and feeling as well as from the rational workings of the mind. Human memory is nothing like the so-called "memory" of computers which is simply the capacity to retrieve data. Human memory represses, distorts, projects, embellishes. It works through the mind, the senses, the feelings. Creative thought is supple, unpredictable, fluent, mysterious—in short, not at all computer-like. As Kuhn has shown, even scientific thought, at least in its higher reaches, is not at all computational.[17] The great scientific discoveries have proceeded through astonishing leaps of the imagination, through intuitions, through flashes of insight rather than through either the accumulation of empirical data or the workings of an apparently objective rationality.

Ideas do not grow out of empirical observation nor from raw data; they are not based on information. Information may shape and color our ideas but certainly cannot constitute them. Ideas are created by a consciousness in search of meaning. We cannot think without ideas. As Roszak observes, ideas actually generate information rather than vice versa, as is so often thought. The mind works with ideas not information. Ideas contain, define, and produce information but are by no means identical with it.

> Every fact grows from an idea; it is the answer to a question we could not ask in the first place if an idea had not been invented which isolated some portion of the world, made it important, focused our attention, and stimulated enquiry.[18]

17 See T. Kuhn, *The Structure of Scientific Revolutions* (Chicago: Chicago University Press, 1963).

18 T. Roszak, *The Cult of Information*, p. 126.

Information can only be gathered and organized in response to questions which are governed by ideas and values: "In the long run, no ideas, no information."[19]

One of the most fundamental questions, one which is all too frequently ignored in the general enthusiasm for information, is "What is worth knowing?" It is also well to remember that there are many problems which cannot be addressed let alone solved by any amount of information. As Frithjof Schuon has remarked, "That which is lacking in the present world is a profound knowledge of the nature of things";[20] that ignorance certainly can not be remedied by information of any kind whatsoever.

If we accept a recent definition of knowledge as the capacity to interpret and "to establish relevant relationships or connections between facts, data, and other information in some coherent form and to explain the reasons for those generalizations"[21] then the word "knowledge" cannot properly be applied to any of the computer's capacities. Computers are incapable of anything even resembling intuition or imagination or human sympathies of any kind. The computer cannot possibly generate ideas or values or meanings. Likewise computers are utterly incapable of interpretation. Interpretation, if it is to mean anything, must mean the making of judgments—a esthetic, moral, ideological, intellectual. Learning should consist, among other things, in becoming familiar with and learning to handle a diversity of interpretations—interpretations of the human condition, of the social order, of art, of philosophy and science, of the natural world, and so on. There can, by definition, be no exclusively correct interpretation of anything.

To speak and write of computers offering us "interpretations" is a nonsense: "The prospect of machine interpretation is not only whimsical; it is absurd. Interpretation belongs to a living mind in exactly the same way that birth belongs solely to a living body."[22] Let us also not forget the lesson in Plotinus's dictum of nearly two and a half thousand years ago, no less true now that it was then: "Knowing demands the organ fitted to the object."

19 T. Roszak, *The Cult of Information*, p. 128.

20 F. Schuon, "No Activity Without Truth" in *The Sword of Gnosis*, ed. J. Needleman (Baltimore: Penguin, 1974), p. 28.

21 D. Bell, "Gutenberg and the Computer," *Encounter*, May 1985, p. 17.

22 T. Roszak, *The Cult of Information*, p. 154.

Computers in the Classroom

An eminent American educationalist, Dr. Ernest Boyer, articulates a common hope when he writes that

> in the long run, electronic teachers may provide exchanges of information, ideas, and experiences more effectively . . . than the traditional classroom or the teacher. The promise of the new technology is to enrich the study of literature, science and mathematics, and the arts through words, pictures, and auditory messages.[23]

I am much more sympathetic to Theodore Roszak's response to this claim:

> My own taste runs to another image: that of teachers and students in one another's face-to-face company, perhaps pondering a book, a work of art, even a crude scrawl on the blackboard. At the very least, that image reminds us of how marvelously simple, even primitive, education is. It is the unmediated encounter of two minds, one needing to learn, the other wanting to teach. . . . Too much apparatus, like too much bureaucracy, only inhibits the natural flow. Free human dialogue, wandering wherever the agility of mind allows, lies at the heart of education.[24]

I cannot claim to be familiar with much of the research done on the educational use of computers. However, the evidence with which I am familiar[25] and my own experience suggest that when computers are used as a teaching tool several things are bound to happen: an inordinate amount of time is spent on overcoming technical difficulties and on mastering the software; students work largely in isolation from each other; contact between student and teacher is most often about procedural problems; almost inevitably the mastery of the software and of the machine come to be seen not as means towards some more significant educational end, but as ends in themselves. It is as if the filing cabinet, the counting machine, and the typewriter had been transformed

23 Boyer quoted in T. Roszak, *The Cult of Information*, pp. 77-78.

24 T. Roszak, *The Cult of Information*, pp. 79-80 (emphasis mine).

25 For instance, C. Beattie, "Packaging Computer Knowledge: The Further Education Classroom" in *Breaking into the Curriculum: The Impact of Information Technology on Schooling*, ed. J.F. Schostak (London: Methuen, 1988), p. 177-199.

from useful but humble tools into the very object of study. Similarly the ability to manipulate data through a mastery of techniques comes to be grossly over-valued.

The technology also comes to determine the kind of tasks put in front of students. It has been claimed that "the computer can be as much associated with play, fun, imagination, sharing ideas, self-expression as it can with rational information manipulation and the routine mindless repetition of predefined outputs. . . . [T]he difference depends upon how the computer is used and interpreted."[26] This strikes me as a very sanguine view indeed. It is much more likely that the computer is indeed the last step in a process which began with the scientific revolution of the seventeenth century. Clearly the mystique of the computer and of computer-based paradigms derives in part from the philosophical traditions of empiricism and rationalism noted at the start of this essay.

> ["Smart" machines] have a seductive appeal to the scientific imagination, which has freely borrowed them as models of the universe at large, often reshaping our experience of the world to make it fit that model. And in this there can be the real danger that we fall prey to a technological idolatry, allowing an invention of our own hands to become an image that dominates our understanding of ourselves and all nature around us.[27]

One need not look far for examples. An eminent American psychologist: "Many psychologists have come to take for granted in recent years . . . that men and computers are merely two different species of a more abstract genus called 'information processing systems.'"[28] Ugh!

The triumph of Cartesianism and of a materialistic ideology of science has meant

> the expulsion from scientific thought of all considerations based on value, perfection, harmony, meaning, beauty, purpose, for such considerations are now regarded as merely subjective and so as irrelevant to a scientific understanding of the real "objective" world—the

26 J.F. Schostak, *Breaking into the Curriculum*, p. 18.

27 T. Roszak, *The Cult of Information*, p. 55.

28 George Miller quoted in J. Weizenbaum, *Computer Power and Human Reason*, p. 158

world of quantity, of reified geometry, of a nature that is impersonal and purely functional.[29]

Those modes of thought and understanding which go beyond the logical and the mechanical, already radically devalued by modern scientism, will be even further diminished by our infatuation with the computer. The perfect computer-driven classroom project may well be the production of the phone book or a railway timetable—a vast amount of data, highly organized into a "user-friendly" package! The surrender to scientific paradigms of knowledge leads to a kind of learning bleached of all questions of taste and value, and "strips human thought of its most intimately personal qualities—its ethical vision, its metaphysical resonance, its existential meaning."[30]

Recall a short scene from Charles Dickens' novel *Hard Times* in which his abhorrence of a rigorously utilitarian and information-based education is most forcefully expressed. The scene is set in the classroom of a school devoted to the Gradgrind system of education. Sissy Jupe, a young girl who has spent most of her life in a traveling circus and who has an intimate experience of horses, is unable to satisfy Mr. Gradgrind's demand for a definition of a horse. The star pupil in the class is a robotic boy named Bitzer who has no direct experience of horses. He is able to supply the necessary definition. It goes this way:

> "Quadruped. Gramnivorous. Forty teeth, namely twenty-four grinders, four eye teeth, and twelve incisive. Sheds coat in spring; in marshy countries, sheds hoofs too. Hoofs hard, but requiring to be shod with iron. Age known by marks in mouth." Thus (and much more) Bitzer.[31]

This, surely, needs no comment.

Where in the domain of the computer is the place for metaphor, allegory, symbol, myth, analogy? How is a computer to engender these value-laden, unpredictable, and intensely personal modes of thought

29 P. Sherrard, *The Rape of Man and Nature: An Enquiry into the Origins and Conse-quences of Modern Science* (Colombo: Sri Lanka Institute of Traditional Studies, 1987), p. 69.

30 T. Roszak, *The Cult of Information*, p. 159.

31 C. Dickens, *Hard Times* (first published 1854) (Harmondsworth: Penguin, 1969), p. 50.

and experience? What becomes of questions concerning meaning, beauty, ethics, value? How are we to use a computer in the teaching of Homer? I have yet to see cogent answers to such questions.

Nor do I find much to commend the argument that computers allow students to take control of their own learning. Within a limited arena they may well do so. But on this issue I agree with the observations of the American poet Wendell Berry:

> The responsibility to decide what to teach the young is an adult responsibility. When adults transfer this responsibility to the young, whether they do it by indifference or as a grant of freedom, they trap themselves in a kind of childishness. In that failure to accept responsibility, the teacher's own learning and character are disemployed, and, in the contemporary industrialized education system, they are easily replaced by bureaucratic and methodological procedures, "job market" specifications, and tests graded by machines.[32]

There is a good deal of talk about the ways in which computers might "liberate" teachers from some of the tasks which they presently carry out. It is much more likely that in the long run the real consequence of this kind of process will be the destruction of the academic and teaching profession.

> For computer scientists, it is no doubt exciting to ask: "Can we invent a machine that does what a teacher does?" But there is another question one might ask: "Why should we want to invent a machine to do that in the first place?" There was never any difficulty in answering that question where the machine was intended to take over work that was dirty, dangerous, or back-breaking. Teaching is hardly any of these.[33]

Nor will it do to see in the computer an answer to the problems of incompetent teaching, student alienation, boredom, and the like. If

32 W. Berry, *Home Economics: Fourteen Essays* (San Francisco: North Point Press, 1987), p. 86.

33 T. Roszak, *The Cult of Information*, p. 70. See also R. Sworder, "Are We the Last Academics?" in *Academia Under Pressure: Theory and Practice for the 21st Century*, ed. M.S. Parer (Churchill, Victoria: Higher Education and Research Development Society of Australia, 1992), pp. 233-236.

teachers do not have the energy, the imagination, or the expertise to engage their students, or if students are too alienated or distracted or demoralized to respond, then this is the problem to be addressed and solved "from inside the experience of the teachers and the students. Defaulting to the computer is not a solution; it is surrender."[34] I am reminded of a Cobb cartoon in which a robot standing in front of a bank of computer-like machines addresses a begowned graduate, clutching his newly acquired degree: "Haven't you heard? The Industrial Revolution is over . . . we won. . . ."

I do not have space here to canvas the ways in which the move towards technology-centered teaching might be connected to the view of education held by the federal government. It is no secret that the universities are increasingly being straitjacketed into a model derived from industrial production.[35] It does not take much imagination to see how these trends might be related. Nor can I here examine the ways in which the computing industry has penetrated the educational systems in most industrialized countries. The agenda of developing a more or less universal computer "literacy" can perhaps more properly be seen as a drive to make everyone computer-dependent. The marketing of hi-tech in the educational arena has been highly aggressive, sophisticated, and cynical. This massive intrusion has only rarely been challenged from within the education system: more often it has been greeted with either mindless enthusiasm or meek surrender. Let us also not forget that computers are expensive to manufacture, to service, and to replace. Like most modern appliances they have a built-in obsolescence which demands constant up-dating—thus a cycle of endless consumption characteristic of our whole industrial system. Nowhere is the lure and hypnotic glamour of the new more apparent than in the domain of the computer.

The computer was once well described as "a solution in search of a problem." The computer is all too often a false solution to a real problem or an apparently real solution to a false problem. Our technological fundamentalism constitutes the real problem.

34 T. Roszak, *The Cult of Information*, pp. 79-80.

35 See B. Huppauf, "Universities in the Grip of the Electronic Age," *Meanjin*, 42, 1987.

CHAPTER 10

Frithjof Schuon on Culturism

Genius is nothing unless determined by a spiritual perspective.
Frithjof Schuon[1]

One manifestation of the anti-traditional outlook, is the cult of genius and the phenomenon of what Frithjof Schuon calls "culturism." In "To Have a Center," one of his most arresting essays in which he directly addresses some specifically modern cultural movements, Schuon articulates his governing theme:

> We live in a world which on the one hand tends to deprive men of their center, and on the other hand offers them—in place of the saint and the hero—the cult of the "genius." Now a genius is all too often a man without a center, in whom this lack is replaced by a creative hypertrophy. To be sure, there is a genius proper to normal, hence balanced and virtuous, man; but the world of "culture" and "art for art's sake" accepts with the same enthusiasm normal and abnormal men, the latter being particularly numerous . . . in that world of dreams or nightmares that was the nineteenth century.[2]

That many of these nineteenth century geniuses led unhappy and desperate lives only adds to their prestige and strengthens the "seduction, indeed the fascination, which emanates from their siren songs and tragic destinies." The "unbridled subjectivism" and the "split and heteroclite psychism"[3] of many of the century's geniuses often induced melancholy and despair, sometimes psychopathology and insanity. Now, Schuon readily concedes that profane genius can, "in any human climate," be "the medium of a cosmic quality, of an archetype of beauty

---

1 F. Schuon, *Art from the Sacred to the Profane: East and West*, ed. C. Schuon (Bloomington, IN: World Wisdom, 2007), p. 41.

2 F. Schuon, *To Have a Center* (Bloomington, IN: World Wisdom Books, 1990), p. 8. A Virgil, a Dante, a Fra Angelico furnish examples of normal men blessed with a creative genius.

3 F. Schuon, *To Have a Center*, p. 9.

or greatness," in which case we can respect at least some of its productions even though they lie outside tradition. As he writes elsewhere:

> Modern art—starting from the Renaissance—does include some more or less isolated works which, though they fit into the style of their period, are in a deeper sense opposed to it and neutralize its errors by their own qualities.[4]

However, what we most often witness in the last few centuries is a "useless profusion of talents and geniuses" driven by a "humanistic narcissism with its mania for individualistic and unlimited production."[5] Humanism promotes a certain dynamism and a "fruitless moral idealism" which "depends entirely on a human ideology."

Schuon goes on to illustrate his theme with reference to the lives and productions of a gallery of nineteenth century artists, among them Beethoven, Wagner, Rodin, Nietzsche, Wilde, Gauguin, Van Gogh, Ibsen, Bizet, Balzac, Dickens, Tolstoy, and Dostoevsky—all figures whose prodigious talents were turned astray by an impoverished environment, which is not to deny the traces of incidental beauty and grandeur which can be found in many of their works. Let us briefly consider Schuon's remarks on a few representative cases. Firstly, Beethoven:

> Despite the fact that Beethoven was a believer, he was inevitably situated on the plane of humanism, hence of "horizontality." And though there was nothing morbid about him, we note the characteristic disproportion between the artistic work and the spiritual personality; characteristic, precisely, for genius arising from the cult of man, thus from the Renaissance and its consequences. There is no denying what is powerful and profound about many of Beethoven's musical motifs, but, all things considered, a music of this sort should not exist; it exteriorizes and hence exhausts possibilities which ought to remain inward and contribute in their own way to the contemplative scope of the soul. In this sense, Beethoven's art is both an indiscretion and a dilapidation, as is the case with most post-Renaissance artistic manifestations.[6]

4 F. Schuon, *Art from the Sacred to the Profane*, p. 15.

5 F. Schuon, *To Have a Center*, p. 10.

6 F. Schuon, *To Have a Center*, pp. 12-13.

And all this despite the fact that Beethoven, compared to other geniuses, was "a homogeneous man, hence 'normal', if we disregard his demiurgic passion for musical exteriorization." Schuon also notes that

> Whereas in Bach or Mozart musicality still manifests itself with faultless crystallinity, in Beethoven there is something like the rupture of a dam or an explosion; and this climate of cataclysm is precisely what people appreciate.[7]

Rodin provides an instance of another "powerful and quasi-volcanic" genius, "direct heir to the Renaissance" in his titanesque "carnal and tormented" productions, reminiscent of ancient naturalism and the "sensual cult of the human body."[8] Victor Hugo, on the other hand, is no more than a "bombastic and long-winded spokesman of French romanticism" who "puffs himself up and finally becomes hardened in the passionate projection of himself"[9] (a story repeated many times in modern "culture"!). There are others, like Ibsen and Strindberg, who become spokesmen for "a thesis that is excessive, revolutionary, subversive, and in the highest degree individualistic and anarchic":

> This kind of talent—or of genius, as the case may be—makes one think of children who play with fire, or of Goethe's sorcerer's apprentice: these people play with everything, with religion, with the social order, with mental equilibrium, provided they can safeguard their originality; an originality which, retrospectively, shows itself to be a perfect banality, because there is nothing more banal than fashion, no matter how clamorous.[10]

To turn to one of the more formidable figures of the century, Nietzsche was yet another "volcanic genius":

> Here, too, there is a passionate exteriorization of an inward fire, but in a manner that is both deviated and demented; we have in mind here, not the Nietzschean philosophy, which taken literally is with-

---

7 F. Schuon, *To Have a Center*, p. 13n.

8 F. Schuon, *To Have a Center*, pp. 13-14. In some sense Rodin is heir to the "blustering and carnal paintings of a Rubens" (*Art from the Sacred to the Profane*, p. 39).

9 F. Schuon, *To Have a Center*, p. 20.

10 F. Schuon, *To Have a Center*, p. 20.

out interest, but his poetical work, whose most intense expression is in part his *Zarathustra*. What this highly uneven book manifests above all is the violent reaction of an *a priori* profound soul against a mediocre and paralyzing cultural environment; Nietzsche's fault was to have only a sense of grandeur in the absence of all intellectual discernment. *Zarathustra* is basically the cry of a grandeur trodden underfoot, whence comes the heart-rending authenticity—grandeur precisely—of certain passages; not all of them, to be sure, and above all not those which express a half-Machiavellian, half-Darwinian philosophy, or minor literary cleverness. Be that as it may, Nietzsche's misfortune, like that of other men of genius, such as Napoleon, was to be born after the Renaissance and not before it; which indicates evidently an aspect of their nature, for there is no such thing as chance.[11]

Goethe, a well-balanced man with a "lofty and generous" mind, was another victim of the epoch "owing to the fact that humanism in general and Kantianism in particular had vitiated his tendency towards a vast and finely-shaded wisdom" and made him, paradoxically, "the spokesman of a perfectly bourgeois 'horizontality.'"[12]

The nineteenth century novelists furnish many instances of "a problematic type of talent led astray from its true vocation": whereas in medieval times narratives were inspired by myths, legends, and religious and chivalrous ideals, in the modern novel they become "more and more profane, even garrulous and insignificant." Their authors lived only a vicarious existence through their characters: "A Balzac, a Dickens, a Tolstoy, a Dostoevsky lived on the fringe of themselves, they gave their blood to phantoms, and they incited their readers to do the same . . . with the aggravating circumstance that these others were neither heroes nor saints and, besides, never existed." Furthermore:

> These remarks can be applied to the whole of that universe of dreams which is called "culture": flooded by literary opium, siren songs, vampirizing, and—to say the least—useless production, people live on the fringe of the natural world and its exigencies, and consequently on the fringe—or at the antipodes—of the "one thing needful." The nineteenth century—with its garrulous and irrespon-

---

11 F. Schuon, *To Have a Center*, p. 15.
12 F. Schuon, *To Have a Center*, p. 16.

sible novelists, its *poètes maudits*, its creators of pernicious operas, its unhappy artists, in short with all its superfluous idolatries and all of its blind allies leading to despair—was bound to crash against a wall, the fruit of its own absurdity; thus the First World War was for the *belle époque* what the sinking of the Titanic was for the elegant and decadent society that happened to be on board, or what Reading Goal was for Oscar Wilde, analogically speaking.[13]

Then, too, there are the "unhappy painters," such as Van Gogh and Gauguin, both "bearers of certain incontestable values" but whose work, "despite the prestige of the style," is marred by "the lack of discernment and spirituality." They also dramatize the tragedy of "normally intelligent men who sell their souls to a creative activity which no one asks of them . . . who make a religion of their profane and individualistic art and who, so to speak, die martyrs for a cause not worth the trouble."[14] (Gauguin is a particularly interesting case, given the fact that Schuon's own paintings are somewhat reminiscent, in both subject matter and style, of Gauguin's.) In another essay Schuon alludes to artworks which, to some degree, escape the limitations and distortions of the age:

> Of famous or well-known painters the elder Brueghel's snow scenes may be quoted and, nearer to our day, Gauguin, some of whose canvases are almost perfect, Van Gogh's flower paintings, Douanier Rousseau with his exotic forests akin to folk painting, and, among our contemporaries, Covarrubias with his Mexican and Balinese subjects. We might perhaps also allude to certain American Indian painters whose work shows, through a naturalistic influence, a vision close to that of the ancient pictography. Conversely, equivalents of the positive experiments of modern art can be found in the most varied of traditional art, which proves not only that these experiments are compatible with the universal principles of art, but also that—once again—"there is nothing new under the sun."[15]

Returning to "To Have a Center": Schuon goes on to describe the depredations of humanism and the cult of genius in several other fields

13 F. Schuon, *To Have a Center*, p. 17.
14 F. Schuon, *To Have a Center*, p. 19.
15 F. Schuon, *Art from the Sacred to the Profane*, p. 15.

of "cultural production," including the theatre, philosophy, and the darker recesses of Romanticism, as well as discussing the ostensible lack of "culture" (as it is understood in the modern West) amongst non-literate peoples. It is worth taking close note of the following remarks:

> A particularly problematic sector of culture with a humanist background is philosophical production, where naive pretension and impious ambition become involved in the affairs of universal truth, which is an extremely serious matter; on this plane, the desire for originality is one of the least pardonable sins. . . . The most serious reproach we can make concerning the general run of these "thinkers" is their lack of intuition of the real and consequently their lack of a sense of proportion; or the short-sightedness and lack of respect with which they handle the weightiest questions human intelligence can conceive, and to which centuries or millennia of spiritual consciousness have provided the answer.[16]

The brief account above perhaps suggests that Schuon makes a blanket condemnation of modern culture; this is not quite the case. What *is* unequivocally condemned is a kind of humanistic ideology of "culturism"—but Schuon remains acutely sensitive to those qualities of intelligence and beauty which still appear in various artworks, despite the mediocre and spiritually stifling cultural milieu in which they appear, and which bear witness to the artist's nobility of soul even when this is compromised by the false idol of "art for art's sake." Readers who turn to the essay in full will find there a carefully nuanced treatment of the subject. However, if "it is not easy to have completely unmixed feelings on the subject of profane 'cultural' genius," Schuon's general case against humanistic culture is implacable:

> Humanistic culture, insofar as it functions as an ideology and therefore as a religion, consists essentially in being unaware of three things: firstly, of what God is, because it does not grant primacy to Him; secondly, of what man is, because it puts him in the place of God; thirdly, of what the meaning of life is, because this culture limits itself to playing with evanescent things and to plunging into them with criminal unconsciousness. In a word, there is nothing more in-

16 F. Schuon, *To Have a Center*, pp. 21-22.

human than humanism, by the fact that it, so to speak, decapitates man.[17]

*

All of the "-isms" that have been under discussion as well as countless other modernist ideologies with which they consort, amount to bogus philosophies because they betray our real nature. And these ideologies are everywhere in the contemporary world. It is for this reason that Schuon writes, "It is necessary to reject the modern world, its errors, its tendencies, its trivialities."[18] Of the countless passages in his writings which refute these degraded views of the human condition and which affirm our real nature, here is one with which to conclude:

> Man is spirit incarnate; if he were only matter, he would be identified with the feet; if he were only spirit, he would be the head, that is, the Sky; he would be the Great Spirit. But the object of his existence is to be in the middle: it is to transcend matter while being situated there, and to realize the light, the Sky, starting from this intermediary level. It is true that the other creatures also participate in life, but man synthesizes them: he carries all life within himself and thus becomes the spokesman for all life, the vertical axis where life opens onto the spirit and where it becomes spirit. In all terrestrial creatures the cold inertia of matter becomes heat, but in man alone does heat become light.[19]

17 F. Schuon, *To Have a Center*, p. 37.

18 Frithjof Schuon, unpublished writings, courtesy of World Wisdom.

19 F. Schuon, *The Feathered Sun: Plains Indians in Art and Philosophy* (Bloomington, IN: World Wisdom Books, 1990), p. 16.

CHAPTER 11

The Past Disowned:
The Political and Postmodern Assault on the Humanities

Almost all the words standing for learning, seriousness, and reverence have in fact been compromised. . . .

Raymond Williams[1]

Real art has the capacity to make us nervous.

Susan Sontag[2]

When all have become the breakers of idols, the protector of graven images is the true revolutionary.

T.S. Eliot[3]

In almost any recent period it is not difficult to find claims about the crisis in higher education: it is permanently contested territory. The present debate is signaled by an avalanche of books, papers, articles, and conferences concerned with the future of the whole tertiary system in Australia, and, perhaps to an even greater degree, in the USA and UK. The current crisis seems particularly acute to those who believe that the intellectual and cultural values embodied in the traditional ideal of the university should not be discarded into the rubbish bin of the past. We have recently seen some of the effects of the political centralization and bureaucratization of the tertiary sector. The utilitarian model of the university, harnessed to the needs of the national economy and clothed in such repellent jargon as "product accountability" and "the knowledge industry," is fraught with all manner of hazards. We are living in a period of naked educational functionalism: nothing is an end in itself but only a means. Our real business, it seems, is no longer the educating of the human person but the training of a

---

1 R. Williams, *Culture and Society: 1780-1950* (Harmondsworth: Penguin, 1961), p. 135.

2 "Against Interpretation" in *A Susan Sontag Reader*, ed. E. Hardwick (Harmondsworth: Penguin, 1983), p. 99.

3 T.S. Eliot quoted in G.H. Bantock (ed.), *T.S. Eliot and Education* (London: Faber, 1970), p. 109.

Graduate, a Specialist, a Careerist, the making of a particular cog for The Economy. How far we have come from that view so eloquently expressed by Newman when he wrote:

> [K]nowledge is, not merely a means to something beyond it, or the preliminary of certain arts into which it naturally resolves, but an end sufficient to rest in and pursue for its own sake.[4]

Utilitarianism is the order of the day and it is every bit as ugly as that educational Gradgrindery which Dickens excoriated in *Hard Times*. Here, however, I wish to focus specifically on the current situation of the humane disciplines in the Academy, particularly the study of literature.

The Liberal View of the Humanities

The liberal view of education rested on the notion of an intellectual and cultural tradition to which every educated person should have access, a tradition which we can now see stretching from Homer to Joyce, from the Old Testament prophets to Bob Dylan, a tradition which, in the words of a contemporary commentator, "can embrace everything from Hildegard von Bingen to Cowboy Junkies."[5] This heritage was seen to be important for several reasons: firstly because it enshrined works of the highest intellectual, aesthetic, and moral qualities, works which illumined the question of what it means to be human. It was assumed that Sophocles and the Bible and Shakespeare had something of more or less universal interest to offer, that our human potentialities had been immeasurably enriched by these works. The tradition was also important because, historically, it had shaped the culture to which most of us belong. It provided us with a treasure-house of myths, symbols, images, motifs, and narratives, a collective repository gradually enlarged and handed down from generation to generation. The task of the student of the humanities in particular was, in the first place, to pursue a disinterested understanding of what such philosophers and painters and writers had to say about the human condition. Such a study could free us from the tyranny of the ephemeral, the transient,

---

4 Quoted in B. Spurr, "The New Idea of the University," *Quadrant*, April 1990, p. 43.

5 R. Wood, "Servants and Slaves: Brown Persons in Classical Hollywood Cinema," *CineAction!*, 32, 1993, p. 84.

the merely fashionable, enabling us to transcend the narrow limits of our own historical moment and cultural location. As Matthew Arnold wrote in those oft-quoted but now maligned words:

> [C]ulture is the great help out of our present difficulties; culture being the pursuit of our total perfection by means of getting to know, on all matters which most concern us, the best that has been said and thought in the world; and through this knowledge, turning a stream of fresh and free thought upon our stock notions and habits. . . .[6]

Today such an ideal is, in many quarters, in serious disrepute: to attempt to reanimate it is likely to provoke a positive orgy of polemical sloganeering. We can, I think, discern two persistent motifs, related but distinct, in the widespread repudiation of the Arnoldian view of a humane education. For purposes of convenience we can dub these as the "political" and the "postmodernist."

The Political Critique

The key to the first assault on the liberal view of the humanities lies in the word "political," signaling matters related to the exercise of power. The nub of the case is that the traditional view of a humane education is part of an intellectual-cultural-institutional complex of factors whose covert purpose is the maintenance of a particular set of social power relations. Whatever the lofty rhetoric in which the ideal was clothed the real function of this kind of education, it is argued, was and is political. The vocabulary of these critics is by now monotonously familiar. The most frequently leveled charges: "hierarchicalism," "elitism," "sexism," "racism," "cultural chauvinism," "canonic monumentalism." The liberal view of education, it is said, is an exclusivist weapon in the hands of a small, white, male elite, a glorification of a cultural and political tradition which disenfranchised women, children, slaves, and ethnic minorities, one that justifies class oppression, patriarchalism, and imperialism, a cultural inheritance which is worshipped as some kind of static monument and which incorporates "repressive politics" in its canonic texts and in the ways in which these texts are taught. These charges are not new. Over a century ago Matthew Arnold found it necessary to defend culture against the charge that it was "an engine

---

6 M. Arnold, *Culture and Anarchy* (first published 1869) (Cambridge: Cambridge University Press, 1935), p. 6.

of social and class distinction, separating its holder, like a badge or title, from other people who have not got it."[7]

Take a couple of comparatively temperate examples of this kind of political view. Thus Henry Giroux, an American professor of education:

> How we read or define a "canonical" work may not be as important as challenging the overall function and social uses the notion of the canon has served. Within this type of discourse, the canon can be analyzed as part of a wider set of relations that connect the academic disciplines, teaching, and power to considerations defined through broader, intersecting political and cultural concerns such as race, class, gender, ethnicity, and nationalism. What is in question here is not merely a defense of a particular canon, but the issue of struggle and empowerment. . . . The notion of the liberal arts has to be reconstituted around a knowledge-power relationship in which the question of curriculum is seen as a form of cultural and political production grounded in a radical conception of citizenship and public wisdom.[8]

Another representative example, from Professor Linda Kerber, recent President of the American Studies Association:

> Freed from the defensive constraints of cold-war ideology, empowered by our new sensitivity to the distinctions of race, class, and gender, we are ready to begin to understand difference as a series of power relationships involving domination and subordination, and to use our understanding of power relationships to reconceptualize our interpretation and our teaching of American culture. . . .[9]

The Chairperson of the National Endowment for the Humanities in America has observed that

> Viewing humanities texts as though they were primarily political documents is the most noticeable trend in academic study of the

7 *Culture and Anarchy*, p. 43. True culture, in Arnold's view, far from being a socio-economic "badge," is "an inward condition of the mind and the spirit" (Ibid., p. 48).

8 Quoted in J. Searle, "The Storm Over the University," *New York Review of Books*, 36:19, December 6, 1990, p. 36.

9 From *Chronicle of Higher Education*, March 29, 1989, quoted in S. Hook, "Is Teaching 'Western Culture' Racist or Sexist?" *Encounter*, September-October, 1989, p. 19.

humanities today. Truth and beauty and excellence are regarded as irrelevant; questions of intellectual and aesthetic quality dismissed.[10]

This kind of agenda is characteristic of what Richard Rorty termed the "new cultural left," one which would like to make Humanities departments "staging areas for political action."[11] The study of the humanities, under this view, should be recognized as a form of "cultural and political production," and should become a forum for self-conscious "politicization" and "consciousness raising," a springboard for radical political activity. Thus the "orgiastic massacre of ancestors" goes hand-in-hand with the Godardian fantasy of a "return to zero."

Relativism, Deconstructionism, and the Flight into Theory
Similarly, the very notion of a disinterested pursuit of knowledge is now, in many quarters, seen to be discredited. The American Council for Learned Societies recently released a study entitled *Speaking for the Humanities*:

> Over the past two decades, traditional assumptions about ways of studying the humanities have been contested in large measure because a number of related disciplines—cultural anthropology, linguistics, psychoanalysis, the philosophy of language—were undergoing major changes that inevitably forced humanists to ask basic questions about their methods and very definition of their fields. . . . The challenge to claims of intellectual authority . . . issues from almost all areas of modern thought—science, psychology, feminism, linguistics, semiotics, and anthropology. . . .

Or again:

> As the most powerful modern philosophies and theories have been demonstrating, claims of disinterested objectivity, and universality are not to be trusted and themselves tend to reflect local historical conditions. . . .[12]

10 Per P. Brooks: "Western Civ at Bay," *Times Literary Supplement*, January 25, 1991, p. 5.

11 Richard Rorty in an address at George Mason University, Fairfax, Virginia, March 1, 1989, quoted in S. Hook, "Is Teaching 'Western Culture' Racist or Sexist?" p. 19.

12 *Speaking for the Humanities*, quoted in J. Searle, "The Storm Over the University," p. 39.

One of the most potent schools of thought which has obscured the traditional ideal of the humanities is what can loosely be called postmodernist theory, that mesmeric light-show of ideas generated by European *illuminati* such as Lacan, Derrida, Barthes, Baudrillard, Lyotard, Foucault, and Kristeva. Psychoanalytical theory, linguistics, structural anthropology, semiology, and feminist theory have indeed all contributed to a dazzling display of intellectual pyrotechnics.

Postmodernism has been notoriously difficult to define and has "acquired a wide range of different and often contradictory meanings."[13] The term has been applied to aesthetics, to political ideology and sociology, to popular culture.[14] Jean-Francois Lyotard memorably sketched the post-modernist life-style thus: "One listens to reggae, watches a western, eats McDonald's food for lunch and local cuisine for dinner, wears Paris perfume in Tokyo and 'retro' clothes in Hong Kong."[15] As another commentator says, "Postmodernism as a cultural movement (not as an ideology, theory, or program) has a simple enough message: anything goes."[16] The postmodernist theoretical discourse is not dissimilar: it is indifferent to consistency, continuity, and "wholeness"; it stigmatizes all epistemological, moral, and aesthetic "universals" and affirms *difference*; it exhibits "an incredulity about metanarratives";[17] it abhors "coherence" and dismantles and collages styles, genres, forms; it decomposes "history" and the "past" as a given datum and treats it as a "metafictional narrative"; it disdains originality and favors an ironic stance. "*Pastiche* is the *lingua franca* of postmodernism: apolitical, ahistorical, promiscuous."[18] Postmodernist theory repudiates the

13 R. Felski, "Feminism, Realism and the Avant-Garde" in *Post-Modern Conditions*, ed. A. Milner, P. Thomson & C. Worth (Clayton: Center for General and Comparative Literature, Monash University, 1988), p. 67

14 See B. Frankel, "The Cultural Contradictions of Postmodernity" in A. Milner et al., *Post-Modern Conditions*, esp. pp. 95-96.

15 Per Todd Gitlin, "Style for Style's Sake," *The Weekend Australian*, January 21-22, 1989, "Weekender," p. 9.

16 A. Heller, "Existentialism, Alienation, Postmodernism: Cultural Movements as Vehicles for Change in Patterns of Everyday Life" in A. Milner et al., *Post-Modern Conditions*, p. 7.

17 J. Rundell, "Marx and the 'Postmodern' Image of Society" in A. Milner et al., *Post-Modern Conditions*, p. 157.

18 M. Hollway, "Blu-Tack and Temples: Artistic Practice in the Eighties: A Postmodernist View" in A. Milner et al., *Post-Modern Conditions*, p. 191.

"transparency" of art and disavows the traditional privileging of "high art" over "popular culture." It presents "a field of tension which can no longer be grasped in terms of categories such as progress and reaction, Left vs. Right, present vs. past, modernism vs. realism, abstraction vs. representation. . . ."[19] A heady brew indeed—hardly surprising that it has proved to be so intoxicating!

As for postmodernism within the Academy it is difficult not to share Andrew Milner's view that

> What postmodernism provides us with is . . . an index of the range and extent of the Western intelligentsia's own internal crisis, that is, its collective crisis of faith in its own self-proclaimedly adversarial and redemptive functions.[20]

We do not have time here to enter the labyrinthine maze of postmodernist critical theory and to track our way through the corridors of this intellectual Disneyland, with seductive but elusive attractions on all sides. Let us rather, for the moment, set our sights on one target—the "death of the author." As John Caughie has recently reminded us

> The challenge to the concept of the author . . . has been decisive in contemporary criticism and aesthetic theory. . . . [T]he result has been a reconsideration of the text . . . as a structured play of forces, relations, and discourses, rather than as a site of final, unified meanings, authorized by their source.[21]

In postmodernist critical discourse "the author," "the artist," "the work," even "meaning," "cognition," "reality" itself, "dissolve" or "deconstruct" or "decompose" into chimera or mirages. We now talk rather of "texts," "discourses," "games," "images," "simulations," "consumptions," and "readings." The literary work becomes a kind of epiphenomenon

---

19 A. Huyssen, "Mapping the Postmodern," *New German Critique*, 33, 1984, quoted in R. Felski, "Feminism, realism and the avant-garde," p. 68.

20 A. Milner, "Postmodernism and Popular Culture," *Meanjin*, 49:1, November 1990, pp. 37-38.

21 J. Caughie (ed.), *Theories of Authorship: A Reader* (London: Routledge & Kegan Paul, 1981), p. 1

of "reading," the "project" or "production" of the "reading subject."[22]

> We now know [wrote Roland Barthes in 1968] that a text is not a line
> of words releasing a single "theological" meaning (the "message" of
> the Author-God) but a multi-dimensional space in which a variety
> of writings, none of them original, blend and clash. The text is a tis-
> sue of quotations. . . .[23]

Semiotic theory, drawing on linguistic and perception theory and
on Lacanian psychoanalytic models, views any text—a novel, a film, an
advertisement, even a building or a city landscape—as a complex set
of fluid relations between authors (as "subject-positions"), texts, and
readers. The meaning of a text is not set in concrete by an intentional
author but is created anew at every "reading." Those stylistic/thematic
properties which we read off the text and which we ascribe to an author are, Foucault tells us, "projections of our way of handling texts";
in a fundamental sense the "author is in fact created by the reader."[24]

Post-structuralist semiotic criticism undertakes to "open out" the
text as a *process* "obedient to a certain history and to certain 'orders
of discourse' rather than to the personality and self-expression of the
author."[25] The task of criticism is no longer the "construction of the
author" but the explication of the discursive organization on which the
text is founded and which "negotiates its relationship with its historical
audience." Critical attention moves away from an illusory expressive
author onto the structures, codes, and conventions, the language of
the discursive mode in question, onto *signifying practices*. Any overt
concern with intentional meaning becomes a kind of "philistinism."[26]

Under pressure from these kinds of ideas the study of literature
increasingly turns away from the *criticism of works* to the *construction*

22 For a brief discussion of some of these points see D. Bennett, "Wrapping up Postmodernism: The Subject of Consumption versus the Subject of Cognition" in A. Milner et al., *Post-Modern Conditions*, pp. 15-36.

23 R. Barthes, *Image, Music, Text*, ed. S. Heath, (London: Fontana, 1977), p.146. For a
brief but iridescent account of Barthes' work see S. Sontag, "Writing Itself: On Roland
Barthes" in *A Susan Sontag Reader*, pp. 425-446.

24 S. Crofts, "Authorship and Hollywood," *Wide Angle*, 6:1, 1984, p. 17.

25 J. Caughie, *Theories of Authorship*, p. 1.

26 S. Sontag, "Against Interpretation," p. 96.

of theory.[27] By "criticism" I refer to a personal engagement, one that is both intense and open-ended, both mental and emotional, intellectual and moral, with a work of literature or art or philosophy, a work which the critic approaches *on its own terms* and in an initial state of intellectual humility and receptivity. The critic *allows the work to speak* and is willing to learn *from* the work rather than immediately plunging into some kind of "deconstruction." As Mircea Eliade reminds us

> A work of art reveals its meaning only insofar as it is regarded as an autonomous creation; that is, insofar as we accept its mode of being—that of an artistic creation—and do not reduce it to one of its constituent elements . . . or to one of its subsequent uses. . . .[28]

The lexicon of abuse favored by the postmodernist theorists is illuminating: one can hardly do worse than be labeled a "humanist," a "moralist," a "traditionalist," a "romantic," perhaps worst of all in the literary field, a "Leavisite"!

The Barthesian announcement of the death of the author is only one fragment in the kaleidoscopic glitter of postmodernist deconstructionism. We have dwelt on it here to throw into sharp relief the "deconstructive" impulses of postmodern theorizing and to illustrate its corrosive affects on one particular discipline. One might equally well refer to Foucault's assault on the idea of a continuous and intelligible past which has sabotaged the study of history, or to Derrida's subversion of the idea of truth, perhaps the final step of continental philosophy into an unbridled relativism, if one might so paradoxically express it.

Defending the Liberal View
(a)*Politics*
In formulating some sort of response to the political critique I make three preliminary points. Firstly, the critique reifies its own image of the tradition, an image which often seems to be willfully ignorant. One

---

27 On this subject see two amusing essays, "French Letters: Theories of the New Novel" and "The Hacks of Academe" by Gore Vidal in *Matters of Fact and of Fiction* (New York: Vintage Books, 1978), pp. 65-98.

28 M. Eliade, "A New Humanism" in *The Quest: History and Meaning in Religion* (Chicago: University of Chicago Press, 1969), p. 6.

can look into the tradition at almost any point to see that the tradition itself, is in large measure, subversive, skeptical, critical. We need think only of Socrates, Thucydides, and Euripides to choose three contemporaneous classical examples. We find in the works of such authors the most searching inquiry into the prevailing values, ideas, and assumptions of the day, a profound criticism of the "dominant ideology" if you will. There is no more devastating attack on the ethos of pragmatic power politics and imperialism than we find in Thucydides, no more penetrating exposure of religious and political conservatism than we find in the plays of Euripides, no more relentless stripping away of cliché and conformist thinking than we find in Socrates. To label such thinkers and such works as "hegemonic," "elitist," and "chauvinist," as being intent on legitimizing the political *status quo*, is simply not to have read them and is to indulge in a kind of political reductionism which is ignorant, facile, and deeply cynical. (To take note of the fact that all these thinkers are male, that they belonged to a particular elite, and to press questions about the relationship of their work and ideas to their social position is altogether another matter.) No properly constituted radicalism should find it necessary to resort to this kind of simplistic sloganeering deployed most frequently by people who have only the most nebulous notion of the tradition on which they so recklessly pass judgment.

Such political reductionism is all the more seductive in a climate where cynicism about the past is taken for an emblem of "sophistication." Kathleen Raine's characterization of the reductionist mentality as that frame of mind which "sees in the pearl nothing but the disease of the oyster" could hardly find more fitting illustrative material than in these ideologically generated "critiques." To resort to jejune caricatures of the culture of the past is also to misunderstand what a tradition is all about: all of the great cultural traditions include within themselves a variety of viewpoints and value-systems. As Roger Sworder has recently observed, "What one has in a tradition is quite as antinomian as establishmentarian."[29] The Western cultural tradition, whatever else might be said about it, has been continuously self-critical and often aware of the limits of its own ethnocentrism.[30]

29 R. Sworder, "The Value of the Traditional Disciplines," *Education Monitor*, 2:1, Spring 1990, p. 27.

30 See S. Hook, "Is Teaching 'Western Culture' Racist or Sexist?" p. 15. In a specifically

When one speaks of a cultural tradition one is indeed implying certain intellectual, moral, and imaginative continuities rather than a random aggregation of disparate bits and pieces. It is for good reason that many writers have turned to organic metaphors when trying to describe the growth of traditions. However, this by no means implies that the tradition is monolithic—in terms of ideology or, indeed, in any other terms.

Secondly, it is not without irony that the values to which the political "radicals" so often appeal derive from the tradition which they are so intent on dismantling: social justice, intellectual freedom, toleration of diverse points of view, skepticism, the search for Utopia—these are all recurrent motifs in our cultural heritage. These censorious debunkers often seem quite oblivious to the fact that these values have been articulated, elaborated, and argued about within the tradition the study of which they are intent on replacing with some fashionable assemblage of ideologically acceptable and contemporary ("relevant") materials. Many radicals seem to have no notion that the movements to which they adhere actually "arose as continuations of or as reactions to the cultural environment that spawned them, and can only be fully understood when so contextualized." As John Penwill so neatly put it, "No matter how radical the ideology, the past is always already present as intertext."[31] The iconoclasts apparently imagine that it is only a handful of modern ideologues who can lay claim to positive moral and political values. A more brazen impertinence can hardly be imagined. They are akin to adolescents who want to pretend that they have no parents!

literary context it is also worth noting the following suggestive remarks, "[L]iterature as an institution, understood not as individual works but as the norms governing their production and reception, has always possessed its own self-criticism in the form of parodistic self-reflexion. The function of parody may be defined as the critique of representation of life in literature and as such the immanent self-consciousness of literature as institution, for parody must necessarily foreground and estrange both the forms of production and the norms of reception" (D. Roberts, "*Marat/Sade*, or the Birth of Postmodernism from the Spirit of the Avant-Garde" in A. Milner et al., *Postmodern Conditions*, p. 41). This kind of self-criticism, both literary and philosophical, can, incidentally, be found in many different traditions—the Indian and the Chinese to name two.

31 J. Penwill, "Editorial," in H. Oldmeadow, "Mircea Eliade and Carl Jung: 'Priests Without Surplices'?" *Studies in Western Traditions Occasional Papers 1*, Department of Arts, La Trobe University Bendigo, 1995, p. viii.

Thirdly, a good deal of what passes for "political critique" is, in fact, vacuous sloganeering. Take "hierarchicalism": the charge could only be obviated if we are willing to say that studying any one thing is neither more nor less valuable than studying any other thing—and indeed this is the point of view taken in some literature, media, and popular culture courses. This kind of anarchism might, at first blush, look daring but in the end it is nothing more than an abdication, the abandonment of *any* pedagogical ethic. To believe that no one thing is any more or less worth studying than another is to make a mockery of education as such. Any education worth the name should teach students to discriminate between the good and the bad, the authentic and the spurious, the enriching and the meretricious. By all means let us argue strenuously and at length about the kinds of *values* involved in this process, *including political ones*, but let us not succumb to the nonsense that there is no essential difference between Dostoevsky and *Dallas*, or between Kafka and a Kleenex ad.

In criticizing some of the simple-minded excesses of the political critique I do not want to suggest that the charges of elitism, Eurocentricism, sexism are entirely fanciful or ludicrous: they are serious and have to be addressed. Too often those intent on protecting the embattled ideal of a liberal education evade these charges by trivializing them.[32] Some of the agenda of the "cultural left" can certainly be accommodated *within* the traditional liberal ideal of education. No one, surely, would want to argue against recuperating works which have been ignored because they were by women or against recovering women's role in our intellectual and cultural history, against developing more respectful and open attitudes to other cultural traditions and civilizations, against being alert to questions about power relations and the political functions of art and of ideas. None of these laudable aims impel us to throw our whole cultural tradition onto the garbage dump of human history, nor to succumb to a rampant political reductionism so fashionable in some quarters. The contemporary literary critics whose work I most admire—George Steiner, Raymond Williams, Irving Howe, Susan Sontag amongst them—have shown how one can both simultaneously respect *and* incisively interrogate the European

---

32 Some of the sillier claims made by "conservatives" such as Bloom, Roger Kimball, and others are well exposed in P. Brooks, "Western Civ at Bay," *Times Literary Supplement*, January 25, 1991.

cultural tradition: such critics certainly do not evade the most pro-
foundly disturbing political questions. Good criticism is often political
in this sense. However, the wholesale politicization of the teaching of
the humanities under the aegis of certain social-ideological priorities
is another matter. To aestheticize *or* to politicize literary studies is to
reduce and trivialize them. Recall the ludicrous spectacle of a group of
French feminists petitioning the Minister of Culture, in the early '80s,
to ban *Madame Bovary* on the grounds of its purported misogyny, a
move which might have robbed generations of readers of one of the
most searching and poignant depictions of the social and psychological predicaments of women in the nineteenth century.

Robert Hughes remarks on the one-dimensional ideological approach to literature which now holds sway in many universities:
"Through it one enters a strange, nostalgic, Marxist never-never land,
where all the most retrograde phantoms of Literature as Instrument of
Social Utility are trotted forth." He cites the recent *Columbia History of
the American Novel* which pronounces Harriet Beecher Stowe a better
novelist than Melville

> because she was a woman and "socially constructive," because *Uncle
> Tom's Cabin* helped rouse Americans against slavery . . . whereas the
> captain of the Pequod was a symbol of laissez-faire capitalist indi-
> vidualism with a bad attitude to whales.[33]

As Hughes so acutely remarks, "one of the first conditions of freedom is to discover the line beyond which politics may not go. . . ."[34] But
let us not fall into another snare: to imagine that our cultural traditions
and the way they are studied somehow transcend political questions.
As Robin Wood has argued, the judgment of an artistic work must be
at once "moral, aesthetic, and political, inseparably. . . ."[35] This strikes
me as judicious.

Let us also not fudge another central issue: to insist that literature
and art and philosophy should always and only be viewed through political spectacles amounts to *a denial of the spiritual* which is either

---

33 R. Hughes, *The Culture of Complaint* (London: Harper Collins, 1994), p. 98.

34 R. Hughes, *The Culture of Complaint*, p. 98.

35 R. Wood, "Creativity & Evaluation: Two Film Noirs of the Fifties," *CineAction!*, 21-
22, Summer-Fall 1990, p. 16.

ignored altogether or turned into some kind of epiphenomenon, as if most of the greatest works of the past have not been primarily spiritual dramas concerned with the fundamental questions of human existence. How apposite Coleridge's warning of nearly two hundred years ago seems in the present climate! He reminds us that without elevation "above the semblances of custom and the senses to a world of spirit" our "organic life is but a state of somnambulism."[36]

The contempt for the spiritual characterizes much of both the radical political outlook and postmodernist theory. We remember, for instance, Barthes disdain for the idea that literature might set out "to express the inexpressible"—this Barthes dismisses as a "literature of the soul." Literature's proper purpose, he asseverates, should be "to unexpress the expressible," which is to say that it should problematize our familiar perceptions and conferrals of meaning.[37] Indeed one might say that a scorning of the spiritual is a calling-card of the modern outlook generally, so far have we moved from any kind of normal civilization in which, necessarily, "it is the spiritual, not the temporal, which culturally, socially, and politically is the criterion of all other values."[38]

(b) Relativism and Postmodernism

The epistemological objections to the liberal ideal of a disinterested pursuit of truth are more difficult to counter. However a good deal of the confusion will evaporate like morning dew if we recognize a simple but important distinction at the outset. Part of the problem is that two related but quite separate issues have been conflated. The positivist rubric of "objectivity" is now quite rightly in tatters: Kuhn, Rorty, and others have shown how the apparently objective basis of the scientific disciplines themselves is illusory (never mind the more absurd preten-

---

36 It is, he says, "only the elevation of the spirit which affords the sole anchorage in the storm, and at the same time the substantiating principle of all true wisdom, the satisfactory solution of all the contradictions of human nature, of the whole riddle of the world. This alone belongs to and speaks intelligibly to all alike, the learned and the ignorant, if but the heart listens" (*The Friend* [1818], quoted in R. Williams, *Culture and Society*, p. 83).

37 See J. Culler, *Barthes* (Glasgow: Fontana, 1983), p. 47.

38 F. Schuon, "Usurpations of Religious Feeling," *Studies in Comparative Religion*, 2:2, 1968, p. 66.

sions of a positivist sociology or a behaviorist psychology).[39] However, this and the *ideal* of a *disinterested* pursuit of knowledge are two quite different matters.

As a recent American commentator has written:

> It is one of the clearest symptoms of the decadence of the academy that ideals that once informed the humanities have been corrupted, willfully misunderstood, or simply ignored by the new sophistries that have triumphed on our campuses. We know something is gravely amiss when teachers of the humanities confess—or, as is more often the case, when they boast—that they are no longer able to distinguish between truth and falsity. We know something is wrong when scholars assure us—and their pupils—that there is no essential difference between the disinterested pursuit of knowledge and partisan proselytizing, or when academic literary critics abandon the effort to identify and elucidate works of lasting achievement as a reactionary enterprise unworthy of their calling. And indeed, the most troubling development of all is that such contentions are no longer the exceptional pronouncements of a radical elite, but have increasingly become the conventional wisdom in humanities departments of our major colleges and universities.[40]

The assassination of the very idea of truth and falsity can probably be traced back to Nietzsche but Messieurs Derrida, Foucault, Barthes, Lyotard, and Baudrillard have been his enthusiastic latter-day accomplices. Indeed, the very idea of knowledge itself has been seen in some quarters as nothing more than "a persistent self-delusion." Foucault's *The Study of Things*, one of his admirers tells us, "proclaims the eclipse of man as a ground of thought."[41]

At this juncture it is perhaps worth floating a few general remarks about the current vogue for the "postmodernist" theorists. (For our present purposes it is unnecessary to make fastidious discriminations between "deconstructionists," "postmodernists," "semioticians," and

---

39 See T. Kuhn, *The Structure of Scientific Revolutions* (Chicago: University of Chicago Press, 1970), and R. Rorty, *Philosophy and the Mirror of Nature* (Princeton: Princeton University Press, 1979).

40 R. Kimball, *Tenured Radicals: How Politics Has Corrupted Our Higher Education* (1990), quoted in J. Searle, "The Storm Over the University," p. 37.

41 J.G. Merquior, *Foucault* (London: Fontana, 1985), p. 55.

"post-structuralists," nor to concern ourselves with distinguishing various materialist, psychoanalytical, and feminist permutations.) Perhaps deconstructionism is so popular amongst intellectuals because it places a premium on cleverness, on mental facility and agility, on a kind of mental dexterity that allows all manner of captivating sleights-of-hand. Cleverness yes, but intelligence? Certainly one searches in vain for any kind of *contemplative* intelligence which, in Seyyed Hossein Nasr's words, "differs as much from mental virtuosity as the soaring flight of an eagle differs from the play of a monkey."[42] Paris post-'68 is, whatever else might be said of it, not a *milieu* conducive to contemplative intelligence of any kind!

Postmodernist theory demands nothing in terms of a commitment to any particular set of values or beliefs: it is avowedly amoral. No one should be deceived by the fact that it is apparently most congenial to "radicals" who are attracted by the postmodernist repudiation of both tradition and modernism. Certainly it seems to provide some sort of haven for leftist intellectuals disenchanted by recent events in Eastern Europe, the Soviet Union, and China. The apparent radicalism of postmodern theory is in fact somewhat illusory: much postmodernist theorizing amounts to a disallowance of the so-called "grand narratives" of radical political ideology—Marxist, feminist, anarchist, or whatever—and a repudiation of the values and aspirations of transformative social practice.[43] Frederic Jameson argued in a now celebrated essay that postmodernism theory is an ideological construct which replicates and reinforces the imperatives of a global, multinational, consumerist capitalism.[44] Certainly there have been attempts to marry postmodernist theoretical discourse and political radicalism: such enterprises have, to say the least, been attended by ambiguous results.[45]

42 S.H. Nasr, *Ideals and Realities of Islam* (London: Allen & Unwin, 1975), p. 21.

43 For some interesting discussion of postmodernist theory *viz.* oppositional social thought see B. Agger, *The Decline of Discourse: Reading, Writing, and Resistance in Postmodern Capitalism* (New York: Falmer Press, 1990), esp. Ch. 1.

44 See F. Jameson, "Postmodernism and the Consumer Society" in H. Foster (ed.), *Postmodern Culture* (London: Pluto Press, 1983), pp. 111-125. See also A. Milner et al., *Postmodern Conditions*, pp. xii-xv and S. Gunew, "Postmodern Tensions: Reading for (Multi)Cultural Difference," *Meanjin*, 49:1, November 1990, pp. 21ff.

45 Whilst on the subject of "grand narratives" we might usefully recall an observation made recently by Ron Gilbert: "[I]n the postmodernist critique the space previously occupied by the master narrative—a power function—is replaced by postmodernism

Deconstructionist literary practice seems often to rest on a commitment to little more than ingenuity, inventiveness, pyrotechnics,
complexity, a highly sophisticated and seductive plausibility—in short,
to sophistry. Indeed, at times it seems as if theory has become a kind of
enclave to which one most easily gains admittance by writing obscufatory and opaque prose heavily littered with references to the European
oracles of the moment. One need only take the most cursory glance at
the forums of postmodernist literary theory to see that one of the most
binding taboos is that on the writing of plain English. As well as con-
ferring an aura of the recondite and the enigmatic the arcane jargon
of postmodernist theory is a covert device of *exclusion*. Obversely, to
refer in anything other than the most stringently disparaging terms to
"old-fashioned" critics such as Leavis is immediately to ostracize oneself, to betray an apparent ignorance of the latest French *avatar*. In any
case, has not Roland Barthes told us that "repressive discourse is the
discourse of good conscience, liberal discourse"?[46] Certainly any talk
of the "good," the "beautiful," and the "true" is likely to be thrown out
of court as being part of this "repressive discourse." This leaves us in
precisely the situation described by Kathleen Raine when she writes,

> Poets of the imagination write of the soul, of intellectual beauty, of
> the living spirit of the world. What does such work communicate to
> readers who do not believe in the soul, in the spirit of life, or in any-
> thing that can be called "the beautiful"? . . . [S]uch terms of quality
> become . . . "meaningless," because there is nothing for which they
> stand. . . .[47]

I do not claim that this peculiarly French constellation of theory
has nothing whatever to offer. Foucault's "archaeology" of the past, for

itself. Postmodernism's authority, like that of the systems it displaces, is constituted
by its own canon, symposia, publications, and forms of credentialization" ("Endings,"
Meanjin, 49:1, November 1990, p. 45). The postmodernist "canon" would include, at
the least, the following: R. Barthes, *The Semiology of Signs: Writing Degree Zero, S/Z,*
and *The Pleasure of the Text*; J. Baudrillard, *Simulations*; J. Derrida, *Of Grammatology*
and *Writing and Difference*; M. Foucault, *The Order of Things* and *Discipline and Pun-
ish*; J-F Lyotard, *The Postmodern Condition*.

46 R. Barthes, *Image, Music, Text*, p. 209.

47 From K. Raine, "Premises and Poetry," quoted in H. Smith, "Excluded Knowledge:
A Critique of the Modern Western Mind Set," *Teachers College Record*, 80:3, February
1979, p. 438.

instance, has been a useful corrective to an historiography tyrannized by what we might call "progressive and continuous linearity," and has opened up new historical landscapes for "excavation." The somewhat phosphoric work of Roland Barthes has detonated some exciting fireworks in the field of media and "popular culture" studies. Semiotic theorists such as Christian Metz have liberated the study of film and other visual media from excessively literary modes of analysis. Much postmodernist writing is audacious and doubtless many of the shocks it administers are therapeutic. It is not the substantial (if somewhat treacherous) achievements of postmodernist analysis that one wants to deny but rather the notion that postmodernist theory has now established its primacy over other modes of analysis and discourse. More specific to our concerns here is the need to resist the ruinous notion that the postmodernist preoccupation with contemporaneity and with popular culture can and should now replace the study of the tradition, that a widespread "cultural anesthesia" is both inevitable and desirable, and that one might as well study *Dynasty* as Dante on the grounds that at least the former is contemporary and not a relic of "museum art." All of this can easily lead us into a kind of ghastly celebration of a meaningless present, exiled from the past, bereft of any vision of the future. We would do well to heed Wendell Berry when he writes,

> Contemporaneity, in the sense of being "up with the times," is of no value. Wakefulness to experience—as well as to instruction and example—is another matter. But what we call the modern world is not necessarily, and not often, the real world, and there is no virtue in being up-to-date in it.[48]

In our secularized, pluralistic, and multicultural society the question of moral values and of moral authority is indeed problematic. Nietzsche, Heidegger, and their followers have force-marched us into a kind of moral relativism wherein talk about "good" and "evil" becomes an embarrassment.[49] But as George Steiner has remarked,

---

48 W. Berry, *Standing by Words: Essays* (San Francisco: Northpoint Press, 1983), p. 13.

49 Moral relativism is one of Allan Bloom's central targets in his critique of contemporary American higher education in *The Closing of the American Mind: How Higher Education has Failed Democracy and Impoverished the Souls of Today's Students* (Harmondsworth: Penguin, 1987). Martha Nussbaum has launched one of the more persuasive ripostes, "Undemocratic Vistas," *New York Review of Books*, November 5, 1987.

A neutral humanism is either a pedantic artifice or a prologue to the inhuman. . . . It is a matter of seriousness and emotional risk, a recognition that the teaching of literature, if it can be done at all, is an extraordinarily complex and dangerous business, of knowing that one takes in hand the quick of another human being. . . . To teach literature as if it were some kind of urbane trade . . . is to do worse than teach badly. To teach it as if the critical text were more important than, more profitable than the poem . . . is worst of all.[50]

The postmodernist response to the moral challenges of literature and its teaching seems to be one of simple evasion or a retreat into glib talk about moral and cultural relativism or, to use more faddish terminology, "perspectivism." On this subject one can again do no better than recall the words of Frithjof Schuon, this time on the "contradiction of relativism":

Relativism reduces every element of absoluteness to a relativity while making a completely illogical exception in favor of this reduction itself. Fundamentally it consists in propounding the claim that there is no truth as if this were truth or in declaring it to be absolutely true that there is nothing but the relatively true; one might as well say that there is no language or write that there is no writing.[51]

The ironic stance, so characteristic of postmodernist writing, becomes a kind of refuge. A "playful" detachment and an apparent "moral neutrality" become a cover for moral nihilism (and, it might be said, for a political impotence, though this issue is rather more perplexing). It is no accident that postmodernist self-definitions are almost entirely negative. The Parisian pontificators are, veritably, the monks of negation! It has been observed that postmodernist critics

are against tradition for it is an oppressive authority, they are equally against modernism for it "has sold out to the arts of the museum." And whenever interpreters venture any further and try to establish positive principles by which to identify the postmodernist art work

---

50 G. Steiner, "To Civilize Our Gentlemen" in *Language and Silence: Essays 1958-1966* (Harmondsworth: Penguin, 1969), pp. 89-90.

51 F. Schuon, *Logic and Transcendence: A New Translation with Selected Letters* (Bloomington, IN: World Wisdom, 2009), p. 6.

and distinguish it from what is not postmodernist, they invariably end up empty-handed.[52]

The same can be said of postmodernist theory. Insofar as all this impinges on the debate about education what we are inevitably left with (sooner rather than later) is a situation in which there is not only no agreement about what constitutes an educated human person but one in which there is not even an intelligible debate centering on competing visions of such an ideal.[53] It is simply erased from the agenda.

Perhaps the most conspicuous impact of postmodernist theory in literature studies is the displacement of the artist, and to some extent, the eclipse of the very idea of art if by that term we imply a made object which intentionally proclaims a coherent and meaningful vision of life. The theorist now usurps the artist: theory takes priority over art. The study of the novel, for example, is largely replaced by the study of "novel theory" or by one of its sub-genres such as "narratology." The novel itself becomes little more than a platform from which to construct a theoretical edifice. Interpretation, freed from the demands of a hermeneutic which focuses on authorial intention, does indeed become, as Foucault insists, an "infinite task,"[54] or, in Agnes Heller's phrase, "a boundless pluralism."[55] Such theory subverts any and every hermeneutic and in any particular work meaning is obscured, perhaps obliterated, by the preoccupation with certain formal and discursive properties.[56] This kind of thinking and its implications needs to be examined much more critically if it is to be resisted. As Rita Felski has recently written:

> [T]he idea that the formal properties of the literary text negate, transcend, deconstruct, or otherwise problematize its substantive content is revealed as the product of the modern understanding of art and needs as such to be critically examined in relation to the ideo-

52 F. Feher, "The Pyrrhic Victory of Art in its War of Liberation: Remarks on the Postmodernist Intermezzo" in A. Milner et al., *Postmodernist Conditions*, p. 85.

53 See A. Bloom, *The Closing of the American Mind*, p. 337.

54 Per J.G. Merquior, *Foucault*, p. 74.

55 See A. Heller, "Existentialism, Alienation, Postmodernism," p. 7.

56 One thinks, for instance, of a recent article about *Wuthering Heights* devoted entirely to the place in the text of the letter *h*.

logical function which it serves. Thus entire academic industries are based upon the exegesis of the experimental literary or artistic text, which acquire an enigmatic aura, that can only be deciphered by the expert: "in a way analogous to religion, the work of art alludes mysteriously to a superior but now essentially opaque and unknowable order."[57]

As Berry has observed, in this kind of climate, the study of literature

ceases to be a meeting ground of all readers of a common tongue and becomes only the occasion of a deafening clatter about literature. Teachers and students read the great songs and stories to learn about them, not from them. The texts are tracked as by the passing of an army of ants, but the power of songs and stories to affect life is still little acknowledged, apparently because it is little felt.[58]

Another bizarre sign of the times is the spectacle of some novelists now clearly no longer writing for any kind of public audience but only for the critics.[59] Witness too some of the more absurd and symptomatic contentions recently made in defense of "Helen Demidenko." One might observe in passing that the so-called Demidenko affair revealed nothing if not the frivolity, trendiness, and moral and political bankruptcy of much of the Australian literary establishment—although we hardly needed this particular fiasco to make that plain.[60]

57 R. Felski, "Feminism, Realism and the Avant-Garde," p. 62. The internal quote is from B. McBurney, "The Postmodernist Transvaluation of Modernist Values," *Thesis Eleven*, 12, 1985.

58 W. Berry, "The Loss of the University" in *Home Economics: Fourteen Essays* (San Francisco: North Point Press, 1987), p. 79.

59 See Gore Vidal's essay "American Plastic: The Matter of Fiction" in *Matters of Fact and of Fiction*, pp. 99-126.

60 In 1994 Helen Demidenko received the Miles Franklin Prize, Australia's most prestigious literary award for *The Hand that Signed the Paper*, a novel apparently based on her own family's experiences of Stalinist purges in the Ukraine. After the awarding of the prize and the accompanying critical fanfare, the Ukrainian identity of "Helen Demidenko" and the experiences on which the novel was ostensibly based were exposed as fraudulent. Robert Manne and others also denounced the poisonous anti-Semitism of the novel, something which had apparently escaped the attention of crit-

The Proper Place of the Humanities and Our Attitude to the Past

Before concluding let me briefly affirm what I take to be the primary functions of the humanities. Let me firstly admit that I see no realistic alternative to the "Great Books" approach in the study of the humanities, most decisively in the study of literature. One can profitably argue about the canon, interrogate it, change it, enlarge it, revise it. No serious critic of literature has ever supposed the canon to be fixed, inscribed on a tablet of gold, inviolate and static for all time.[61] Such a notion is simply a straw-man set up by those wishing to disable humanistic approaches to the study of literature. But to reject the very idea of the canon is to cut oneself off from the treasury of the past and to live only by the fashionable dictates of an impoverished present.

It is one of the glories of the human condition that we can make of ourselves what we will. In one sense we are what we believe ourselves to be. One of the invaluable and irreplaceable functions of the humane disciplines was to expose the student to various images of the human condition, images and metaphors which spoke both to our ancestors and to ourselves across the barriers of time and space.[62] Such study taught students to understand the profound language of image, symbol, and myth, those imaginative, non-mechanistic, and qualitative modes of experience and understanding before which the modern mentality so often stands baffled. It *is* still possible to hear the voices of Homer or Meister Eckhart or William Blake, or indeed, if we are prepared to make the necessary effort, of Lao Tzu and Black Elk or the sages who composed *The Upanishads*. The problem is not that they have nothing to say to us: nothing could be more childish, more impudent than such a belief. Nor, whatever the deconstructionists might

ics and the Miles Franklin judges. Much controversy ensued with some of the more trendy post-modernist critics continuing to defend the novel. See R. Manne, *The Culture of Forgetting: Helen Demidenko and the Holocaust* (Melbourne: Text Publishing, 1996), and R. Manne, "The Strange Case of Helen Demidenko," http://www.australianhumanitiesreview.org/archive/demidenko/manne.1.html.

61 See D. Parker, "Is There a Future for English Literature?" *Quadrant*, September 1990, p. 48.

62 For two articles in which this idea is developed much more fully and in which a more extended affirmation of the role of the humanities is canvassed, see R. Sworder, "A Manifesto for the Humanities," *Quadrant*, June 1988, pp. 35-39 and "The Value of the Traditional Disciplines," *Education Monitor*, 2:1, Spring 1990, pp. 25-28.

aver, is the problem that such voices from the past do not mean what they say or that they mean what they do not say. No, the problem is that we no longer care to *listen*. We are far too busy concocting theories *about* them; we are more interested in listening to our own voices babbling about the past rather than in hearing those voices direct.

Speaking of the "old criticism," George Steiner says this:

> [It] is engendered by admiration. It sometimes steps back from the text to look upon moral purpose. It thinks of literature not in isolation but as central to the play of historical and political energies. Above all, the old criticism is philosophic in range and temper.[63]

Against this, today, we have what Robert Hughes and Paul Ricouer have respectively called the "culture of complaint" and the "Age of Suspicion."[64] At a time when skepticism, moral nihilism, a runaway relativism, and a posture of suspicion and incredulity are taken as badges of sophistication, we would do well to reflect on the words of Frithjof Schuon when, in another context, he writes this:

> Those who reproach our ancestors with having been stupidly credulous forget in the first place that one can also be stupidly incredulous, and in the second place that the self-styled destroyers of illusion live on illusions that exemplify a credulity second to none; for a simple credulity can be replaced by a complicated one, adorned with the arabesques of a studied doubt that forms part of the style, but it is still credulity; complication does not make error any less false, nor stupidity less stupid.[65]

The reasons for this kind of attitude to the past, sometimes openly contemptuous but more often condescending, are complicated. The tyranny of Cartesian rationalism, the triumph of a materialistic scientism, the philosophical legacy of the so-called Enlightenment, the stranglehold of evolutionary theory, the alienation from traditional modes of experience and understanding, the tenacious attachment to

---

63 G. Steiner, *Tolstoy or Dostoevsky* (Harmondsworth: Penguin, 1967), p. 13.

64 See R. Hughes, *The Culture of Complaint* and B. Nichols (ed.) *Movies and Methods: An Anthology*, Vol. 2 (Berkeley: University of California Press, 1985), p. 8.

65 F. Schuon, *Light on the Ancient Worlds: A New Translation with Selected Letters* (Bloomington, IN: World Wisdom, 2006), p. 83.

preposterous notions about "progress," the smug and credulous complacency engendered by the trivialities which pass as "the wonders of modern technology" and the materialistic values which make such an attitude possible, have doubtless all played their malefic part in creating attitudes to the past which variously pride themselves on being "progressive," "realistic," "humane," "scientific," "enlightened," and "up to date" but which so often are in reality naive, ignorant, impertinent, and, perhaps above all, intensely sentimental. Such attitudes usually signal little more than a surrender to both the silliest and the darkest prejudices of our own times which can hardly be better summed up than in René Guénon's phrase "the reign of quantity."

A proper study of any of the humane disciplines can help to detach us from some of the more obvious absurdities of our own time and give us a chance to experience the deepest understandings of our ancestors. George Steiner's thesis about the failure of European humanism to avert the Holocaust has too often been deployed as a polemical instrument to ridicule the idea that the study of literature can have *any* positive moral effect.[66] Certainly Steiner's argument is a powerful and deeply disturbing one but it does not force us to the conclusion that the study of the humanities must necessarily and always be morally impotent. There *are* still credible claims to be made for the liberating and humanizing effects of literary studies. David Parker writes of "the power of literature and art to illuminate our experience, extend our imagination, face us with ethical questions about how to think, sympathize, and behave." He goes on to add the salutary qualification that,

> Whether we actually change into more thoughtful, imaginative, humane people will depend on a number of things—one of which might be whether or not our teachers foregrounded such ethical issues and encouraged us to ponder and to discuss them in their full presented complexity; or whether they encouraged us merely to be intoxicated by art's "beauty"; or taught us that literature referred to nothing beyond itself.[67]

The study of the humane disciplines can also have all manner of

---

66 See several of the essays in *Language and Silence*. See also Roger Sworder's comments on this issue in "A Manifesto for the Humanities," pp. 37-8

67 D. Parker, "Is There a Future for English Literature?" p. 49.

specific benefits for the university as a whole. Disciplinary specializa-
tion and compartmentalization have produced a situation in which

> the various disciplines have ceased to speak to each other; they have
> become too specialized, and this overspecialization, this separation,
> of the disciplines has been enabled and enforced by the specializa-
> tion of their languages. As a result, the modern university has grown,
> not according to any unifying principle, like an expanding universe,
> but according to the principle of miscellaneous accretion, like a fur-
> niture storage business.[68]

It is not too much to suggest that the humane disciplines are the
only ones which can provide the "unifying principle" which they still
do, even in their etiolated form, in the USA where in most universities they at least have the good sense to insist that all tertiary students
spend at least one year studying humanities-type courses.

The humanities can also help us to resist the idolatry of science
and the overvaluation of those intellectual ideals and quasi-scientific
modes of enquiry which are, in fact, most inimical to the proper study
of the humanities: positivist empiricism, a chimerical "objectivity,"
quantification, the sophisticated manipulation of data. It is no accident
that such ideals and modes irresistibly suggest the computer. The cul-
tic status of the computer is indeed a sign of the times. The other side
of this particular coin is, of course, the disavowal of the imagination
without which no proper study of the humanities can proceed.

Finally, I return to the title of my essay. Above and beyond all
these, more pernicious than any of these specific threats, is that frame
of mind which congratulates itself above all else on being "modern"
(or even "postmodern"!) and which establishes its credentials by a dis-
missive attitude to the past. The consequences of such an attitude are
incalculable but the destruction of the humane disciplines is surely one
of them.

I conclude with what seem to me to be some entirely apposite
words which were written in reference to the general *Zeitgeist* of the
twentieth century but which are sharply pertinent to some of the issues
we have been exploring. The lengthy quotation is vindicated by the fact
that it penetrates to the heart of the matter. Frithjof Schuon:

---

68 W. Berry, "Loss of the University," p. 76.

A monstrous expenditure of mental ability is incurred in setting out opinions that have no relation to intelligence; people who are not well endowed intellectually by nature learn how to play at thinking and cannot even get on without some such imposture, while people who are well endowed are in danger of losing their power of thinking by falling in with the trend. What looks like an ascent is really a descent; ignorance and lack of intelligence are at ease in a wholly superficial refinement, and the result is a climate in which wisdom takes on the appearance of naivety, of uncouthness and of reverie. . . . In our days everyone wants to appear intelligent . . . but since intelligence cannot be extracted from the void, subterfuges are resorted to, of which one of the most prevalent is debunking, which enables an impression of intelligence to be conveyed at small cost, for all one need do is assert that the normal reaction to a particular phenomenon is "prejudiced" and that it is high time it was cleared of the "legends" that surround it; if the ocean could be made out to be a pond or the Himalayas a hill, it would be done. . . . This strategy is followed especially in dealing with evident and universally known things. . . .[69]

These are words we cannot ponder without profit.

---

69 F. Schuon, *Light on the Ancient Worlds*, pp. 108-109.

CHAPTER 12

Eckhart Tolle's *The Power of Now*

Jettison the ego, still the incessant chatter of the mind, abandon the mind-created "pain body," live in the present moment, be a channel for the Divine. What do I need? Well, for starters, a copy of Eckhart Tolle's *The Power of Now*,[1] the book which, with a little help from Oprah, inaugurated Tolle's career as "spiritual teacher" and has since taken up permanent residence in the best-seller charts, along with the more recent *A New Earth* (2005). Tolle is now a hugely popular speaker on the "spirituality" lecture/seminar/workshop/retreat circuit. Business has never been better!

Many readers will be familiar with the outer facts of the Eckhart Tolle phenomenon. He was born Ulrich Tolle in Germany in 1948. He spent some time as a youth in Spain and studied literature, languages, and philosophy at London and Cambridge universities, enrolling in but never completing doctoral studies. Until his thirtieth year, Tolle tells us, he lived in a state of "continuous anxiety" and suffered from "suicidal depression" (p. 3). His life was altered by a "profoundly significant" transformative experience which awakened him to his real nature as "the ever-present *I am*." Later, he writes, he learned to enter "that inner timeless and deathless realm" and to dwell in states of "indescribable bliss and sacredness." After his "epiphany" he finds himself with "no relationships, no job, no home, no socially defined identity," but with a sense of "intense joy" (p. 5). He spends a lot of time in parks. Somewhere along the line he takes on the name of the great medieval mystic. In the mid-'90s he meets Ms. Constance Kellough, a marketing executive, management consultant, and "wellness expert" who soon publishes *The Power of Now* on her start-up imprint, Namaste. Sales remain modest until 2002 when Oprah Winfrey's acclamation of *The Power of Now* as "one of the most important books of our times" lifts Tolle out of the general ruck of New Age teachers and, virtually overnight, turns his books into chart-toppers. *The Power of Now* has since

---

1 E. Tolle, *The Power of Now: A Guide to Spiritual Enlightenment* (Novato, CA: Namaste Publishing & New World Library, 2004). All intertextual citations are to this work.

been translated into upwards of thirty languages, and sold over five million copies. Tolle lives in Vancouver with his business partner, Kim Eng, now also a teacher of sorts. Beyond this sketchy biographical outline further details are remarkably scarce. (Tolle: "I have little use for the past and rarely think about it" [p. 3].)

Tolle's books, five in number, have been variously described as "New Age mystical texts," "self-help manuals," "spiritual classics," and the like. He belongs with those many contemporary "spiritual teachers" without any firm commitment to a particular religious tradition—Deepak Chopra and Shakti Gawain might serve as examples. He also shares some ground with those "self-help" teachers who draw on psychotherapy and transpersonal psychology, and sometimes on successful business and advertising techniques. (One may mention such figures as Dale Carnegie, Norman Vincent Peale, Wayne Dyer, Louise Hay, and Richard Carlson.)

Tolle writes in a simple and often quite engaging style, and weaves together teachings from and allusions to the world's great religious traditions. Among his favorite sources we find the spiritual classics of Taoism and Zen Buddhism, Rumi, the New Testament and *A Course in Miracles*. One can find reverberations of traditional teachings throughout his writing and much of what he says is quite unexceptional, often nicely put. He has also acknowledged a considerable debt to the teachings of Barry Long (1926-2003), the Australian journalist and self-styled "tantric master." Asked in an interview about the influences on his work, Eckhart Tolle identified the great Advaitin sage of Arunachala, Ramana Maharshi, and the Indian iconoclast and counter-culture "guru," Jiddu Krishnamurti (also a formative influence on Long, and on Deepak Chopra). His own work, Tolle claims, is a synthesis of these two influences—a case of mixing gold and clay! The fact that Tolle registers no sense of dissonance here, that he can apparently situate these two figures on the same level, just as he can without embarrassment juxtapose *A Course in Miracles* and the teachings of Jesus and the Buddha, alerts us to one of the most troubling aspects of his work—not only the conspicuous failure to discern between the authentic and the spurious but also the lack of any sense of the different levels at which such figures and their teachings might be situated, a lack of any sense of proportion. One might say the same of his treatment of "the mind" in which he fails to differentiate its many functions or to understand that all manner of modes and processes might come under this term;

for Tolle the mind seems to be no more than a rather mechanical accomplice to the ego. Moreover, the ego-mind is the root of all our trou-
bles. Now, of course, there is an echo of traditional teachings here—but
in Tolle's hands, the idea is robbed of all nuance and qualification, and
his writing on the subject often degenerates into rhetorical sleight-of-
hand. "Being" is another word bandied about in cavalier fashion.

Tolle's general philosophical position as modern day magus can
be summed up this way: non-dualistic, a-religious, vaguely "Eastern"
but with pretensions to universality, tinged with "spiritual evolutionism" (one of the calling cards of New Age teachers), and directed towards an inner transformation bringing peace and joy. He promotes
a "new consciousness" to liberate us from the fetters of the analytical
and ratiocinative mind which is the principal instrument of the ego.
Associated with the ego-mind is the "pain body" in which reside all
manner of negativities (hatred, jealousy, rage, bitterness, guilt, and so
on—some echoes of Wilhelm Reich here). Both our individual and
collective ills derive from the false but tyrannical constructions of the
ego-mind and its associated "pain-bodies." We must break out of "inherited collective mind-patterns that have kept humans in bondage to
suffering for eons" (p. 6). Readers familiar with the genre will readily
understand the kind of fare on offer through the most cursory glance
at Tolle's chapter headings: "You Are Not Your Mind," "Consciousness:
The Way Out of Pain," "Moving Deeply into the Now," "Mind Strategies
for Avoiding the Now," etc. Tolle's central message is signaled by the
title of the book under review. Here is a characteristic passage:

> Realize deeply that the present moment is all you ever have. Make
> the Now the primary focus of your life. Whereas before you dwelt
> in time and paid brief visits to the Now, have your dwelling place in
> the Now and pay brief visits to past and future when required to deal
> with the practical aspects of your life situation. Always say "yes" to
> the present moment (p. 35).

This theme was popularized in counter-cultural "spirituality" by
books such as Douglas Harding's *On Having No Head* (1961), Alan
Watts' *The Book on the Taboo Against Knowing Who You Are* (1966),
and Ram Das' *Be Here Now* (1971). Of course, it has many antecedents, both in orthodox religious teachings, particularly Buddhist, and
in their modern dilutions and counterfeits.

There is no doubt that Tolle, and others like him, answer—or seem to answer—to a widespread spiritual hunger in the contemporary Western world. There is also no gainsaying the fact that Tolle is a writer of considerable intelligence and charm, and some insight—his ruminations on the tyrannical regime of "time," for instance, are not without interest (see Chapter 3). Nor, as far as I can see, is there reason to suspect Tolle of being a charlatan who shamelessly fleeces his followers in the manner of a Rajneesh or a Jim Bakker; this is not to ignore the fact that his writings are finely calibrated to an affluent Western market with an apparently insatiable appetite for the quick "spiritual" fix, especially of the "self-help" and "you can have it all now" variety.

In the early 1970s Whitall Perry examined various "prophets" of "new consciousness," among them Gerald Heard, Aurobindo, Gopi Krishna, Alan Watts, and Krishnamurti. Among the characteristics he discerned in their teachings, in varying degree, were the following (here enumerated for easy reference):

> I. a patent individualism, II. a scientific and moralistic humanism, III. evolutionism, IV. a relativistic "intuitionism," V. inability to grasp metaphysical and cosmological principles and the realities of the Universal domain, VI. a mockery (latent or overt) of the sacred, VII. a prodigal dearth of spiritual imagination, VIII. no eschatological understanding, IX. a pseudo-mysticism in the form of a "cosmic consciousness."[2]

Let us consider these charges in relation to Eckhart Tolle who, in many respects, follows in the footsteps of the figures with whom Perry was concerned—quite self-consciously so in the case of Krishnamurti. On the basis of the book in front of us, the charges most easily sustained are IV, V, VII, VIII, and IX. The case is more complicated with reference to I and to III, while he can be declared (more or less) innocent of VI—though some will think this lenient.

The most disabling limitation of Tolle's work, from which much else inevitably follows, is "the inability to grasp metaphysical and cosmological principles": thence, no real understanding of either Intellection or Revelation, no comprehension whatever of the multiple

2 W. Perry, "Anti-Theology and the Riddles of Alcyone," *Studies in Comparative Religion*, 6:3, 1972, p. 186.

states of Being, not even a glimmer of understanding of Tradition or orthodoxy, no awareness of the metaphysical basis of the "transcendent unity of religions." As Frithjof Schuon and others have so often insisted, there can be no effective spiritual therapy without an adequate metaphysic; this is to say that an efficacious spiritual method must be rooted in a doctrine which can never be exhaustive but must be sufficient. To put it even more simply, a *way* of spiritual transformation, such as is provided by all integral traditions, must be informed by an adequate *understanding* of Reality. In the case of Eckhart Tolle we have neither doctrine nor method—only a jumble of ideas, perceptions, and reflections, some insightful, some attractive, many no more than the prejudices of the age dressed up in "spiritual" guise. Throw in a few passing nods towards a heterogeneous collection of techniques ransacked from Zen, yoga, Sufism, Christianity, and modern psychology. Tolle's work actually confronts us with a case of what Schuon has called "the psychological imposture" whereby the rights of religion are usurped, the spiritual is degraded to the level of the psychic, and contingent psychic phenomena are elevated to the boundless realm of the Spirit. This kind of psychism, infra-intellectual and anti-spiritual, is endemic in New Age movements. And, to be sure, whatever distinctive features Tolle's work might evince, it belongs firmly in this camp.

No doubt some people have found a measure of guidance and temporary relief from their immediate problems in Tolle's books, though it is difficult to imagine them leading to any long-term transformation. After all, one does not harvest figs from thistles. Perhaps Tolle's books, for all their limitations, have served to direct some seekers towards deeper and more authentic sources of wisdom. This is to take the most charitable view possible. On the other hand, there is a good deal here to set off the alarm bells. Consider, for instance, this claim, one which has doubtless been swallowed whole by many Tolle enthusiasts:

> This book [*The Power of Now*] can be seen as a restatement for our time of that one timeless spiritual teaching, the essence of all religions. It is not derived from external sources, but from the one true Source within, so it contains no theory or speculation. I speak from inner experience... (p. 10).

A review of this scope does not allow us to dismantle this claim, nor to demonstrate its implications and possible ramifications—though these should be clear enough. In our time there have been many who have laid claim to some essential wisdom, surpassing traditional religious forms. By now we should be wary of all such claims when they are apparently based on nothing more than "inner experience" and when traditional criteria are either flouted or ignored. Tolle's work as a whole should be subjected to the most severe interrogation in the light of Tradition.

III. East and West

Every initiative taken with a view to harmony between different cultures and for the defense of spiritual values is good, if it has as its basis a recognition of the great principial truths and consequently also a recognition of tradition or of the traditions.

FRITHJOF SCHUON

CHAPTER 13

Ananda Coomaraswamy
and the East-West Encounter

Every tradition is necessarily a partial representation of the truth in-
tended by tradition universally considered. . . .

Ananda Coomaraswamy[1]

One of the most remarkable figures of recent times was Ananda Kent-
ish Coomaraswamy, born in Sri Lanka (then Ceylon) in 1877 of a Tamil
father and an English mother. By nativity and temperament alike he
belonged to both East and West. He was educated in England but returned often to Sri Lanka where he founded the Ceylon Reform Movement of which he was the inaugural President. The Society dedicated
itself to the preservation of traditional arts and crafts and to resist-
ing "the thoughtless imitation of unsuitable European habits and customs." In 1905, mindful of the destructive consequences of European
imperialism, Coomaraswamy wrote these prophetic words:

Why do we not meet the wave of European civilization on equal
terms? . . . Our Eastern civilization was here two thousand years ago;
shall its spirit be broken utterly before the new commercialism of the
West? Sometimes I think the eastern spirit is not dead, but sleeping,
and may yet play a greater part in the world's spiritual life.[2]

Coomaraswamy went on to become a peerless authority on Asian art
and, in his later years, one of the most influential exponents of the perennial philosophy which informs the world's great traditions.

In one of his essays Coomaraswamy refers to the "impotence and
arrogance" implicit in the well-known refrain, "East is East and West
is West, and never the twain shall meet." This proposition, he writes, is

---

1 A.K. Coomaraswamy, "Sri Ramakrishna and Religious Tolerance" in *Light from the
East: Eastern Wisdom for the Modern West,* ed. H. Oldmeadow (Bloomington, IN:
World Wisdom, 2007), p. 235.

2 Manifesto of the Ceylon Reform Society, quoted in R. Lipsey, *Coomaraswamy, Vol. 3:
His Life and Work* (Princeton: Princeton University Press, 1977), p. 22.

one "to which only the most abysmal ignorance and the deepest dis-couragement could have given rise."[3] As an art historian, philosopher, linguist, and hermeneutist, Coomaraswamy himself undertook a mas-sive labor to dispel the West's "most abysmal ignorance" about Eastern traditions. In this heroic enterprise he followed the trail blazed by René Guénon, the French metaphysician who, early in the last century, gave us the first authoritative European exegesis of some of the pivotal doc-trines and texts of both India and China. In the half-century since their passing, various clichés about the East have circulated in the West, per-haps the most pervasive of these turning on the well-worn contrast of a "materialistic" West and a "spiritual" East—but let us not forget that clichés, no matter how facile, do not spring from nowhere. The con-temporary debate about East and West is swarming on one side with advocates for Western-style "Progress," and on the other with those prone to romanticize the "East" as the last bastion of an ill-defined "spirituality." In order to dispel some of the confusion and the rhetori-cal fog which has accumulated around this subject, we can do no better than turn to Coomaraswamy and Guénon.

The now familiar tropes about "East" and "West" sometimes imply a series of immutable differences between essentialized geo-cultural monoliths. It is not always understood that the contrasts to which at-tention is so often drawn arise, largely, from the preservation of tradi-tion in the East, and its destruction in the West. As Coomaraswamy remarks,

> "East and West" imports a cultural rather than a geographical an-tithesis: an opposition of the traditional or ordinary way of life that survives in the East to the modern and irregular way of life that now prevails in the West. It is because such an opposition as this could not have been felt before the Renaissance that we say that the prob-lem is one that presents itself only accidentally in terms of geogra-phy; it is one of times much more than of places.[4]

3 A.K. Coomaraswamy, "The Pertinence of Philosophy" in *What is Civilisation? And Other Essays* (Cambridge: Golgonooza Press, 1989), p. 19.

4 A.K. Coomaraswamy, "East and West" in *The Bugbear of Literacy* (Bedfont: Peren-nial Books, 1979), p. 80. See also Letter to Sidney Gulick, July 1943, in *Selected Letters of Ananda K. Coomaraswamy*, ed. R.P. Coomaraswamy & A. Moore Jr. (Delhi: Oxford University Press, 1988), p. 69.

If it indeed be the case, as Coomaraswamy and Guénon insisted, that the spiritual malady of the modern world is to be explained by its indifference or hostility to the lessons of tradition, then it follows that the East may have a vital role to perform in any remedy. As he made clear in his essay "Oriental Metaphysics," Guénon believed that it was only in the East that various sapiential traditions remained more or less intact. It was to these, particularly Advaita Vedanta as the fullest possible expression of metaphysical doctrine, that the West must turn to recover its sense of timeless truths which have been obscured in modern times. Guénon also stressed that any traditional society, such as still survived in the East, is oriented to spiritual ends whilst any anti-traditional society, found everywhere in the modern West, is necessarily governed by values inimical to our spiritual welfare. T.S. Eliot somewhere remarked that the health of any civilization can be gauged by the number of saints it nurtures. We should be in no doubt that, whatever contaminations modernity might have brought to Asia in the last two centuries, the East preserves something of the spiritual effulgence which has characterized it since primordial times—one need only mention Paramahamsa Ramakrishna, Ramana Maharshi, and Anandamayi Ma, to restrict ourselves to India and to leave aside the Tibetan adepts, Chinese sages, and Zen masters of the Far East.

It is important not to confuse the Eastward-looking stance of figures like Guénon and Coomaraswamy with the sentimental exoticism nowadays so much in vogue. Coomaraswamy reminds us that

> If Guénon wants the West to turn to Eastern metaphysics, it is not because they are Eastern but because this is metaphysics. If "Eastern" metaphysics differed from a "Western" metaphysics, one or the other would not be metaphysics.[5]

One of Guénon's translators made the same point in suggesting that if Guénon turns so often to the East it is because the West is in the position of the

> foolish virgins who, through the wandering of their attention in other directions, had allowed their lamps to go out; in order to rekindle the

5 A.K. Coomaraswamy, "Eastern Wisdom and Western Knowledge" in *The Bugbear of Literacy*, pp. 72-73.

sacred fire, which in its essence is always the same wherever it may
be burning, they must have recourse to the lamps still kept alight.[6]

In other words, a turn to the spiritual heritage of the East need not
signal an abandonment of the West but might, rather, prefigure the
recuperation of those riches in our own traditions which have been
neglected but which can never truly be destroyed. It is sometimes only
with the aid of traditions much less ravaged by the onslaughts of modernity that we can appreciate what lies closer to hand. Furthermore,
such a rediscovery will help us to understand that metaphysical wisdom, the *sophia perennis*, is indeed always fundamentally the same,
albeit that the vestments in which it is clothed will vary from religion
to religion. Again, recall the prescient words of Coomaraswamy:

> [T]he only possible ground upon which an effective *entente* of East
> and West can be accomplished is that of the purely intellectual wis-
> dom that is one and the same for all times and for all men, and is
> independent of all environmental idiosyncrasy.[7]

Somewhat paradoxically, the diversity of religious doctrines and
practices only goes to prove the point. Properly understood, this mul-
tiplicity will be seen as a function of the diversity of mankind and of
those manifold Revelations in which all traditions originate, each being attuned to the receptivities and affinities of the human collectivity
in question. From each Divine dispensation—the descent of the Koran or the revelation of the Vedas, to choose an example from each
hemisphere—issues a doctrine and a method. The doctrine provides
an adequate but not exhaustive account of the nature of Reality, and
the method marks out a spiritual way whereby, through an alchemy of
the soul, we may conform ourselves with the one Reality (by whatever
name it might be called). The inter-relationships of the world's integral
religious traditions, and the interplay of their esoteric and exoteric dimensions, was the principal concern of the third of the "great trium-
virate" of twentieth century perennialists, Frithjof Schuon. Schuon's
work ranges through the vast domain of religious forms from all parts

6 Quoted in G. Eaton, *The Richest Vein: Eastern Tradition and Modern Thought* (London: Faber & Faber, 1949), p. 199.

7 A.K. Coomaraswamy, "Pertinence of Philosophy," p. 19.

of the globe, and he too has had a decisive role to play in bringing the spiritual heritage of the East within a Western purview.

The outlook espoused by Guénon, Coomaraswamy, and Schuon—an outlook still very much alive in parts of the East—stands at right angles to the prevailing ideologies of the modern West. One illustration must suffice. For the modern mind, shaped by a profane scientism, the words "matter" and "reality" are often more or less synonymous. Furthermore, in common parlance the word "reality" is generally without gradations; the notion that something might be "relatively real," and that this kind of "reality" is as nothing in the face of the Absolute, is more or less incomprehensible to the modern mind. In the East, and for anyone who understands the first thing about Tradition, nothing could be more absurd. To take as Real that ambiguous tissue of fugitive relativities which constitutes the spatio-temporal world is indeed to be ensnared in *maya*!

CHAPTER 14

Frithjof Schuon on Eastern Traditions

Truth is one and it would be vain to refuse to look for it except in one particular place, for the Intellect contains in its substance all that is true, and truth cannot but be manifested wherever the Intellect is deployed in the atmosphere of a Revelation.

Frithjof Schuon[1]

What matters in a religion is its central affirmation, its qualitative content, which is indispensable for man and of which the peripheral arguments are like a protective enclosure.

Frithjof Schuon[2]

The passage from one Asiatic tradition to another—Hinduism, Buddhism, Taoism—is a small thing, seeing that the metaphysical content is everywhere clearly apparent and even throws into relief the relativity of "mythological" diversities.

Frithjof Schuon[3]

While much of Frithjof Schuon's work has been devoted to the religious forms of the Abrahamic traditions, his metaphysical expositions, like those of Guénon, are rooted in Advaita Vedanta, and this for a very simple reason: Vedanta "is the most direct possible expression of gnosis"[4] and "an intrinsic esoterism."[5] From his youthful days Schuon evinced a particular affinity with Eastern religious forms, both doc-

1 F. Schuon, *Light on the Ancient Worlds: A New Translation with Selected Letters* (Bloomington, IN: World Wisdom, 2006), p. 121.

2 F. Schuon, *Spiritual Perspectives and Human Facts* (Bloomington, IN: World Wisdom, 2007), p. 71.

3 F. Schuon, *In the Tracks of Buddhism* (London: Allen & Unwin, 1968), p. 82.

4 F. Schuon, *Gnosis: Divine Wisdom, A New Translation with Selected Letters* (Bloomington, IN: World Wisdom, 2006), p. 61n. Similarly, "The doctrine of the Vedantists is incontestably metaphysical in the highest possible sense; it transmits every essential truth" (F. Schuon, *Light on the Ancient Worlds*, p. 75).

5 F. Schuon, *Survey of Metaphysics and Esoterism* (Bloomington, IN: World Wisdom Books, 2000), p. 118.

trinal and artistic. In a 1982 letter to Leo Schaya, Schuon wrote of the years following his move as a sixteen year-old to Paris:

> For about ten years I was completely spellbound by Hinduism, without however being able to be a Hindu in the literal sense. . . . I lived no other religion but that of the Vedanta and the *Bhagavad Gita*; this was my first experience of the *religio perennis*.[6]

Soon after his arrival in Paris in 1923 he was introduced to Guénon's *Introduction to the Study of the Hindu Doctrines, Man and His Becoming According to the Vedanta*, and *East and West*, which he read with the greatest interest and enthusiasm.[7] Here is a passage from a letter written in 1929:

> I feel Hindu, like a branch of this soul or of this spirituality, which spreads from the burning *Gopurams* of the Ganges to the red-gold shadows of the silent *Gompas* . . . as far as Angkor Wat and the Shivaite harmony of Mongolia and Cambodia, and which is still alive in pious Bali. This kinship is a fact and not a voluntary monomania; it corresponds to natural laws, to an elective affinity.[8]

Think, too, of Schuon's remark that "Being *a priori* a metaphysician, I have had since my youth a particular interest in Advaita Vedanta, but also in the method of realization of which Advaita Vedanta approves."[9] It was only because of the insurmountable barrier of caste that Schuon could not embark directly on this path—hence the turn towards Sufism. He also felt a particular affinity with both Buddhism

6 Schuon, letter to Leo Schaya, August 11, 1982, quoted in J-B. Aymard & P. Laude, *Frithjof Schuon: Life and Teachings* (Albany, NY: State University of New York Press, 2004), p. 10.

7 Schuon said of these works, "Guénon was the first European who dared to affirm in the West the superiority of the Hindu spirit over the modern Western spirit, and, in the name of Eastern spirituality and that of the ancient West, dared mercilessly to criticize modern civilization. . . . He expounded all the fundamental data that it is necessary to know in the West in order to understand India" (Schuon quoted in J-B. Aymard & P. Laude, *Frithjof Schuon: Life and Teachings*, p. 142n).

8 Schuon quoted in M. Fitzgerald, *Frithjof Schuon: Messenger of the Perennial Philosophy* (Bloomington, IN: World Wisdom, 2010), p. 26.

9 Schuon quoted in M. Fitzgerald, *Frithjof Schuon: Messenger of the Perennial Philosophy*, p. 27.

and Taoism, finding the latter "peerless and unique."[10] From his earliest years Schuon was also fascinated by the arts of the Far East. In an unusual personal reference in one of his works he tells of coming face to face, as a child, with a Buddha figure in an ethnographical museum, a traditional representation in gilded wood, flanked by statues of the Bodhisattvas Seishi and Kwannon, which seemed "to have emerged from a celestial river of golden light, silence, and mercy." Of the encounter with "this overwhelming embodiment of an infinite victory of the Spirit" Schuon writes, *"veni, vidi, victus sum"* ("I came, I saw, I was conquered").[11]

These biographical fragments remind us, firstly, of the axial place of Vedantic metaphysics in Schuon's work, and secondly, that Schuon was a *jnanin* whose intellectuality and aesthetic sensibility were not bound by those limits normally imposed by birth, culture, and formal religious affiliation. It is for this reason, among others, that Schuon's expositions of Eastern doctrines and practices have been hailed by the most exacting authorities from within those traditions. Here we will consider four Oriental traditions, isolating a few features which are accented in Schuon's writings, paying most attention to his account of Hinduism for reasons foreshadowed above.

The Hindu Tradition

In the context of Schuon's work as a whole, three aspects of the Hindu tradition deserve particular attention: Vedantic metaphysics; the caste system and its typology of spiritual dispositions; and the four paths or yogas. Before proceeding it might be as well to note Schuon's caution that

> Hinduism, while it is organically linked with the *Upanishads*, is nonetheless not reducible to the Shivaite and Shankarian Vedantism, although this must be considered as the essence of the Vedanta and thus of Hindu tradition.[12]

Unlike the Christian perspective, "The Hindu perspective begins with Reality, not with man; the fall is one cosmic accident among thou-

10 Unpublished writings, courtesy of World Wisdom.

11 F. Schuon, *Treasures of Buddhism* (Bloomington, IN: World Wisdom, 1993), p. 8.

12 F. Schuon, *Spiritual Perspectives*, p. 99.

sands of others."[13] It envisages things "primarily in relation to divine principle,"[14] which is to say that Hinduism is *primarily* a metaphysic rather than a spiritual method: it starts from a gnosis which is rooted in an unwavering discernment of the distinction between the Absolute and the relative, between *Atman* (or *Brahman*) and *maya*. This knowledge was revealed through the rishis of yore in the *Vedas*, and was most systematically and lucidly articulated in the *Upanishads*—the "end of the *Vedas*," Vedanta.

> The Vedanta stands out among explicit doctrines as one of the most direct formulations possible of what constitutes the very essence of our spiritual reality.... The Vedantic perspective finds its equivalents in the great religions which regulate humanity, for truth is one.[15]

The doctrine which governs the Vedanta and which is reaffirmed throughout the *Upanishads* is the identity of the Self (*Atman*) and Ultimate Reality (*Brahman*) which, insofar as it can be said to have attributes, is *Sat-Cit-Ananda* (Being-Consciousness-Bliss). The supreme goal, for man, is the realization of the Self; the surest path to this realization is *jnana* yoga, the way of knowledge. The world of space-time relativities is *maya*—from one point of point, illusion; from another, divine play (*lila*)—which both veils and discloses the Absolute, outside of which there is nothing:

> There is nothing unrelated to this Reality; even the "object" which is least in conformity with it is still it, but "objectified" by *maya*, the power of illusion, resulting from the infinity of the Self.[16]

> *Maya* is at once light and darkness: as "divine art" it is light inasmuch as it reveals the secrets of *Atma*; it is darkness inasmuch as it hides *Atma*. As darkness it is "ignorance," *avidya*.[17]

Maya encompasses the whole of the manifested realms, not only

---

13 F. Schuon, *Spiritual Perspectives*, p. 55.

14 F. Schuon, *Spiritual Perspectives*, pp. 58-59.

15 F. Schuon, *Spiritual Perspectives*, p. 99.

16 F. Schuon, *Spiritual Perspectives*, pp. 101-102.

17 F. Schuon, *Spiritual Perspectives*, p. 105.

the material and animic world: she is also "affirmed already *a fortiori* 'within' the Principle; the divine Principle 'desiring to be known'—or 'desiring to know'—condescends to the unfolding of its inward infinity, an unfolding at first potential and then outward or cosmic."[18] The Intellect is the microcosmic "crystallization" of *Atma* so that man may be "integrated within the subjective and thus returned to the divine Subject."[19] *Tat tvam asi*: That art thou.

A modern Hindu saint who is the very embodiment of the timeless truth of the Vedanta is Ramana Maharshi, of whom Schuon writes in these terms:

> In Sri Ramana Maharshi one meets ancient and eternal India again. Vedantic truth—that of the *Upanishads*—is reduced to its simplest expression but without any betrayal: it is the simplicity inherent in the Real, not the artificial and quite external simplification that springs from ignorance.

> The spiritual function that consists in an "action of presence" found its most rigorous expression in the Maharshi. In these latter days Sri Ramana was as it were the incarnation of what is primordial and incorruptible in India in opposition to modern activism; he manifested the nobility of contemplative "non-action" in opposition to an ethic of utilitarian agitation, and he showed the implacable beauty of pure truth in opposition to passions, weaknesses, betrayals.

> The great question "Who am I?" appears in his case as the concrete expression of a "lived" reality, if one may put it this way, and this authenticity gives each word of the Maharshi a perfume of inimitable freshness—the perfume of Truth, which incarnates itself in the most immediate way.

> The whole Vedanta is contained in Sri Ramana's question: "Who am I?" The answer is the Inexpressible.[20]

A more or less infallible litmus test of the modern mentality is the attitude to the Indian caste system, almost universally misunderstood

18 F. Schuon, *Light on the Ancient Worlds*, p. 76.

19 F. Schuon, *Spiritual Perspectives*, p. 102.

20 F. Schuon, *Spiritual Perspectives*, p. 129.

and castigated in the West. Here we can offer no more than a few general remarks on this vexed subject. It is of paramount importance to understand the principles which, on the one hand, give rise to caste systems such as we find within Hinduism, and on the other, elsewhere preclude them in favor of religious egalitarianism. The four *varnas* within the Hindu caste system, sanctioned by Scripture, are based on a division of man's understanding of the Real. The caste system, Schuon insists,

> is founded on the nature of things or, to be more exact, on one aspect of that nature, and thus on a reality which in certain circumstances cannot but manifest itself; this statement is equally valid as regards the opposite aspect, that of the equality of men before God. In short, in order to justify the system of castes it is enough to put the following question: does diversity of qualifications [spiritual and intellectual] and heredity exist? If it does, then the system of castes is both possible and legitimate. In the case of an absence of castes, where this is traditionally imposed, the sole question is: are men equal, not just from the point of view of their animality which is not in question, but from the point of view of their final end? Since every man has an immortal soul this is certain; therefore in a given traditional society this consideration can take precedence over that of diversity of qualifications. The immortality of the soul is the postulate of religious "egalitarianism," just as the quasi-divine character of the intellect—and hence of the intellectual elite—is the postulate of the caste system.[21]

Schuon goes on to elucidate some of the differences between the "leveling" outlook of Islam and Christianity (and one might here add Buddhism) and the hierarchical categories of the Hindu *varnas*, which identify those fundamental tendencies which divide men. For the moment all that needs to be further said is that the four levels of the caste hierarchy, and the two groupings "outside" (i.e. the *sannyasi* and the *chandala*), correspond with differing spiritual temperaments or dispositions, determined by the law of heredity which is so little understood in the modern West.

Hinduism is a primordial tradition which embraces a diver-

21 F. Schuon, *Language of the Self* (Bloomington, IN: World Wisdom Books, 1999), p. 113.

sity of spiritual possibilities, "an uncommon wealth of doctrines and methods"[22]—to an even greater extent than many other traditions. We remember that the great spiritual universes centered on each of the integral traditions will provide, in one way or another, for the needs of all human types and for the exigencies of the cyclic circumstances prevailing at the time—hence such phenomena as the "theistic" Buddhism to be found in the Pure Land schools of the Far East, and, by the same token, the "non-theism" which appears within theistic esoterism.[23] But even taking this principle into account, the Hindu tradition has been able to accommodate an extraordinary diversity. Truly Hinduism is a compendium of spiritual possibilities. As Martin Lings has observed:

> An advantage of Hinduism as a basis for the exposition of universal truth is the comprehensive breadth of its structure. On the one hand, like Judaism and Islam, it depends on direct revelation and makes a rigorous distinction between what is revealed and what is merely inspired. On the other hand, like Christianity, it depends on the *Avatara*, that is, the descent of the Divinity into this world.[24]

It is no surprise, then, that Hinduism should offer its adherents several pathways to *moksha* (liberation), the most pertinent of which are those of *jnana*, *bhakti*, and *karma* yoga—the ways of knowledge, devotion, and action (or work) respectively. *Jnana* yoga is the path of plenary esoterism, directed towards full realization of the Self, which comes from intellection. The spiritual disciplines of the *jnanin* are meditation, contemplative prayer, study, and various techniques and austerities which purify the mind, free it from the distractions of the

---

22 F. Schuon, *Treasures of Buddhism*, p. 19.

23 See F. Schuon, *Treasures of Buddhism*, pp. 17-20. Thomas Merton speaks of this tradition: "the Christian contemplative . . . is called mainly to penetrate the wordless darkness [void] and apophatic light of an experience beyond concepts, and here he gradually becomes familiar with a God who is 'absent' and as it were 'non-existent' to all human experience" (Merton quoted in W.H. Shannon, *Thomas Merton's Dark Path: The Inner Experience of a Contemplative* [New York: Farrar, Strauss & Giroux, 1988], p. 11). See also T. Merton, *Contemplation in a World of Action* (New York: Doubleday, 1973), p. 186.

24 M. Lings, "The World of Today in the Light of Tradition" in *In Quest of the Sacred: The Modern World in the Light of Tradition*, ed. S.H. Nasr & K. O'Brien (Oakton, VA: Foundation for Traditional Studies, 1994), p. 196.

ego, and release it from the bonds of ignorance so that the veil of *maya* becomes completely transparent and only the Real remains. This is the path to be followed by Brahmins, which is to say those blessed with an intelligence attuned to the Real. The path of *bhakti* harnesses man's will and his emotions and brings about a spiritual alchemy through devotion to one of the deities "personifying" *Brahman*, pre-eminently Shiva and Vishnu, or one of the *avataras*, amongst whom Krishna is the most popular and who extols the paths of both *bhakti* and *karma* yoga in one of India's most exalted Scriptures, the *Bhagavad Gita*.[25] *Karma* yoga is the way of action or work done in a spirit of selfless detachment and without any concern for the fruits thereof. Both *bhakti* and *karma* yoga offer a way which can be practiced by anyone, no matter how modest their intellectual endowments, and is thus suited to the majority of adherents, whilst *jnana* must remain the preserve of a spiritual elite, institutionalized in India in the caste of the Brahmins. *Raja* yoga is a system of psycho-spiritual techniques through which, under the guidance of a properly qualified guru, the psyche is cleansed and one is enabled to find in the *guha*, the innermost chamber of the heart, the supreme Self, "that great Purusha, of the color of the sun, beyond all darkness" (*Shvetashvatara Upanishad*).

Buddhism
Schuon opens his book on Buddhism with these salutary remarks which, if heeded, will immediately erase many outlandish notions that have accumulated around this subject in the modern West:

> Whoever sets out to define a spiritual phenomenon situated in the almost heavenly era of the great Revelations has to beware of assessing it according to the impoverished categories of later ages or, still worse, those belonging to the inbuilt profanity of the "free-thinking" world. Buddhism . . . is anything but a purely human ideology; were it such, its quality as a way of enlightenment or salvation would be unintelligible. To deny the celestial character of Shakyamuni and his

---

25 Described so memorably by Emerson as "the first of books; it was as if an empire spoke to us, nothing small or unworthy, but large, serene, consistent, the voice of an old intelligence which in another age and climate had pondered over and disposed of the same questions which exercise us" (quoted in E. Sharpe, *The Universal Gita: Western Images of the "Bhagavadgita", A Bicentenary Survey* [London: Duckworth, 1985], p. 24).

Message is after all tantamount to saying that there are effects without a cause.[26]

This tradition's status, so to speak, is a subject which has caused
untold confusion—amongst the adherents of the other religions,
amongst those who champion atheism and agnosticism, amongst
many Western converts, and even, in these later times, amongst practitioners within the Buddhist homelands whose thinking has been
adulterated by modern influences. No doubt these misapprehensions
arise from many different sources, but four are immediately apparent:
firstly, from a Hindu viewpoint Buddhism presents itself as a heterodoxy; secondly, Buddhism is problematic from the viewpoint of any
exoteric theism; thirdly, the spiritual methodology of Buddhism rests
on the metaphysic of the Void, misunderstood as a kind of nihilism of
which, it is thought, the doctrine of no soul (*anatma*) is another scan-
dalous instance; lastly, many Westerners attracted to Buddhism, often
unaware of its close affinities with the Christian tradition which they
have rejected, laud it as "rational," "empirical," "scientific," "humanistic," and the like, and disavow its religious "trappings." Such folk often
assert that Buddhism is a "way of life" or a "philosophy" rather than a
"religion." What does Schuon say about these matters?

On the question of Buddhism's relation to the Hindu tradition out
of which it emerged:

> The first question to be asked concerning any doctrine or tradition is
> that of its intrinsic orthodoxy: that is to say one must know whether
> that tradition is consonant, not necessarily with another given tradi-
> tionally orthodox perspective, but simply with Truth. As far as Bud-
> dhism is concerned, we will not ask therefore whether it agrees with
> the letter of the *Veda* or if its non-theism—and not "atheism"!—is
> reconcilable in its expression with Semitic theism or any other, but
> only whether Buddhism is true in itself; which means, if the answer
> is affirmative, that it will agree with the Vedic spirit and that its non-
> theism will express the Truth, or a sufficient and efficacious aspect
> of the Truth, whereof theism provides another possible expression,
> opportune in the world it governs.[27]

26 F. Schuon, *In the Tracks of Buddhism*, p. 17.

27 F. Schuon, *Treasures of Buddhism*, p. 18.

No doubt, from a certain viewpoint, Buddhism might be understood as a reaction against various excesses, corruptions, and degenerations within the Hindu tradition, just as Christianity can be seen
as a reaction against Judaic legalism and pharisaism. But to think of
the Buddha as a "reformer" is to misunderstand him and his message.[28] The Buddha is "renunciation, peace, mercy, and mystery," the
last being "the essence of truth which cannot adequately be conveyed
through language."[29]

On the vexed question of Buddhism's non-theism and its "negative" metaphysic, Schuon writes this:

> "Extinction" or "Voidness" is none other than Selfhood, a word
> which Buddhism, however, refrains from defining or even naming;
> the whole doctrine of anatma is calculated to prevent any concep-
> tual and therefore restrictive attribution being applied to the Divine
> Suchness which, being free from all otherness, alone is wholly Itself.[30]

Likewise:

> If Buddhism denies the outward, objective, and transcendent God,
> this is because it puts all its emphasis on the inward, subjective, and
> immanent Divinity—called *Nirvana* and *Adi-Buddha* as well as oth-
> er names—which moreover makes it impermissible to describe Bud-
> dhism as atheistic.[31]

Then again:

> If it be admitted that "the kingdom of Heaven is within you," there
> is no logical cause for reproaching Buddhism with conceiving the

28 F. Schuon, *Treasures of Buddhism*, pp.17-18.

29 F. Schuon, *Art from the Sacred to the Profane: East and West* (Bloomington, IN:
World Wisdom, 2007), p. 99.

30 F. Schuon, *In the Tracks of Buddhism*, p. 65. Elsewhere Schuon writes this: "No
doubt, the Buddhist *Nirvana* is nothing other than the Self, *Atma*; but whereas for the
Hindus the starting point is that reflection of the Self which is the 'I,' for the Buddhists
on the contrary the starting point is entirely negative and moreover purely empirical:
it is the *Samsara* as the world of suffering, and this world is merely a 'void,' *shunya*"
(F. Schuon, *To Have a Center* [Bloomington, IN: World Wisdom Books, 1990], pp.
135-136).

31 F. Schuon, *Esoterism as Principle and as Way* (London: Perennial Books, 1981), p. 141.

Divine Principle in this respect alone. The "Void" or "Extinction" is God—the supra-ontological Real and Being seen "inwardly"—within ourselves; not in our thought or in our ego, of course, but starting from that "geometrical point" within us whereby we are mysteriously attached to the Infinite.[32]

Buddhism's non-theism is one expression amongst many of the Truth:

Buddhism, inasmuch as it is a characteristic perspective and independently of its various modes, answers to a necessity: it could not but come to be, given that a non-anthropomorphic, impersonal, and "static" consideration of the Infinite is in itself a possibility; such a perspective had therefore to be manifested at a cyclic moment and in human surroundings that rendered it opportune, for wherever the receptacle is, there the content imposes itself.[33]

Furthermore, Buddhism is "a 'Hinduism universalized,' just as Christianity and Islam—each in its own way—are a Judaism rendered universal, which is to say detached from its particular ethnic environment and made accessible to men of all manner of racial origins."[34] Whilst it be true that Buddhism rests on a metaphysic which is in no essential way different from that of the Vedanta, it would be a grave mistake to infer that thereby it "does not represent as spontaneous and autonomous a reality as do the other great Revelations."[35] Concerning the well-known polemic of Shankara against Nagarjuna, Schuon says this:

The antagonism between Shankara and Nagarjuna is of the same order as that between Ramanuja and Shankara, with this difference,

---

32 F. Schuon, *Treasures of Buddhism*, p. 22; Schuon continues, "Buddhist 'atheism' consists in a refusal to objectivize or to exteriorize dogmatically the 'God within.'" However it is also true, as Schuon points out, that "such an objectivizing does occur on occasion in a 'provisional' sense in the merciful message of *Amitabha*, but the very possibility of such an objectivizing proves precisely that Buddhism is in no way 'atheistic' in the privative sense of the word."

33 F. Schuon, *Treasures of Buddhism*, p. 19.

34 F. Schuon, *Treasures of Buddhism*, pp. 19-20.

35 F. Schuon, *Treasures of Buddhism*, p. 19.

however: when Shankara rejects the Nagarjunian doctrine, it is because its form corresponds—independently of its real content and spiritual potential—to a more restricted perspective than that of the Vedanta. When on the other hand Ramanuja rejects the Shankarian doctrine, it is for the opposite reason: the perspective of Shankara surpasses that of Ramanuja, not merely by its form, but in its very foundation.

In order truly to understand Nagarjuna, or the Mahayana in general, it is necessary to take account of two facts before everything else: first that Buddhism presents itself essentially as a spiritual method and therefore subordinates everything to the methodic point of view and second that this method is essentially one of negation.[36]

"Buddhism does not begin with the notion of the ego as do the religions of Semitic origin but with the wholly empirical reality of suffering."[37] Dialectically and methodically, it is founded on the experience of human suffering; it is a spiritual way directed to the cessation of such suffering:

> The doctrines of the Buddha are only "celestial mirages" intended to catch, as in the golden net, the greatest possible number of creatures plunged in ignorance, suffering, and transmigration, and . . . it is therefore the benefit of creatures and not the suchness of the Universe which determines the necessarily contingent form of the Message. . . . Buddhism, within the framework of its own wisdom, goes beyond the formal "mythology" or the "letter" and ultimately transcends all possible human formulations, thus realizing an unsurpassable contemplative disinterestedness as do the Vedanta, Taoism, and analogous doctrines.[38]

It follows that the wishful claims sometimes made by Orientalists and Western converts that Buddhism is simply a "philosophy" or "natural religion" are announcements that the persons in question are seeing Buddhism refracted through modern prejudices.

Buddhism comprises an immense spiritual universe in which

36 F. Schuon, *Spiritual Perspectives*, p. 109.

37 F. Schuon, *Spiritual Perspectives*, p. 56.

38 F. Schuon, *Treasures of Buddhism*, pp. 107-108.

we find an encyclopedic range of religious forms and practices, as is evident in the very different inflections given to the Buddha's saving message in the Theravada, Vajrayana, Zen, and Pure Land branches of the tradition. On these great branches and the various schools and sects contained therein, Schuon has written with characteristic percipience. These writings are all the more illuminating, and sometimes startling, given that Buddhism has received comparatively little attention within the perennialist school. As is well-known, Guénon himself for many years harbored the notion that Buddhism was no more than a Hindu heterodoxy until he was set right by Ananda Coomaraswamy and Marco Pallis, who, after Schuon, are the two foremost perennialist authorities on this tradition.

Notes on the Chinese Tradition and Shinto
The pre-Buddhist Chinese tradition, with its Confucian and Taoist branches, belongs to the traditional family of Mongoloid shamanism, as does Shintoism, each of these resting on doctrines of

> a complementary opposition of Heaven and earth and a cult of Nature, the latter being envisaged under the aspect of its essential causality and not of its existential accidentality; they are also distinguished by a certain parsimony in their eschatology.[39]

The religious heritage of China covered the Far East and included lands beyond the present national boundaries, encompassing ancestorism, shamanism, Taoism, and Confucianism, and later assimilating Buddhism and giving it a distinctive expression through the Ch'an/Zen and Pure Land schools. Rather than untangling this skein from either an historical or a doctrinal point of view, we will here confine ourselves to noting a few of Schuon's observations about Confucianism, which has stamped so many aspects of Chinese culture, and Taoism, the most

---

39 F. Schuon, *The Feathered Sun: Plains Indians in Art and Philosophy* (Bloomington, IN: World Wisdom Books, 1990), pp. 22-23. This "parsimony," Schuon explains, derives from several factors, including the fact that the eschatological element is manifested in the cult of the emperor (and of heroes and ancestors), and the emphasis in warrior traditions on deeds rather than words. In this perspective "the act, as a decisive affirmation of the immortal person, seems almost sufficient unto itself; the act is the character and the character is salvation, in a certain sense" (F. Schuon, *Treasures of Buddhism*, p. 179).

metaphysical and mystical branch of the Chinese heritage.⁴⁰ These re-flections will also illuminate, sometimes obliquely, other aspects of the whole tradition which will not come within our immediate purview.

As is so often the case, Schuon is able to condense the essential and distinctive features of a tradition into a short and decisive formulation which tells us more than a whole shelf of Orientalist tomes. In the case of Confucianism he starts from the outer social framework:

> Confucianism divides men into rulers and ruled. From the former it requires a sense of duty and from the latter filial piety. Here we see that the social Law is in no wise detached from the spiritual meaning of the whole tradition; inevitably it has concomitant spiritual elements which concern man as such, that is, man envisaged independently from society.

This, it might be noted in passing, gives the lie to one of the most fatigued of Western clichés about Confucianism—that it is no more than "a system of social ethics" which, we are told, performs a "conservative" ideological function in the Chinese social formation. But to return to Schuon's remarks:

> Indeed every man rules or determines something that is placed in some way in his keeping, even if it is only his own soul, which is made up of images and desires; on the other hand every man is governed or determined by something that in some way surpasses him, even if it is only his Intellect. Thus each man bears in himself the double obligation of duty in relation to the inferior and piety in relation to the superior, and this double principle lends itself to incalculable applications: it includes even inanimate nature in the sense that anything may serve—with regard to us and according to circumstances—as a celestial principle or as a terrestrial substance.

> Chinese wisdom foresees an application of the universal pair "Heaven-Earth" (*Tien-Ti*) that is first of all social and then personal, and thereby a conformation to the "Ineffable" (*Wu-Ming*) from which the pair proceeds. The point of connection between Confucianism and

---

40 It was René Guénon who first made it perfectly clear to Western readers that these, far from being two different "religions," were complementary dimensions of a single tradition. See R. Guénon, "Taoism and Confucianism," *Studies in Comparative Religion*, 6:4, 1971, pp. 239-250.

Taoism is in the virtues: Confucianism considers their social and human value and Taoism their intrinsic and spiritual quality. Man is the place where Heaven and Earth meet. Egoism must be extinguished between devotion and duty.[41]

The "Great Triad," or ternary, of Taoism, Heaven-Man-Earth (*Tien-Ti-Jen*), provides the scaffold for Taoist metaphysics, cosmology, and spiritual practice.

The ethnic genius of both the Chinese and the Japanese peoples finds one of its most distinctive expressions in the traditional art of the Far East, one which vibrates with those spiritual mysteries which lie beyond the reach of discursive thought and verbal formulation. Mystery may be revealed "in an illuminating flash through a symbol, such as a key word, a mystic sound, or an image whose suggestive action may be scarcely graspable"—so it is with the Zen *koans* which are "verbal symbols calculated to provoke an ontological breach in our carapace of ignorance," and with the "mysterious and transparent atmosphere of Taoist and Zen landscapes" which witness the fact that "no peoples have been more successful in visualizing the mystery of things."[42]

> Far-Eastern painting has an aerial grace, the inimitable charm of a furtive and precious vision; by compensation, the terrifying presence of dragons, genii, and demons adds to the art of the Far East a dynamic and flamboyant element.[43]

Taoist landscape paintings "exteriorize a metaphysic and a contemplative state: they spring, not from space, but from the 'void,'" and constitute "one of the most powerfully original forms of sacred art."[44]

It only remains to make a few fragmentary but suggestive remarks about Shinto, the mythological and shamanistic tradition indigenous to Japan. Firstly, it is as well to banish the common error of supposing that Shinto ancestorism replaced the Divinity with the ancestors, which overlooks the fact that "the Divinity itself is conceived in the Far East as a kind of Ancestor, and one's human ancestors are like a

41 F. Schuon, *Spiritual Perspectives*, pp. 62-63.

42 F. Schuon, *Art from the Sacred to the Profane*, p. 99.

43 F. Schuon, *Art from the Sacred to the Profane*, p. 101.

44 F. Schuon, *Art from the Sacred to the Profane*, p. 103.

prolongation of the Divinity."[45] It is for this reason that "the ancestor is at once the origin and the spiritual or moral norm":

> He is, for his descendants, the essential personality, that is to say the substance of which they are like the accidents; and piety consists precisely in viewing him thus and in seeing in him but the bridge connecting them—his descendants—with the Divine. . . . Ancestors are the human imprints of angelic substances and, for that reason, also of divine Qualities; to be true to them is to be true to God.[46]

The cult of the Emperor is a particular expression of the same principle.

The spiritual affinities between Shinto and other forms of "Hyperborean Shamanism" are evident in "many mythological, and even vestimentary similarities," in the cult of Nature, and in "their thirst for freedom, their contempt for luxury, their taciturnness and other similar characteristics"[47]—the comparisons with the American Indians are too obvious to need laboring. These affinities also go to explain why Shinto was so easily able to assimilate Far Eastern forms of Buddhism (especially the ideal of the *Bodhisattva*), also remembering that "The passage from one Asiatic tradition to another—Hinduism, Buddhism, Taoism—is a small thing, seeing that the metaphysical content is everywhere clearly apparent."[48]

---

45 F. Schuon, *Treasures of Buddhism*, p. 173.

46 F. Schuon, *Treasures of Buddhism*, p. 176.

47 F. Schuon, *Treasures of Buddhism*, p. 177.

48 F. Schuon, *In the Tracks of Buddhism*, p. 82.

CHAPTER 15

Ex Oriente Lux:
Eastern Religions, Western Writers

Sanskrit literature will be no less influential for our time than Greek
literature was in the fifteenth century for the Renaissance.

Schopenhauer[1]

In the Orient we must seek the highest Romanticism.

Frederick Schlegel[2]

In the early nineteenth century Hegel remarked that "Without being
known too well, [India] has existed for millennia in the imagination
of the Europeans as a wonderland. Its fame, which it has always had
with regard to its treasures, both its natural ones, and, in particular,
its wisdom, has lured men there."[3] Eusebius relates the time-honored
anecdote that Socrates himself was visited in Athens by an Indian who
asked him about the nature of his philosophizing. When Socrates re-
sponded that he was studying the problems of human life, his inter-
locutor laughed and explained that it was impossible to understand
human matters without considering the divine.[4] India is mentioned a
good deal in the classical literature from Herodotus onwards and we
know that ancient philosophers and theologians such as Pythagoras,
Diogenes, Plotinus, and Clement took a close interest in the learning of their Eastern counterparts. We remember that Alexander the
Great's entourage in his Eastern campaigns included several distinguished philosophers, historians, and writers wishing to learn more
about the intellectual and spiritual life of the Eastern barbarians, and

---

1 Schopenhauer quoted in S. Batchelor, *The Awakening of the West: The Encounter of Buddhism and Western Culture* (Berkeley: Parallax Press, 1994), p. 255.

2 Schlegel quoted in S. Batchelor, *Awakening of the West*, p. 252.

3 Hegel quoted in W. Halbfass, *India and Europe: An Essay in Philosophical Under-standing* (Delhi: Motilal Banarsidass, 1990), p. 2.

4 The anecdote apparently goes back to the Aristotelian Aristoxenes; see W. Halbfass, *India and Europe*, p. 8.

we are told that Alexander himself conversed with the gymnosophists, as the Greeks called them—the naked sages of India.[5]

Sarvepalli Radhakrishnan, the eminent Indian philosopher and first President of India, has written of the West's attraction to "the glamour of the exotic," and has remarked that "The East has ever been a romantic puzzle to the West, the home of adventures like those of the Arabian Nights, the abode of magic, the land of heart's desire. . . ."[6] Michel Le Bris, a contemporary commentator, has characterized the East as it exists in the European imagination as

> That Elsewhere, that yearned for realm where it was supposed that a man might get rid of the burden of self, that land outside time and space, thought of as being at once a place of wandering and a place of homecoming.[7]

But, of course, this is only one facet of a very complex phenomenon. At least since the time of the classical historians and playwrights the East has also been depicted not only as exotic, mysterious, and alluring but as sinister, dark, threatening. Stephen Batchelor has put the matter in psychological terms:

> In the European imagination Asia came to stand for something both distant and unknown yet also to be feared. As the colonizing powers came to identify themselves with order, reason, and power, so the colonized East became perceived as chaotic, irrational, and weak. In psychological terms, the East became a cipher for the Western unconscious, the repository of all that is dark, unacknowledged, feminine, sensual, repressed, and liable to eruption.[8]

Then too, there is another persistent strain in European attitudes, one which we can mark in the frankly contemptuous remarks by one of the most pompous stuffed shirts of the nineteenth century, to wit, the one-time colonial administrator and historian Thomas Babbington

5 See W. Halbfass, *India and Europe*, p. 12.

6 S. Radhakrishnan, *Eastern Religions and Western Thought* (New York: Oxford University Press, 1959), p. 251.

7 Quoted in J.J. Clarke, *Oriental Enlightenment: The Encounter Between Asian and Western Thought* (London: Routledge, 1997), p. 19.

8 S. Batchelor, *Awakening of the West*, p. 234.

Macaulay. None of us will be unfamiliar with his characterization of Indians as "lesser breeds without the law" even if we be unaware of the provenance of that deeply offensive phrase. Perhaps less well-known, but no less characteristic, was his dismissal of Hinduism as a web of "monstrous superstitions" and of the ancient Sanskrit Scriptures as "less valuable than what may be found in the most paltry abridgments used at preparatory schools in England." He scorned Indian

> medical doctrines which would disgrace an English farrier—astronomy which would move laughter in the girls at an English boarding-school—history, abounding with kings thirty feet long, and reigns thirty thousand years long—and geography made up of seas of treacle and seas of butter.[9]

The history of intellectual and cultural contact between West and East is a long and complicated one. Here I am concerned only with the relatively recent past—to be more precise, with the last two centuries—and only with the ways in which imaginative writers have engaged in a dialogue with Eastern spirituality. One might approach an investigation of the place of the East in the recent European literary imagination in any number of ways. One might, for instance, organize the inquiry around the impact of particular Asian religious traditions—the Confucianism and Taoism of China, Indian Hinduism and Buddhism, the Zen Buddhism of Japan, and most recently, the Tibetan Vajrayana, to identify them in the order in which they have infiltrated the European imagination. Or one might structure the inquiry around national cultures in the West, and address questions such as: How are we to account for the deep and tenacious German interest in Indian religions, particularly Buddhism, remembering that Germany had no imperial presence or ambitions in the subcontinent? Or again our angle of approach might be determined by a theoretical schema. Most influential of all such theorizations in recent years has been Edward Said's widely-celebrated and massively influential work, *Orientalism*, published in 1978, in which he argued that the Orient was a "system of ideological fictions" whose purpose was and is to legitimize Western cultural and

9 Macaulay quoted in J.J. Clarke, *Oriental Enlightenment*, p. 73, and in E. Sharpe, *The Universal Gita: Western Images of the "Bhagavadgita," A Bicentenary Survey* (London: Duckworth, 1985), p. 17.

political superiority; furthermore, that the Western understanding of the East—Orientalism—has grown out of "a relationship of power, of domination, of varying degrees of complex hegemony."[10] Said's argument, it must be said, is addressed primarily to the European encounter with Islam and with the Middle East, although Said himself extends the case to the Orient in general. His case has become the reigning orthodoxy in the field of post-colonial studies. I believe that a close study of Western engagements in Eastern religion and philosophy in particular exposes certain fundamental weaknesses in Said's argument—which is not to deny the force and cogency of Said's argument within the Middle Eastern domain with which he is principally concerned.

However, for this essay I will isolate five groups of writers who exhibited a close and serious interest in Eastern philosophy and spirituality, one which can be traced in their own imaginative creations. After some general remarks about the group in question I will make some more detailed comments about one or two exemplary figures. The groups in question: the German and English Romantics of the late eighteenth and early nineteenth century; the American Transcendentalists; modernist poets and novelists of the first half of the twentieth century; a group of neo-Vedantins and perennialists who congregated on the American West Coast in the thirties; and finally several writers from those American cultural perturbations known as the Beat movement of the 1950s and the counter-culture of the 1960s.

The German and English Romantics
The Enlightenment *philosophes*, who fall outside our purview, had been much attracted to the Chinese civilization. Many aspects of Chinese thought and culture had become well known in Western Europe, largely through the Jesuit missionaries, and writers like Voltaire, Diderot, Helvetius, Leibniz, and David Hume extolled the virtues of many aspects of Chinese civilization, particularly Confucianism which they understood as a rationally-based and humanistic system of social ethics. So widespread was the interest in and enthusiasm for things Chinese that we might speak of a wave of Sinophilia, if not Sinomania, flowing over Western Europe, particularly France, in the first half of the eighteenth century. However, for reasons which cannot be canvassed here, late in the century the European gaze shifted from China to India.

10 E. Said, *Orientalism* (Harmondsworth: Penguin, 1985), pp. 321, 5.

The beginnings of a serious and informed intellectual interest in the philosophic and religious thought of India can be tied to several specific events in the late eighteenth century: the founding in the 1780s of the Asiatic Society of Bengal by the remarkable William Jones, lawyer, linguist, poet, and scholar, and the publication of the first journal of Oriental studies, *Asiatic Researches*; the publication in 1785 of Charles Wilkins' first English translation of the *Bhagavad Gita*, a book "which was to exercise enormous influence on the mind of Europe and America,"[11] followed in 1801 by Duperron's translation from the Persian into Latin of a number of Upanishads as *Oupnek'hat*;[12] and the rapid emergence of the first generation of Indologists: in this context we might mention figures such as Jones, Wilkins, and Thomas Colebrook, precursors of the great nineteenth century philologists and scholars such as Max Müller.

Among the German Romantics in whom the Eastern scriptures ignited an intense if sometimes temporary excitement were Herder, Goethe, Schelling, Fichte, Schopenhauer, Schleiermacher, Schiller, Novalis, and both Schlegels—a veritable roll call of German Romanticism! Herder was amongst the first of the Romantics to "conscript the Orient in pursuit of the goals of Romanticism."[13] His attitude to India is evinced by such comments as "O holy land [of India], I salute thee, thou source of all music, thou voice of the heart," and "Behold the East—cradle of the human race, of human emotion, of all religion."[14] Many of the German Romantics lauded the Hindu Scriptures, particularly the *Upanishads*: Schelling, for instance, asserted that the "sacred texts of the Indians" were superior to the Bible. In England we can discern various Oriental interests and themes in the work of Southey, Coleridge, Shelley, Byron, and De Quincey, though in some cases the interest was once-removed, mediated by the German Idealists. However, these interests sometimes went quite deep: Shelley's exposition of Vedantic philosophy in *Adonais* might be cited as an example. Edward Said, in somewhat overheated and lurid language, refers to "the virtual epidemic of Orientalia affecting almost every major poet, essayist, and

---

11 E. Sharpe, *Universal Gita*, p. 10.

12 The remarkable story of the translation is told by Stephen Cross in "*Ex Oriente Lux*: How the Upanishads Came to Europe," *Temenos Academy Review*, Issue 2, 1999.

13 J.J. Clarke, *Oriental Enlightenment*, p. 61.

14 J.J. Clarke, *Oriental Enlightenment*, p. 61.

philosopher of the period."[15]

What was the excitement all about? The East in general and India in particular became a site where several Romantic interests could
happily converge: the interest of the early Indologists in the origins
of various European and Indian languages, and the claim that these
may have had a common genesis, became intertwined with new and
burgeoning Romantic conceptions about national and cultural identity, conceptions paralleled in a strange way by the affirmation of a
universal humanity whose lineaments could just as easily be read in
the ancient Hindu Scriptures as in the Judeo-Christian heritage or in
classical Greece.[16] Several German Romantics believed that the origins
of civilization itself were to be found in India. Following Herder, Friedrich Schlegel, for instance, claimed that, "The primary source of all
intellectual development—in a word the whole human culture—is unquestionably to be found in the traditions of the East."[17] Under Schlegel's linguistic and anthropological theories Germanic culture could be
traced back to ancient India: this was, in part, a reaction against a clas-
sicism "indelibly associated with France."[18] We might also note in passing that it was Schlegel who coined the term "Oriental Renaissance" to
describe the contemporary efflorescence of European interest in matters Eastern, and who was responsible for the second translation of
the *Gita* into a European language, in this case Latin.[19] Schlegel also
offers us one instance of a recurrent existential pattern, the immersion
in Eastern thought and spirituality followed by a return to one's own
religious tradition, marked in Schlegel's case by his late conversion to
Catholicism. By way of a final aside we might also note that the young-
er Schlegel, August Wilhelm, occupied the first chair in Indology at a
German university, Bonn.[20]

Romantic philosophers found the monistic teachings of the *Upanishads* to be in close harmony with their own Idealist beliefs. As J.J.
Clarke has remarked,

15 E. Said, *Orientalism*, p. 51.

16 See W. Halbfass, *Indian and Europe*, Ch. 5.

17 J.J. Clarke, *Oriental Enlightenment*, p. 65.

18 J.J. Clarke, *Oriental Enlightenment*, p. 65.

19 S. Batchelor, *Awakening of the West*, p. 252, and E. Sharpe, *Universal Gita*, p. 18.

20 W. Halbfass, *Indian and Europe*, p. 81.

just as Confucianism had offered the *philosophes* a model for a rationalist, deistic philosophy, so the Hinduism of the *Upanishads* offered an exalted metaphysical system which resonated with their own idealist assumptions, and which provided a counterblast to the materialistic and mechanistic philosophy that had come to dominate the Enlightenment period.[21]

Indian values and ideas concerning the unity of all life forms and the world-soul could also be seen to validate Romantic ideas about "the transcendental wholeness and fundamentally spiritual essence of the natural world."[22] As Schlegel claimed, "In the Orient we must seek the highest Romanticism."[23] Some of the Romantics, Blake and Novalis amongst them, nurtured ideas about "a single God for all mankind" and about a universal essence to be found at heart of all the great mythological and religious traditions, an idea which later became current under the term "the perennial philosophy," popularized in the West by another writer whom we shall meet a little later.

Let us look a little more closely at the engagement of one hitherto largely neglected Romantic philosopher, Arthur Schopenhauer. His principal work *The World as Will and Representation*, first appeared in 1818, before Schopenhauer was exposed to Indian influences. But it was not until its reappearance in two volumes in 1844, now densely textured with Indian references, that it really exerted its influence on European intellectual life. Its impact on Wagner and Nietzsche is well-known. Schopenhauer had studied under Fichte and Schleiermacher at university in Berlin but his principal influence was Kant. On Schopenhauer's desk in his study stood two figures: a bust of Kant and a statue of the Buddha.[24]

Schopenhauer, at age twenty-five, was given a copy of Duperron's *Oupnek'hat*. It was a revelation to him: he later praised it as "the most profitable and elevating reading which . . . is possible in the world. It has been the solace of my life, and will be the solace of my death."[25] After his introduction to the *Upanishads* Schopenhauer immediately

21 J.J. Clarke, *Oriental Enlightenment*, p. 61.

22 J.J. Clarke, *Oriental Enlightenment*, Clarke, p. 62.

23 S. Batchelor, *Awakening of the West*, p. 252. See also E. Said, *Orientalism*, p. 98.

24 S. Batchelor, *Awakening of the West*, p. 255.

25 J.J. Clarke, *Oriental Enlightenment*, p. 68.

embarked on the collection and study of such Asian texts as had been translated into European languages, claiming that "Sanskrit literature will be no less influential for our time than Greek literature was in the fifteenth century for the Renaissance."[26]

Schopenhauer believed India was "the land of the most ancient and the most pristine wisdom"[27] from whence could be traced many currents within European civilization, Christianity included. Schopenhauer subscribed to the widely held Romantic belief that Christianity "had Indian blood in its veins" and claimed that "Christianity taught only what the whole of Asia knew already long before and even better," for which reason he believed that Christianity would never take root in India: "the ancient wisdom of the human race," he stated, "will not be supplanted by the events in Galilee. On the contrary, Indian wisdom flows back to Europe, and will produce fundamental changes in our knowledge and thought."[28]

He also affirmed the idea of the underlying unity of the world's great religious and philosophical traditions: "in general," he wrote, "the sages of all times have always said the same."[29] Like many other Romantics, Schopenhauer found in the Eastern Scriptures validation of his own idealist, anti-rationalist agenda but he also discovered in Buddhism resonances with his own particular psychological and ethical interests. The ethical ideal of compassion, foregrounded in Buddhism, and its metaphysic of emptiness, struck a deep chord in Schopenhauer who was one of the first to seriously investigate Buddhism as a coherent philosophical system. He can be seen as a transitional figure in the movement of interest away from Hinduism towards Buddhism in the middle of the nineteenth century. Wilhelm Halbfass has summed up Schopenhauer's encounter with Eastern philosophy this way:

> [H]e showed an unprecedented readiness to integrate Indian ideas into his own European thinking and self-understanding, and to utilize them for the illustration, articulation, and clarification of his own teachings and problems. With this, he combined a radical critique of some of the most fundamental presuppositions of the Judeo-

26 S. Batchelor, *Awakening of the West*, p. 255.

27 J.J. Clarke, *Oriental Enlightenment*, p. 68.

28 J.J. Clarke, *Oriental Enlightenment*, p. 69.

29 W. Halbfass, *India and Europe*, p. 111.

Christian tradition, such as notions of a personal God, the uniqueness of the human individual, and the meaning of history, as well as the modern Western belief in the powers of the intellect, rationality, planning, and progress.[30]

The American Transcendentalists

Soon after the appearance of the revised edition of *The World as Will and Representation*, in the winter of 1846 and on the other side of the Atlantic, Henry David Thoreau watched a group of Irishman (whom he called "Hyperboreans"!) carve massive blocks of ice out of Walden pond, ice bound for the southern states and for India. Their labors sparked in Thoreau's imagination another scene:

> Thus it appears that the sweltering inhabitants of Charleston and New Orleans, of Madras and Bombay and Calcutta, drink at my well. In the morning I bathe my intellect in the stupendous and cosmogonal philosophy of the *Bhagavat Geeta*, since whose composition years of the gods have elapsed, and in comparison with which our modern world and its literature seem puny and trivial; and I doubt if that philosophy is not to be referred to a previous state of existence, so remote is its sublimity from our conceptions. I lay down the book and go to my well for water, and lo! there I meet the servant of Bramin, priest of Brahma and Vishnu and Indra, who sits in his temple on the Ganges reading the *Vedas*, or dwells in the root of the tree with his crust and water jug. I meet his servant come to draw water for his master, and our buckets as it were grate together in the same well. The pure Walden water is mingled with the sacred water of the Ganges.[31]

One is reminded of Blake's meetings with Old Testament prophets in the backstreets of London. Thoreau, like the other American transcendentalists, met with ancient India in her scriptures and in his own imagination, never traveling far outside his native New England.

Like the German Romantics, the New Englanders derived much of their knowledge of India from the heroic labors of the early Oriental-

---

30 W. Halbfass, *India and Europe*, p. 120. For a detailed account of the affinities and discontinuities between Schopenhauer's thought and Buddhism, see P. Abelsen, "Schopenhauer and Buddhism," *Philosophy East and West*, 43, 1993, pp. 255-278.

31 From *Walden* (1854) in *The Portable Thoreau*, ed. C. Bode (New York: Viking Press, 1964), pp. 538-539.

ists—William Jones, Wilkins, Colebrook, Duperron. William Emerson for instance, liberal Bostonian cleric and father of Ralph Waldo, was an avid reader of *Asiatic Researches* which he covered with extensive annotations.[32] Thoreau's first encounter with an Eastern text was in Emerson's library—Jones's *Laws of Manu* which, said Thoreau, "comes to me with such a volume of sound as if it had been swept unobstructed over the plains of Hindustan."[33] The *Gita* which Thoreau read under the trees every morning at Walden, had only first arrived in Concord in 1843, Wilkins' translation given to Emerson as a gift. Let us glance at the Eastern enthusiasms of the three key imaginative writers in American Transcendentalism: Emerson, Thoreau, and Whitman. We might, by way of shorthand, describe their interests as theological and metaphysical, practical and poetic respectively. By way of a context here is John Clarke's useful summation of the Transcendentalist agenda:

> The underlying philosophy of New England transcendentalism . . . represented a commitment to ancient and universal ideas concerning the essential unity and ultimately spiritual nature of the cosmos, combined with a belief in the ultimate goodness of man and the supremacy of intuitive over rational thought. Its deeply spiritual outlook was one which sought to go beyond creeds and organized religions in favor of a religious experience deemed to be universal. It represented in many ways a continuation and development of ideas of the European Romantic movement, especially those of Goethe, Wordsworth, Coleridge, and Carlyle, and like Romanticism, was inspired by neo-platonic and mystical traditions. It can also be seen as a reaction against Lockean materialism, utilitarianism, and Calvinistic Christianity. . . .[34]

For Emerson the Hindu Scriptures in particular were a mine of metaphysical and philosophical insights which corroborated and sometimes shaped his own emergent philosophy, underpinned by the idea of the universal world-soul and the underlying unity of God, man, and nature for which he found plentiful Indian sanctions. "We lie in the lap of an immense intelligence," he wrote, "which makes us organs

---

32 R. Fields, *How the Swans Came to the Lake: A Narrative History of Buddhism in America* (Boston: Shambhala Publications, 1992), p. 56.

33 R. Fields, *How the Swans Came*, p. 59.

34 J.J. Clarke, *Oriental Enlightenment*, p. 84.

of its activity and receivers of its truth."[35]

Emerson's enthusiasm for Eastern philosophy and spirituality was more or less restricted to Hinduism and to its primary Scriptures: the *Vedas*, *Upanishads*, and *Gita*. The latter, he confided to his journal, was

> the first of books; it was as if an empire spoke to us, nothing small or unworthy, but large, serene, consistent, the voice of an old intelligence which in another age and climate had pondered over and disposed of the same questions which exercise us.[36]

A Hindu imprint is clearly evident in the poems "Brahma" and "Hamatreya," and in essays such as "Fate," "Plato," "The Over-Soul," "Illusions," and "Immortality." The first four lines of "Brahma," for instance, are almost a paraphrase of Krishna's words to Arjuna in the *Gita*:

> If the red slayer thinks he slays,
> Or if the slain thinks he is slain,
> They know not well the subtle ways
> I keep, and pass, and turn again

Compare with: "He who deems This to be a slayer and he who thinks This to be slain, are alike without discernment; This slays not neither is it slain."[37]

Emerson's attitude to Buddhism oscillated between the ambivalent and the hostile. In particular, what he understood as the Buddhist idea of *nirvana* was repugnant to him. The idea of annihilation, he wrote, froze him with its "icy light":

35 R. Fields, *How the Swans Came*, p. 58. On Emerson's engagement with Hindu doctrines see S. Nagarajan, "Emerson and Advaita: Some Comparisons and Contrasts," *American Transcendental Quarterly*, 3:4, 1989, pp. 325-336; R.B. Goodman, "East-West Philosophy in Nineteenth Century America: Emerson and Hinduism," *Journal of the History of Ideas*, 51:4, 1990, pp. 625-645; and G. Ferrando, "Emerson and the East" in *Vedanta for Modern Man*, ed. C. Isherwood (New York: New American Library, 1972), pp. 351-356.

36 E. Sharpe, *Universal Gita*, p. 24.

37 *Bhagavad Gita* II.19. On "Brahma" see K.N. Chandran, "The Pining Gods and Sages in Emerson's 'Brahma,'" *English Language Notes*, 27:1, pp. 55-57.

This remorseless Buddhism lies all around, threatening with death and night. . . . Every thought, every enterprise, every sentiment, has its ruin in this horrid Infinite which circles us and awaits our dropping into it.

In another journal entry "the Sage of Concord" summarized Buddhism as "Winter. Night. Sleep."[38]

Thoreau, the "Yankee Diogenes" as some of his contemporaries called him, was less interested in metaphysical speculation and more concerned with the practical ideal of a simple, spiritual life; he was much more enthusiastic about Buddhism whilst he shared Emerson's enthusiasm for the *Gita* of which he wrote, "the reader is nowhere raised into and sustained in a higher, purer, or rarer region of thought than in the Bhagavat-Geeta."[39] Thoreau adopted as his motto "*Ex Oriente Lux*"—Light comes from the East. In the "Ethnical Scriptures" column of *Dial*, the principal organ of the Transcendentalists, Thoreau presented his own translation from Eugene Burnouf's French, of the *Lotus Sutra*, one of the great texts of the Mahayana. The principal lesson Thoreau drew from the Sutra was the necessity for sustained and disciplined meditation, soon to be put into effect during his sojourn at Walden Pond. His temperament was of a much more contemplative turn than Emerson's. Earlier, in 1841 he wrote in his journal that

one may discover the root of the Hindoo religion in his own private history, when, in the silent intervals of the day or the night, he does sometimes inflict on himself like austerities with a stern satisfaction.[40]

As Rick Fields has remarked, Thoreau was perhaps the first American to explore "the nontheistic mode of contemplation which is the

---

38 R. Fields, *How the Swans Came*, p. 60. In recent years there have been several attempts to find some affinities between Emerson's thought and sensibility and Zen Buddhism: see S. Morris, "Beyond Christianity: Transcendentalism and Zen," *The Eastern Buddhist*, 24:2, Autumn 1991, pp. 33-68, and J.G. Rudy, "Engaging the Void: Emerson's Essay on Experience and the Zen Experience of Self-Emptying," *The Eastern Buddhist*, 26:1, Spring 1993, pp. 101-125.

39 E. Sharpe, *Universal Gita*, p. 27.

40 E. Sharpe, *Universal Gita*, p. 30.

distinguishing mark of Buddhism."[41] His friend Moncure Conway compared Thoreau with the *sannyasis* and *yogins* of the Indian forests:

> Like the pious Yogi, so long motionless while gazing on the sun that knotty plants encircled his neck and the cast snake-skin his loins, and the birds built their nests on his shoulders, this poet and naturalist, by equal consecration, became a part of field and forest.[42]

Emerson once famously remarked that Walt Whitman's *Leaves of Grass* was "a mixture of the *Bhagavad-Gita* and the *New York Herald*," the latter being a somewhat yellowish rag of the day. Whitman himself said that he had absorbed "the ancient Hindu poems" as well as some of the cardinal texts of the West—Homer, Aeschylus, Sophocles, Dante, Shakespeare—in preparation for his *magnum opus*. Rick Fields describes the poetic process in Whitman as a kind of "ecstatic eclecticism," borne out by passages such as this, from Whitman's "Song of Myself":

> My faith is the greatest of faiths and the least of faiths,
> Enclosing worship ancient and modern and all between ancient and modern,
> Believing I shall come again upon the earth after five thousand years,
> Waiting repose from oracles, honoring the gods, saluting the sun,
> Making a fetish of the first rock or stump, powowing with the sticks in the circle of obis,
> Helping the lama or Brahmin as he trims the lamps of the idols,
> Dancing through the streets in a phallic procession, rapt and austere in the woods a gymnosophist,
> Drinking mead from the skull-cap, to Shastas and Vedas admirant minding the Koran. . . .[43]

More reminiscences of Blake and anticipations of Ginsberg! In one of his later works, *Passage to India*, Whitman traces a journey not "to

---

41 R. Fields, *How the Swans Came*, pp. 62-63.

42 R. Fields, *How the Swans Came*, p. 64. On the impact of Buddhism on both Thoreau's asceticism and his thought see A.D. Hodder, "'Ex Oriente Lux': Thoreau's Ecstasies and the Hindu Texts," *The Harvard Theological Review*, 86:4, 1993, pp. 403-438.

43 R. Fields, *How the Swans Came*, p. 66.

lands and seas alone" but to "primal thought. . . . Back, back to wisdom's birth, to innocent intuitions."[44]

The Modernists

Before turning our attention to two groups of inter-war writers we must
briefly take note of several key developments, between the time of the
Transcendentalists and the First World War, which promoted the dis-
semination of Eastern influences in the intellectual and cultural life of
the West. Here I can do no more than catalogue these: the growth of a
cluster of Indological disciplines in European universities and the prodigious scholarship of figures such as Max Müller and Paul Deussen;
the popularizing of Eastern mythology and teachings through figures
such as Edwin Arnold, Paul Carus, and Lafcadio Hearn; the proliferation of Eastern texts available in reputable European translations
with the *I Ching* and the *Tibetan Book of the Dead* becoming unlikely
best-sellers; the remarkable growth of the Theosophical Society in four
continents and the popularity of "occult" teachings apparently derived
from Eastern sources—one may mention such formidable figures as
Madame Blavatsky, Alexandra David-Neel, W. Evans-Wentz, and the
Armenian thaumaturge, Georgi Ivanovitch Gurdjieff (a.k.a. "the Tiger
of Turkestan"). The World Parliament of Religions in Chicago in 1893
introduced to the West three figures who were to have a lasting impact:
the charismatic Swami Vivekananda, disciple of the great sage Ramakrishna and apostle of a new universal religion based on ancient Hindu
sources; Anagarika Dharmapala, first of many Theravadin teachers
in the West; and Shoyen Shaku who inaugurated a long line of Zen
Masters who would have a mesmeric effect on Western seekers.[45] In
this context mention should also be made of one of Shoyen Shaku's
pupils who was later to become the single most important figure in the
popularization of Zen in the West and the doyen of East-West bridge-
builders, Daisetz T. Suzuki.

The two groups of writers whom we can, roughly, locate in the
inter-war period, and to whom I now want to turn, briefly, are the
modernist poets and the neo-Vedantins. To understand the appeal of
Eastern cultural forms and religio-philosophical ideas in this period

44 R. Fields, *How the Swans Came*, p. 66.

45 See E.J. Ziolkowski, "The Literary Bearing of Chicago's World's Parliament of Religions," *The Eastern Buddhist*, 26:1, Spring 1993, pp. 10-25.

we must take account of the cultural crisis which engulfed the European intelligentsia. The epochal event, of course, was the Great War but the seeds of the crisis go back at least to the mid-nineteenth century when various subterranean fissures in the European psyche were making themselves felt: one need only mention the names of Kierkegaard, Dostoevsky, Baudelaire, and Nietzsche who each registered some profound inner disturbances which were to culminate in the barbarisms of the twentieth century.[46] Oriental motifs and images, both visual and literary, abound in the work of the *fin-de-siècle* European *avant-garde*. As J.J. Clarke has observed,

> Orientalism . . . helped to give expression and substance to a deep sense of cultural crisis and to loss of faith in the West's idea of progress through scientific rationalism, and to a need for new modes of representation. Responding to the cultural crisis at the turn of the century, modernism meant, in essence, the demand for a new and purified consciousness, one that could replace the discredited tastes and conventions of the Victorian period. . . .[47]

Let us glance at the place of Eastern influences in the work of two modernist poets: Yeats and Eliot.

The influences on Yeats' thought and poetry were many and varied—Celtic mythology, neo-Platonism, Blake, and Swedenborg, amongst the more conspicuous. But Yeats also derived sustenance from the East. In 1887 he joined the recently founded Theosophical Society in London, through which he was introduced to Advaita, the non-dualistic metaphysical teaching of the Vedanta. He found in Vedanta a corroboration of his own rejection of all forms of philosophical dualism which particularly troubled the poet in its theological forms in the West. In the Hindu Scriptures he found "an alliance between body and soul [which] our theology rejects" as well as the "the mind's direct apprehension of the truth, above all antinomies."[48] He was powerfully attracted by the *Upanishads* on a translation of which he collab-

---

46 On this subject see George Steiner's provocative thesis in *In Bluebeard's Castle: Some Notes Towards the Redefinition of Culture* (New Haven, CT: Yale University Press), 1971.

47 J.J. Clarke, *Oriental Enlightenment*, p. 101.

48 J.J. Clarke, *Oriental Enlightenment*, p. 102.

orated with Swami Purohit, a translation, incidentally, in wide circulation in the counter-culture of the 1960s. Under the influence of Pound he became a fervent admirer of the Japanese *No* plays, and through the writings of D.T. Suzuki an enthusiast of Zen Buddhism which he came to regard as the apex of Eastern wisdom in its ability to annihilate all intellectual abstractions.[49] Like Eliot, Yeats was convinced by his studies of Eastern sapiential traditions that Indian wisdom was more accommodating than modern Western philosophy to the "multidimensionality of Truth."[50] In a full-length and highly detailed study, Sankaran Ravindran has argued that Yeats work can be understood as a steady growth in the understanding of the Indian conception of life as a drama played out between the self (the egoic personality) and the Self (*Atman*). Other distinctively Indian ideas about *karma*, transmigration, the four stages of life, and the interdependence of the inner and outer worlds also find expression, often veiled, in Yeats' poetry and in his later prose works.[51]

Mentioning Pound—his *Cantos* exhibit strong Oriental influences derived from his study and translation of Chinese poetry and philosophy. Following the work of the American Orientalist Fenellosa Pound also became entranced by the expressive possibilities of the pictographic Chinese script, charmingly describing his own idiosyncratic poetic exploitation of Chinese characters as "listening to incense."[52]

In 1911 T.S. Eliot embarked on three years intensive postgraduate study at Harvard of Sanskrit, Indian philosophy (particularly logic, ethics, and metaphysics, and Patanjali's *Yoga Sutras*), Pali, and the religious thought of China and Japan.[53] This three-year immersion in Eastern philosophy, metaphysics, and philology left a lasting mark, both on his own spiritual development and on his poetic vision and method.

---

49 J.J. Clarke, *Oriental Enlightenment*, p. 102.

50 S. Ravindran, *W.B. Yeats and Indian Tradition* (Delhi: Konark Publishers, 1990), p. vii.

51 See B.M. Wilson, "'From Mirror to Mirror': Yeats and Eastern Thought," *Comparative Literature*, 34:1, 1982, pp. 28-46.

52 M. Edwardes, *East-West Passage: The Travel of Ideas and Inventions between Asia and the Western World* (London: Cassell, 1971), p. 30.

53 Details of these studies can be found in J. Perl & A. Tuck, "The Hidden Advantage of Tradition: The Significance of T.S. Eliot's Indic Studies," *Philosophy East and West*, 35:2, April 1985, pp. 115ff.

Although Eliot summed up the effect on him of his Indological studies as "enlightened mystification"[54] the impact was sufficiently serious for him to consider, at the time of composing *The Wasteland*, becoming a Buddhist, before committing himself to Anglo-Catholicism.[55] On the evidence of his own testimony it can be argued that Eliot's eventual religious affiliation grew out of his early Indian studies which helped him to escape the intellectual prejudices of his own milieu—a not un-familiar pattern of spiritual growth.[56]

Eastern themes, motifs, and allusions are to be found through-out Eliot's work but particularly in his two poetic masterpieces, "The Wasteland" and *Four Quartets*. The Buddha's "Fire Sermon," the eighth chapter of the *Gita*, and several *Upanishads* figure prominently in these works. Critics have argued about the precise significance and effec-tiveness of Eliot's use of Eastern imagery and Scriptural reference but there is little doubt that they contribute significantly to a sharply dis-tinctive method and poetic vision. Eliot himself explicitly acknowl-edged his poetic debt to "Indian thought and sensibility."[57] The impact of Buddhism is most evident in *Four Quartets* which is pervaded by the premier doctrines of impermanence and suffering, whilst Eliot's treatment of the central theme of time and eternity bears a strong East-ern inflection.[58] We might also note that Eliot's practice of synthesizing themes from Greek, Hindu, and Buddhist as well as Christian sources testifies to his belief in a mystical experience which is of neither East nor West and which transcends religious forms—a characteristically though not exclusively Eastern notion.[59] But Eliot was no "New Age" eclectic: his well-known insistence on the intimate relationship of cul-ture and religion, and on the necessity of the particularities of tradition precluded any sentimental notion of a "distillation" of the "essence" of

54 Eliot quoted in J. Perl & A. Tuck, "Hidden Advantage of Tradition," p.127.

55 S. Spender, "Remembering Eliot" in *T.S. Eliot: The Man and His Work*, ed. A. Tate (Harmondsworth: Penguin, 1971), p. 44.

56 See J. Perl & A. Tuck, "Hidden Advantage of Tradition," p. 115.

57 From *Christianity and Culture* (1949), quoted in J. Perl & A. Tuck, "Hidden Advan-tage of Tradition," p. 127n.

58 The most detailed discussion of the impact of the Eastern Scriptures on Eliot's po-etry is H.E. McCarthy, "T.S. Eliot and Buddhism," *Philosophy East and West*, 2:1, 1952, pp. 31-55. See also E. Sharpe, *Universal Gita*, pp.132-135.

59 J. Perl & A. Tuck, "Hidden Advantage of Tradition," p.121

different religions such as might lead to a new "universal" religion. He also disapproved of those Western appropriations of Eastern religion which ignored or jettisoned "hagiology, rites, and customs."[60]

In the context of the growing European familiarity with the cultural heritage of the Far East, mention should be made of the pioneering translation done by Arthur Waley, a decidedly eccentric Englishman who never visited the East but who achieved a prodigious feat in translating many Chinese and Japanese classics. The appearance of *A Hundred and Seventy Chinese Poems* in 1918 was followed by translations of *The No Plays of Japan* (1923) the medieval Japanese *The Tale of Genji* in six volumes (1923-33), *The Pillow Book of Sei Shonagon* (1928), *The Analects of Confucius* (1938), and *Monkey* (1942), as well as a series of commentaries on Chinese painting, Taoist and Confucian philosophy, and Chinese shamanism.[61] Another slightly later linguist, translator, and commentator who exercised a significant influence in mid-century was R.H. Blythe who moved mid-life to Japan in 1940, and spent the rest of his life there, producing many translations and commentaries. The best known of his works is probably *Zen in English Literature and Oriental Classics*.[62]

By way of a further aside I mention another group of writers who showed some interest in Eastern spirituality in their literary creations: the novelists of the Raj of whom three stand out: Rudyard Kipling, E.M. Forster, and Somerset Maugham. The principal texts are *Kim* (1908), *Passage to India* (1924), and *The Razor's Edge* (1949), each of which offers a peculiar blend of provincial English prejudices and genuine insights.[63]

---

60 J. Perl & A. Tuck, "Hidden Advantage of Tradition," p. 131n.

61 See I. Morris (ed.), *Madly Singing in the Rain: An Appreciation and Anthology of Arthur Waley* (London: Allen & Unwin, 1970). See also A. Waley, *A Half of Two Lives* (London: Weidenfeld & Nicholson, 1982).

62 See R. Aitken, "Remembering R.H. Blythe," *Tricycle: The Buddhist Review*, 7:3, Spring 1998, pp. 22-25, and T. Ferris, "Past Present," *The Nation*, 250:17, April 30, 1990, p. 609.

63 For some recent critical discussion which takes account of the fictional representations of Indian philosophy and spirituality see R. Cronin, "The Indian English Novel: *Kim* and *Midnight's Children*," *Modern Fiction Studies*, 33:2, Summer 1987, pp. 201-213, and K.J. Phillips, "Hindu Avatars, Moslem Martyrs, and Primitive Dying Gods in E.M. Forster's *A Passage to India*," *Journal of Modern Literature*, 15:1, Summer 1988, pp. 121-140.

The California Vedantists and Perennialists

Another constellation of writers of interest to us here was drawn from the generation which followed the great modernists: the principal figures here are Aldous Huxley and Christopher Isherwood whilst the bit players include Romain Rolland and Gerald Heard. Although they share many interests and enthusiasms with the figures whom we have already encountered, these writers are primarily of interest in their attempts to propagate the "perennial philosophy," the foundations of which they believed were most easily and clearly discerned in the Vedanta. These writers were all influenced, one way or another, by the universalist strain in the neo-Hindu movements variously associated with such figures as Vivekananda, Tagore, Aurobindo, and Radhakrishnan.

Huxley is best known in the West for the dystopian *Brave New World* (1932) but the novel which bears the heaviest Eastern impress is the later Utopian novel, *Island* (1962). From an early age Huxley was deeply interested in Eastern religion and philosophy. He made a close study of the work of such Orientalists as Edward Conze, Heinrich Zimmer, and D.T. Suzuki as well as of the great scriptures and spiritual classics of the East. Although not primarily a scholar Huxley was a man of wide learning, who possessed also a real existentialist engagement in Eastern spirituality. In mid-life, in the late 1930s, Huxley moved to California where he became closely associated with the Vedanta Center and, with Isherwood and Heard, edited the magazine *Vedanta and the West*. These writers were convinced that many of the ills of the modern West could be remedied by Eastern values and ideas, most particularly the Vedanta which Vivekananda, patron saint of the American neo-Vedantins, had so eloquently championed at the World Parliament of Religions. Their ideas, along with those of various Hindu gurus with whom they were associated, are most readily met with in two anthologies, edited by Isherwood, which first appeared in the 1940s and have remained in print ever since: *Vedanta for Modern Man* (1945) and *Vedanta for the Western World* (1948).

Isherwood's reputation as a novelist is, I suspect, in well-deserved decline although interest in him as a "personality" does not seem to have abated—note the widespread interest in his interminable diaries! However Isherwood did perform one very honorable service for which he deserves our lasting gratitude: I refer to his biography of the remarkable *Paramahamsa*, Ramakrishna, along with Ramana Maharshi one of the few indubitable Indian saints and sages amidst the veritable plague of so-called swamis, gurus, "enlightened masters," maharishis, "bhagvans," and the like of recent times. Isherwood's *Ramakrishna and His Disciples* (1965) whilst clearly written by an adherent, is informative, judicious, and sensible as well as being finely-attuned to the spiritual modalities in which Ramakrishna's religious "genius" expressed itself. An earlier biographer of Ramakrishna was the French writer Romain Rolland whose *Life of Ramakrishna* (1929) introduced the Bengali saint to a wider Western European audience. Rolland also produced one of the early Western appreciations of Mahatma Gandhi.[64]

However, by far the most significant work to emerge from the Californian coterie was Huxley's *The Perennial Philosophy* which appeared in 1946. The work was an anthology of quotations drawn from the world's sacred texts, strung together by Huxley's commentary which attempts to identify what he rather clumsily calls "the Highest Common Factor" to be found in the world's religions. Whilst not questioning the intelligence, learning, and good will which Huxley bought to this undertaking I must say that his vision of the perennial philosophy is seriously marred by all manner of disabling modern prejudices and assumptions. To give but one example: for all his disquiet about the scientistic ideology of the modern West he himself succumbs to it over and over again. I have elaborated a detailed critique of Huxley's book elsewhere: space precludes me from rehearsing it here.[65] However, at this juncture I must sharply distinguish Huxley and co. from a group to whom we can, in fact, turn for a much more authoritative explication of the *sophia perennis* as it finds expression in the great religious and sapiential traditions of both East and West as well as in the primal mythologies from around the globe: I refer to a group of writers who can be called "traditionalists" and who have engaged my closest interest over a period of twenty-five years and about whom I have written extensively in other places. Three figures tower over this group—René Guénon, Ananda Coomaraswamy, and Frithjof Schuon, each of whom

---

64 R. Rolland, *The Life of Ramakrishna* (Calcutta: Advaita Ashrama, 1929), and *Mahatma Gandhi: The Man Who Became One with the Universal Being* (New York: Century, 1924). For Somerset Maugham's account of his meeting with Ramana see *Points of View* (London: Heinemann, 1958), pp. 56-93.

65 See K. Oldmeadow, *Traditionalism: Religion in the Light of the Perennial Philosophy* (Colombo: Sri Lanka Institute of Traditional Studies, 2000), pp. 158-160.

has played a distinctive and providential role in reanimating the time-less wisdom. However, as they are not in any sense literary writers, they fall outside our ambit here and I shall, with some difficulty, say no more about them but turn to an altogether more flamboyant lot—the beats and hippies of the '50s and '60s, who, for our purposes, I shall treat as belonging to the same family.

But before closing the door on the interwar years I should touch on the work of another writer who only achieved widespread renown after the Second World War—the shadowy and somewhat enigmatic figure of Herman Hesse. Like many others who developed a serious interest in Eastern religion and philosophy and like the author of the present lines, Hesse was the son of missionaries who had spent many years in the East and grew up in a milieu saturated with mementoes of the Orient, some of them lovingly described in several of his au-tobiographical sketches.[66] Hesse made several visits to the East, not entirely happy experiences,[67] but retained throughout his life an abid-ing interest in Eastern spirituality and in a synthesis of religious ideas from East and West. Also central to his intellectual and creative proj-ects was the attempt to affirm and demonstrate the underlying unity of all the branches of the human race. Although Hesse was awarded the Nobel Prize for Literature, largely on the basis of his last novel, *The Glass Bead Game* (1943), the zenith of his acclamation was prob-ably the counter-cultural enthusiasm for his novels among the more serious-minded hippies of the late 60s, particularly *Steppenwolf* (1927) in which the European sense of anxiety and cultural location is dra-matically rendered, and *Siddhartha* (1922) in which Hesse attempted a distillation of what he had learned of Eastern spirituality mingled with what he found most valuable in his own pietistic Protestant back-ground. Incidentally, do not be misled by the many literary histories which tell us that *Siddhartha* recounts the life of the Buddha, an error which might be avoided by actually reading the book! Those who have read the novel will remember the charming portrait of the Buddha, but it is only a vignette in the story of the protagonist who shares one of the Awakened One's several names.

---

66 See particularly "Childhood of the Magician" (1923) and "Life Story Briefly Told" (1925) in *Autobiographical Writings*, ed. T. Ziolkowski (London: Picador, 1975).

67 See R. Freedman, *Herman Hesse: Pilgrim of Crisis* (London: Jonathan Cape, 1979), pp. 149-156, and Hesse's "Remembrance of India" (1916), in *Autobiographical Writings*.

Beats and Hippies

The Beat movement of the 1950s drew on many different cultural streams: Blake and the Romantic poets, American transcendentalism, black musical idioms, and European existentialism. Among their Eastern sources Japanese Zen was pre-eminent but the Beats also evinced a serious interest in aspects of Buddhism at large, Hinduism, and Taoism. By the early '60s when the Beat movement was apparently dying of media hype and before the hippies had appeared, there were also signs of a budding interest in some of the more arcane aspects of Eastern traditions, most notably perhaps the convergence of psychedelic experimentation and the *Tibetan Book of the Dead*.[68] Huxley's earlier experiences with mescaline anticipated the counter-cultural preoccupation with consciousness-altering drugs such as LSD and "magic mushrooms": *The Doors of Perception* became one of the canonical countercultural texts along with the *Tao Te Ching*, Hesse's *Siddhartha*, and various other books of dubious provenance, perhaps most notably Carlos Castaneda's "Don Juan" series.

There were also, in the post-war years, those *litterateurs* who travelled to the East in search of spiritual nutriments but who returned with their hunger unassuaged or who, worse, came to the view that the vaunted spiritual treasures of the Orient were, at best, a mirage, at worst a fraud perpetrated by tricksters who preyed on Western gullibilities. One of the more interesting of this type was Arthur Koestler who visited India and Japan in the '50s, and in *The Lotus and the Robot* (1960) reported his finding that both countries were "spiritually sicker, more estranged from a living faith than the West."[69] Shortly after his return from Japan he also published an excoriating attack on D.T. Suzuki and his work, accusing Zen in general and Suzuki in particular of being woolly-minded, irrational, amoral, hypocritical, and crypto-fascistic. We do not have space to assess Koestler's case here, nor to attend to Suzuki's response. However, something of the flavor of Koestler's admonitions can be tasted in a passage such as this:

---

68 See T. Schwartz, *What Really Matters: Searching for Wisdom in America* (New York: Bantam Books, 1995), Ch. 1, and T. Roszak, *The Making of a Counter Culture: Reflections on the Technocratic Society and its Youthful Opposition* (London: Faber & Faber, 1969), Chs. 4, 5.

69 A. Koestler, *The Lotus and the Robot* (London: Hutchinson, 1960), p. 276.

By virtue of its anti-rationality and amorality, Zen always held a fascination for a category of people in whom brutishness combines with pseudo-mysticism, from Samurai to Kamikaze to beatnik.

Or in his assertion that "It is time for the Professor [i.e., Suzuki] to shut up and for [the] Western intelligentsia to recognize contemporary Zen as one of the sick jokes, slightly gangrened, which are always fashionable in ages of anxiety."[70] These can stand as salutary reminders that not all Western encounters with Eastern spirituality have been rewarded with edifying results.[71] Nor was everyone impressed by those Western writers who became self-styled champions of Eastern spirituality. William Burroughs, for instance, wrote in a letter to Kerouac,

> I have seen nothing from those California Vedantists but a lot of horse shit, and I denounce them without cavil, as a pack of pathetic frauds. Convinced of their own line to be sure, thereby adding self-deception to their other failings.[72]

The outlandish and iconoclastic aspects of the Beats has, until recently, rather obscured what was in many instances a deeply serious and transformative engagement with Eastern spirituality. Orgiastic sexual escapades, monster drug binges, disreputable life-styles, Ginsberg's "Howl," alcoholism, fear and loathing in the suburbs, Burroughs' bizarre killing of his wife, strange happenings of all manner and kind—these are some of the Beat motifs foregrounded in the public perception. But there was also serious intent. Allen Ginsberg recently summed up the Beat agenda this way:

70 Passages from A. Koestler, "Neither Lotus nor Robot" (*Encounter*, February 16, 1960), quoted in L.A. Fader, "Arthur Koestler's Critique of D.T. Suzuki's Interpretation of Zen," *The Eastern Buddhist*, 13:2, Autumn 1980, pp. 54, 56. In *The Lotus and the Robot* Koestler had characterized Zen as "a web of absurd solemnities" (p. 233).

71 In recent years there has been considerable attention paid to the possible connections between various types of "orientalism" and European fascism while the Nazi affiliations of such figures as Heinrich Harrer, Sven Hedin, and the Herrigals have come to public attention. See D. Lopez Jr., *Curators of the Buddha: The Study of Buddhism Under Colonialism* (Chicago: University of Chicago Press, 1995). See also H. Oldmeadow, *Journeys East: Twentieth Century Western Encounters with Eastern Religious Traditions* (Bloomington, IN: World Wisdom, 2004), Ch. 14.

72 Burroughs to Kerouac, August 18, 1954, in *The Letters of William S. Burroughs: 1945-1959*, ed. O. Harris (London: Picador, 1993), p. 226.

What we were proposing was some new sense of spiritual consciousness. We were interested in non-violence, sexual freedom, the exploration of psychedelic drugs and sensitivity. We were aware that
the entire government . . . was corrupt. We were interested in Eastern thought and meditation. We had quite an open heart and open
mind. . . .[73]

We need not look very deeply into the Beat movement to find
considerable evidence of a sustained interest in and, in several cases,
serious commitment to Eastern religious teachings and practices. A
few examples: Gary Snyder spent the best part of ten years in a Zen
monastery in Japan; over a period of several years Jack Kerouac made a
serious study of Eastern religious texts, translated Buddhist scriptures
from French into English, attempted to live like a Buddhist monk, and
wrote an unpublished biography of the Buddha; Phillip Whalen eventually became an ordained Zen monk; Allen Ginsberg took the Three
Refuges and devoted much of his exuberant energy to *dharma* work
over the last twenty-five years of his life. Here too we find, perhaps for
the first time, a significant engagement with Buddhism by women writers, amongst whom we may mention Diane di Prima, Joanne Kryger,
Lenore Kandel, and Anne Waldman who, with Ginsberg and by invitation from Rinpoche Chögyam Trungpa, established the Jack Kerouac
School of Disembodied Poetics at the Naropa Institute, a magnet for all
manner of counter-cultural types in the '70s and beyond. Many of the
Beats as well as countercultural pop "gurus" such as Alan Watts made
pilgrimages to the East—to visit holy sites, to take teachings, to live the
monastic life.[74]

On one level one might suppose that a good deal of the Beat/
counter-cultural infatuation with the exotic, the "oriental," the "mystical," and "magical" was indeed of a sentimental and fashionable order.
Doubtless, there was a good deal of counterfeit spirituality peddled by
false *gurus*, by charlatans and hucksters, as there is today under the
canopy of New Age-ism. But, no question, the interest in Eastern spirituality met some deep yearning for *a vision of reality* deeper, richer,

73 Allen Ginsberg, "Journals Mid-Fifties: 1954-1958: An Interview with Henry Tisch-
ler," http://www.authorsspeak.com/ginsberg.

74 For some account of the various encounters of the Beats with Eastern religion
see C. Tonkinson (ed.), *Big Sky Mind: Buddhism and the Beat Generation* (New York:
Riverhead Books, 1995).

more adequate, more attuned to the fullness of human experience, than the impoverished worldview offered by a scientifically-grounded humanism. The Beat and counter-cultural involvement in Eastern spirituality was not without precedent; nor was it either ephemeral or trivial and, indeed, it is still bearing fruit. The adherence of a rapidly growing and highly significant portion of the Western intelligentsia—artists, writers, philosophers, social activists prominently—to Eastern religious forms (most notably from the Tibetan and Japanese branches of Buddhism), and the assimilation of Asian modes of spiritual experience and cultural expression into Western forms, is one of the more remarkable cultural metamorphoses of the late twentieth century, one as yet barely recognized let alone understood. More particularly, the impact of the Tibetan diaspora on the West, especially the USA, demands more serious attention.

CHAPTER 16

Huston Smith, Bridge-Builder *Extraordinaire*: A Tribute

> Our lives are wrapped in mystery, and a lifetime is hardly sufficient to begin to fathom it.
>
> *Huston Smith*[1]

If Rudolf Otto's *The Idea of the Holy* and William James' *The Varieties of Religious Experience* were two of the most widely read books on religion of the inter-war period, Huston Smith's *The Religions of Man* must surely be the most popular of the second half of the twentieth century. First published in 1958 it has been in print ever since, selling millions of copies and now re-titled *The World's Religions: Our Great Wisdom Traditions*. The hallmarks of Smith's approach to the comparative study of the world's religions were evident from the outset: the conviction that each religion was the custodian of timeless truths and values; the attempt to understand the forms and practices of any particular tradition from the viewpoint of its adherents; an intuitive sympathy which enabled Smith to "tune into" a wide diversity of spiritual modalities; an understanding that the hyper-rationalism of much modern philosophy and the pseudo-scientific methodologies of the so-called social sciences were inadequate tools with which to grasp spiritual realities; and a style of exposition free of the specialized jargon of the disciplines on which Smith drew (most notably philosophy, theology, comparative religion) and one immediately accessible to the intelligent general reader. One might also say that Smith's mode turned on a kind of natural courtesy and respect for the traditions he was exploring, and that he always situated the study of religion within an existential context:

> Religion alive confronts the individual with the most momentous option this world can present. It calls the soul to the highest adventure it can undertake, a proposed journey across the jungles, peaks,

---

1 H. Smith & J. Paine, *Tales of Wonder: An Autobiography* (New York: HarperOne, 2009), p. xx.

and deserts of the human spirit. The call is to confront reality, to master the self. Those who dare to hear and follow this secret call soon learn the dangers and difficulties of its lonely journey.[2]

Clearly, for Smith the study of religion was no mere academic exercise but one of deep *engagement*. He would likely agree with the claim of another inter-religious bridge-builder, Fr. Bede Griffiths, that, "The rediscovery of religion is the great intellectual, moral and spiritual adventure of our time."[3]

Since 1958 Smith's understanding of both the inner unity and the formal diversity of the world's integral religious traditions has been both deepened and sharpened by his encounter with the traditionalist perspective exemplified in the works of such figures as René Guénon, Ananda Coomaraswamy, and Frithjof Schuon. As was clear from the 1991 revisions to *The Religions of Man*, Smith's horizons had also broadened to now encompass the primordial traditions of peoples such as the Native Americans.[4] Within the academic world Smith has been a passionate and eloquent spokesman for the perennialist school, and has engaged many of the deepest problems and issues arising out of the contemporary collision of the forces of tradition and modernity. His essential vocation has been as an *educator* and, to use his own term, a *"religious communicator."* Recently Smith recalled the impact made on him as a fourteen-year old by Kipling's poem, "The Explorer," which includes these lines:

Something hidden, go and find it;
Go and look behind the ranges.
Something lost behind the ranges;
Lost and waiting for you—go!

He writes that the poem still haunts him in his old age.[5] *Exploration*—both intellectual and spiritual—might also be seen as a keynote of Smith's long adventure in the mystery of life.

2 H. Smith, *Religions of Man* (New York: Harper, 1958), p. 11.

3 B. Griffiths, *The Golden String* (London: Collins, 1964), pp. 13-14.

4 See *A Seat at the Table: Huston Smith in Conversation with Native Americans on Religious Freedom* (Berkeley: University of California Press, 2006).

5 See H. Smith, *Tales of Wonder*, pp. xxiv-xxv.

Smith was born in 1919 in Soochow, China.[6] His parents were missionaries and he was to spend the first seventeen years of his life in China—lovingly recounted in his recent autobiography, *Tales of Wonder* (2009). One of his former students, Philip Novak, writes:

> If you would know Huston Smith, start with China. . . . Beholding him, one wonders whether fantastic tales about Chinese magic are not true after all. There is something distantly—and yet distinctly—Asian in his physiognomy. China paused on his skin, it seemed, before proceeding to his marrow. . . . Open the pages of the Analects to Confucius's description of the *chun-tzu* (ideal gentleman) and you touch Huston's fiber. *Chun-tzu* . . . one who possesses a truly human heart, who cherishes the arts of learning and teaching, and who is as concerned to teach by moral example as by intellectual knack.[7]

After his schooling at the Shanghai American School Smith studied at the Central Methodist College in Fayette, Missouri, where his intellectual interests were primarily theological and philosophical. Thereafter he pursued further studies at the prestigious Divinity School at the University of Chicago and at the University of California at Berkeley during which time, partly under the influence of the "Californian Vedantins" (Gerald Heard and Aldous Huxley amongst them) he became more deeply engaged in the study of mysticism. A series of teaching appointments followed at the universities of Denver and Colorado, Washington University in St. Louis, the Massachusetts Institute of Technology (1958-1973), and Syracuse University (1973-1983). Early in his career Smith also served as a chaplain and associate minister in the Methodist Church, improbably combining these duties with the presidency of the St. Louis Vedanta Society! In later years Smith has been one of the prime movers in the establishment of the Foundation of Traditional Studies, based in Washington, D.C. and of which he is the Vice-President.[8] As the editor of a *festschrift* in his honor remarked,

---

6 For biographical details see "Biographical Sketch" in A. Sharma (ed.), *Fragments of Infinity: Essays in Philosophy and Religion, A Festschrift in Honour of Professor Huston Smith* (Bridport: Prism, 1991), pp. xi-xii; M.D. Bryant, "Introduction" in H. Smith, *Huston Smith: Essays on World Religion* (New York: Paragon House, 1993); H. Smith, *Why Religion Matters: The Fate of the Human Spirit in an Age of Disbelief* (San Francisco: HarperCollins, 2001), pp. xiii-xiv; and *Tales of Wonder, passim*.

7 P. Novak, "The Chun-Tzu" in *Fragments of Infinity*, p. 8.

8 See S.H. Nasr, "Homage to Huston Smith on His Eightieth Birthday," *Sophia: The*

Professor Smith's teaching career has been devoted to bridging intellectual gulfs: between East and West, between science and the humanities, and between the formal education of the classroom and
informal education via films and television.[9]

His films and television programs have focused on Hinduism, Buddhism, Sufism, and Tibetan music. In 1996 Bill Moyers hosted a five-
part PBS television series, *The Wisdom of Faith with Huston Smith*.

From Smith's wide-ranging scholarly *oeuvre*, which now includes
fourteen books, we may select three works of signal importance: *The
Religions of Man*, a masterly conspectus of the world's major religious
traditions; *Forgotten Truth: The Primordial Tradition* (1977), in which
he expounds the perennial wisdom which lies at the heart of manifold
sapiential doctrines and religious forms; and *Beyond the Post-Modern
Mind* (1982), which elaborates a critique of the intellectual habits and
prejudices of the prevailing contemporary worldview, particularly as
it finds expression in the Western academic ethos and in the highly
reductive disciplinary specializations which purport to "explain" religious phenomena. As well as these three major landmarks we should
note a recent anthology of some of Smith's most important articles,
Essays on World Religion (1992), which includes many pieces on Asian
subjects. A sample of titles indicates the range of Smith's interests:
"Transcendence in Traditional China," "Tao Now: An Ecological Statement," "A Note on Shinto," "Spiritual Discipline in Zen," "India and the
Infinite," "Vedic Religion and the Soma Experience," "The Importance
of the Buddha," and "Tibetan Chant: Inducing the Spirit."

The most decisive shift in Smith's outlook occurred as a consequence of reading the works of Frithjof Schuon, the master expositor
of the *religio perennis* in modern times. Smith had been introduced
to the works of Guénon, Schuon, and other traditionalists by Seyyed
Hossein Nasr during his time at MIT. Smith:

> I discovered that [Schuon] situated the world's religious traditions in
> a framework that enabled me to honor their significant differences
> unreservedly while at the same time seeing them as expressions of
> a truth, that because it was single, I could affirm. In a single stroke I

Journal of Traditional Studies, 3:2, Winter 1997, p. 7.

9 A. Sharma in *Fragments of Infinity*, pp. xi-xii.

was handed a way of honoring the world's diversity without falling prey to relativism, a resolution I had been seeking for more than thirty years.[10]

The influence of Schuon and Nasr also made itself felt in Smith's ever-deepening interest in mysticism as the esoteric kernel within the exoteric shell of all integral traditions. The perennialist perspective not only placed Smith's understanding of mystical traditions—especially Sufism—on a much firmer footing but also allowed him to honor fully the orthodox religious forms which veil and protect that ultimately formless wisdom which lies at the heart of the *sophia perennis*.

One of the penalties of fame is the exposure to endless invitations to write Prefaces, Forewords, Introductions, and the like. It is a measure of both Smith's international standing and his generosity of spirit to note some of the books which he has helped introduce to a wider audience, many of which have become classics of their kind: Philip Kapleau's *The Three Pillars of Zen* (1967), Dwight Godard's *A Buddhist Bible* (1970), *Zen Mind, Beginner's Mind* (1970) by Shunryu Suzuki, S.H. Nasr's *Ideals and Realities of Islam* (1972), Frithjof Schuon's *The Transcendent Unity of Religions* (1975), Swami Prabhavananda's *The Spiritual Heritage of India* (1979), *On Having No Head* (1986) by D.E. Harding, *A Treasury of Traditional Wisdom* (1986) edited by Whitall Perry, W.T. Stace's *Mysticism and Philosophy* (1987), *The Wheel of Life* (1988) by John Blofeld, and a new edition of *The Way of a Pilgrim and the Pilgrim Continues His Way* (1991).[11]

Whilst the Judeo-Christian tradition in which he was raised has provided Smith with a firm spiritual anchorage his life and work alike testify to his willingness to immerse himself in the religious forms and practices of other traditions, not by way of any kind of syncretism or "universal" religion, but in the search for understanding and for "the light that is of neither East nor West."[12] Religious *experience* has been

10 H. Smith & D.R. Griffin, *Primordial Truth and Postmodern Theology* (Albany, NY: State University of New York Press, 1989, p. 13).

11 For details of these and other works see M.D. Bryant's bibliography, in H. Smith, *Essays on World Religion*, pp. 286-287.

12 A *Newsweek* reviewer of "The Wisdom of Faith with Huston Smith" trivialized Smith as a "spiritual surfer," just as his more academic critics have mistakenly accused him of "eclecticism" and "syncretism." See Rabbi Zalman Schacter-Shalomi & H. Smith, "Spirituality in Education: A Dialogue," in S. Glazer (ed.), *The Heart of Learn-*

a watchword in his writings and amongst his own spiritual encounters we may note his boyhood exposure to a Confucian master, his spell as a Methodist minister, weekly sessions with a Vedantin swami, the practice of yoga and an intensive reading of *The Upanishads* and other Hindu Scriptures in the 1950s, a summer of meditation and *koan*-training in a Myoshinji monastery in Kyoto in the '6os (where he studied under Master Goto Zuigan, developed a close friendship with D.T. Suzuki, doyen of modern Zen scholars, and practiced *zazen* with Gary Snyder), his inquiries into the possible links between drug-induced experiences and mysticism, and his close association with traditionalist Sufis in Iran and the USA. He has been a sympathetic and no doubt exemplary guest in many Houses of the Spirit. As well as moving freely through the corridors of academia (where, it must be said, his ideas encountered some suspicion and skepticism as well as acclaim) he has met countless rabbis, clerics, swamis, Zen masters, lamas, mystics, and the like; by all reports such meetings are marked by that rapport which arises out of the spontaneous and mutual recognition of the radiant spiritual maturity which marks those who have traveled a goodly distance on the path.

As an educator and communicator Huston Smith has always displayed a gift for articulating profound truths in the most simple and accessible language. Here is an example from his recent autobiography, one which also intimates the mystery which, he tells us, can hardly be fathomed in a lifetime.[13] Referring to the cross as "the metaphor I use for understanding human existence," Smith writes:

> Our life in historical or chronological time, measuring and minding, cautious and comparing, forms the horizontal arm of the cross. Our experience of the unqualified, of inner, immeasurable time (or timelessness), is the cross's vertical pole. We live in two kinds of time or perspective simultaneously. The horizontal and the vertical are at once quite distinct and entirely overlapping, and to experience their incongruity and confluence is what it means to be human.[14]

---

ing: *Spirituality in Education* (New York: J.P. Tarcher/Putnam, 1999), p. 228, and S.H. Nasr, "Homage to Huston Smith," p. 7.

13 H. Smith, *Tales of Wonder*, pp. xx.

14 H. Smith, *Tales of Wonder*, p. 41.

In the conclusion to the most recent edition of *The World's Religions* the author observes that we have just survived "the bloodiest of centuries; but if its ordeals are to be birth pangs rather than death throes, the century's scientific advances must be matched by comparable advances in human relations." Such advances depend on our ability to *listen* to voices from all over the planet and to nurture a peace

> built not on ecclesiastical or political hegemonies but on understanding and mutual concern. For understanding, at least in realms as inherently noble as the great faiths of mankind, brings respect; and respect prepares the way for a higher power, love—the only power that can quench the flames of fear, suspicion, and prejudice, and provide the means by which the people of this small but precious Earth can become one to one another.[15]

Huston Smith: scholar, minister, teacher, culture critic, pilgrim, bridge-builder; in each of these roles he has served the cause of interreligious understanding with great distinction and, in the words of one of his students, with "honesty of person, penetrating sensitivity . . . and flowing kindness."[16]

15 H. Smith, *The World's Religions: Our Great Wisdom Traditions* (San Francisco: HarperSanFrancisco, 1991), p. 390.

16 M. Gustin, "Tribute to Huston Smith," in *Fragments of Infinity*, p. 13.

CHAPTER 17

Swami Abhishiktananda on *Sannyasa* and the Monk's Vocation

The call to complete renunciation cuts across all *dharmas* and disregards all frontiers.

Abhishiktananda[1]

Freedom's just another word for nothin' left to lose.

Kris Kristofferson[2]

Monasticism is not situated outside the world; it is the world that situates itself outside monasticism.

Frithjof Schuon[3]

In 1949, at the age of thirty-seven and after two decades in the Kergonan monastery, Father Henri Le Saux, a French Benedictine, left his home country in order to join Fr. Jules Monchanin in establishing a Christian *ashram* in southern India. Over the next quarter of a century, until his death in 1973, Le Saux immersed himself in both the intellectual and spiritual dimensions of Advaita Vedanta, and became known as Swami Abhishiktananda. In his later years he became an itinerant *sannyasi*—one who has renounced all worldly ties.[4] Throughout his years in India Abhishiktananda produced a series of remarkable books in which he recounts his own spiritual experiences and explores various aspects of Hindu and Christian doctrine and spiritual practice. Of the handful of scholars and theologians who have written in

---

1 Abhishiktananda, *The Further Shore* (New Delhi: ISPCK, 1975), p. 7.

2 F. Foster & K. Kristofferson, "Me and Bobby McGee," EMI.

3 F. Schuon, *Light on the Ancient Worlds: A New Translation with Selected Letters* (Bloomington, IN: World Wisdom, 2006), p. 102.

4 Readers interested in the life and work of this remarkable figure are directed to S. du Boulay, *The Cave of the Heart: The Life of Swami Abhishiktananda* (Maryknoll, NY: Orbis Books, 2005), and H. Oldmeadow, *A Christian Pilgrim in India: The Spiritual Journey of Swami Abhishiktananda (Henri Le Saux)* (Bloomington, IN: World Wisdom, 2008).

any detail about Fr. Henri Le Saux/Swami Abhishiktananda, few have given more than cursory attention to his monastic vocation, and to his writings about monasticism. His views on Vedanta and its relationship to Christianity, the Trinity, the *Upanishads*, and on inter-religious dialogue have all commanded far more attention, perhaps because it was in these fields that Abhishiktananda sometimes struck a radical note. However, as a contemporary scholar has observed, "It is doubtful if any Christian monk in the second half of the twentieth century has taken more seriously than Abhishiktananda the deep call to discover and explore experientially the ultimate ground that unites monks of different religious traditions."[5]

A Benedictine Ashram, jointly written by Monchanin and Abhishiktananda and outlining their aspirations for the new Christian *ashram* they were founding, opens with a beautiful statement of the monastic vocation and, in the Christian context, the Orthodox theology which informs it. Despite all the changes in Abhishiktananda's life and thinking over the next twenty-odd years I believe he would have cleaved to these words throughout, even if he may have slightly modified its theological language in his later years. It is worth reproducing here as a simple but powerful reminder of the vocation of the contemplative:

Contemplation stands supreme; viewed either from the standpoint of God or from that of Man, or from that of Holy Church. God has created the universe for His own glory, and out of love, in order to diffuse His intrinsic goodness . . . and to make intelligent creatures sharers in His eternal Bliss. Every creature is then in its own intimate way a manifestation, an ontological witness of God, a "Theophany." Everything reflects, in some measure, the divine attributes, nay participates in the divine Essence and receives its existence from the absolutely Existent. Therefore it cannot but point to God not only as its supreme Source, but especially as to its ultimate Goal. Intelligent creatures, angels and men, were created *ad imaginem et similtudinem Dei* (*Genesis* 1:26), to the image and likeness of God. Man, if we follow the hermeneutics of the Greek Fathers, is made to the image of God by his intelligence and free will, and to His likeness by grace and supernatural gifts. The dignity and happiness of man lie in this very image and likeness. His goal is to know God . . . to seek Him . . . and

5 J. Royster, "Dialogue in Depth: A Monastic Perspective," *Quarterly Review*, 9:2, Summer 1989, p. 78.

to love Him beyond measure. . . . Some at least of the members of society have to be deputed in the name of the rest of their brethren to a life entirely dedicated to the quest for God.[6]

Abhishiktananda's Monastic Vocation, from Kergonan to the Kavery

To claim that Abhishiktananda's vocation as a monk was the pole star of his life is not to evoke some static and unchanging ideal; Abhishiktananda's ideas were forged in the ever-changing crucible of experience, and the way in which he understood both his own vocation and that of the monk in general became ever deeper and, we might say, more universal. Later in life he was able to discern what—beyond all institutional trappings, historical accretions, cultural colorations, and dogmatic formulations—was essential in the life of any monk at any time in any place. In his tribute to Fr. Monchanin he wrote, "The monk simply consecrates himself to God."[7] This ideal never changed, but the way in which Abhishiktananda understood it and sought to live out its implications did indeed change.

From his earliest days in the seminary at Châteaugiron Abhishiktananda was aflame with the desire to know, to love, to serve God. For him the Gospels demanded a life of uncompromising fidelity to God, and from his youth onwards he took with the utmost seriousness those passages in which Jesus summons his disciples "to total renunciation and the way of the Cross." In *The Further Shore* he recalls some of these passages:

> Foxes have holes, and birds of the air have nests; but the Son of man hath nowhere to lay his head. . . . Let the dead bury the dead: but go thou and preach the kingdom of God. . . . No man, having put his hand to the plough, and looking back, is fit for the kingdom of God (*Luke* 9:58-62).

> Go thy way, sell whatsoever thou hast, and give to the poor, and thou shalt have treasure in heaven: and come, take up the cross and follow me. (*Mark* 10:21)

---

6 Abhishiktananda & J. Monchanin, *A Benedictine Ashram* (Douglas: Free Time Press, 1964), pp. 9-10.

7 From Abhishiktananda, "Le Père Monchanin," quoted in A. Rawlinson, *The Book of Enlightened Masters: Western Teachers in Eastern Traditions* (Chicago: Open Court, 1997), p. 148.

Take nothing for your journey, neither staves, nor scrip, neither bread, neither money; neither have two coats apiece. (*Luke* 9:3)

In his youth and early manhood Abhishiktananda's spiritual horizon was bound by provincial Catholic piety as practiced by the French bourgeoisie, and his early years in seminary and monastery seemed to meet the demands of his vocation as he then understood it. But from the outset he believed, as he wrote in a letter of 1929, that "a monk cannot accept mediocrity, only extremes are appropriate for him."[8] By 1934, at the age of twenty-three, he was beginning to feel the call of India—which was nothing other than the invitation to a deeper commitment to his vocation as a monk. As Raimon Panikkar wrote in his "Letter to Abhishiktananda," "you felt the call of India not because you were a Christian, but because you were a monk."[9] Here is Abhishiktananda writing to Fr. Monchanin in 1947 about their plans for a monastic life together in India:

> The point of departure should be the Rule of St. Benedict because it had behind it an extremely reliable monastic tradition which would prevent a headlong plunge into the unknown. But it must be the rule as such . . . with its original character, so flexible and universal. . . . I believe that the Benedictine Rule, in its marvelous profundity and stability, is pliant enough to dominate all these monastic forms. . . . Eighteen years of Benedictine life have deeply bound me to the *sancta regula*. . . . The observance [in the proposed *ashram*] will certainly be very austere, much more so than in our French monasteries. I have no objection to that. On the contrary![10]

These are not the words of a man looking to flee his monastic vows but to live them more fully. On the negative side, he rarely said anything about precisely what fuelled his dissatisfaction with monastic life at Kergonan but here and there he drops suggestive hints. This, for instance, in a letter of December 1964:

---

8 Abhishiktananda, *Swami Abhishiktananda: His Life Told through His Letters* (hereafter *Letters*), ed. J. Stuart (New Delhi: ISPCK, 1989), letter dated 27.10.29, p. 6.

9 R. Panikkar, "Letter to Abhishiktananda," *Studies in Formative Spirituality*, 3:3, 1982, p. 446.

10 Abhishiktananda, *The Eyes of Light*, ed. A. Gzier & J. Lemarie (Denville, NJ: Dimension Books, 1983), letter dated 18.8.47, pp. 13-14.

> Personally I needed years to free myself (if indeed I have done so
> even now) from the infantilism and the lack of a sense of personal
> responsibility which was effectively instilled into me on the pretext
> of obedience.[11]

There is also no doubt that throughout his life he was often frustrated
by ecclesiastical "ritualism, formalism, and intellectualism" which far
from nurturing spiritual experience were a barrier to it.[12]

At the time of his arrival in India Abhishiktananda looked forward
to a coenobitical rather than an eremitical life, but in the wake of his
shattering mystical experiences at Arunachala and Tapovanam, and
his immersion in Upanishadic *advaita*, the life of the *sannyasi*, a life
centered on the "inner mystery," attracted him ever more powerfully:
"The inner mystery calls me with excruciating force, and no outside
being can help me to penetrate it and there, *for myself*, discover the
secret of my origin and destiny."[13] Eventually his ideas about the monk's
vocation fused with the Hindu ideal of *sannyasa*, and in some sense
were subsumed by it. The renunciation to which one was called by *sannyasa* was a more total and self-annihilating ideal than anything which
Abhishiktananda had experienced within the Christian orders, and a
more demanding call to the life of "interiority"—though, in the end,
all ideas of "inner" and "outer" were burnt up in the experience of non-
duality, just as the very "I" which was living out a vocation likewise
disappeared. As early as 1956 he came to the realization that he must
surrender his egoic investments, even in his role as a monk. From his
journal:

> I have not yet managed to achieve it—the "surrender" of my "ego" as
> a Christian, monk, a priest. And yet I must do so. Perhaps it will then
> be given back to me, renewed. But meanwhile, I must leave it be-
> hind—totally—without any hope of its return. And that means abso-
> lute poverty, nakedness, hunger, fasting, a vagrant life without means
> of support, total solitude in heart, in body and in spirit. And still
> more it involves the breaking of all those bonds that are as old as my-
> self, those bonds that are in the most secret recesses of my heart. All

11 Abhishiktananda, *Letters*, letter dated 15.12.64, p. 167.

12 See, for example, Abhishiktananda, *Letters*, letter dated 15.7.66, pp. 182-183.

13 Abhishiktananda, diary entry dated 19.4.56, quoted in R. Panikkar, "Letter to Abhishiktananda," p. 435.

that superego derived from my family upbringing, from my whole training as a young child, as a young man, as a priest, as a monk.

Already he is painfully sensing that a total acceptance of *advaita* and *sannyasa* means moving beyond his attachment to the theological formulations of Christianity:

> If one does not renounce all that one has . . .—even the Jesus whom he has before his eyes. . . . Even the God of Jesus, for that again is an idea which the "ego" possesses, and which prevents the "ego" from disappearing in the abyss.[14]

From Arunachala to Gyansu: Deeper into *Sannyasa*

How did Abhishiktananda understand *sannyasa*? Although Abhishik-tananda recognized that the Indian tradition of *sannyasa* allowed for the practice of *bhakti* he believed that its highest expression entailed complete apophaticism—the giving up of all naming of either God or oneself, the commitment to "infinite silence." From his journal in 1954:

> The *sannyasi* renounces not only the body and everything related to it, the entire domain of the *bahir karana* (renunciation of rights and freedom from all obligations); but also and likewise the entire *an-tahkarana*, the psychic domain, *ahamkara* and *manas*; he renounces the *nama-rupa* (name and form) of himself and of God. *Sannyasa* involves a commitment to the apophatic path.[15]

He doubted whether such an ideal had any equivalent in "ecclesial Christianity" which "does not admit of the possibility of itself being transcended." In this respect he discerned a yawning "abyss" between Christianity and Hinduism in that the latter fulfilled itself in tran-scending its own religious forms, "in orienting the best of its adepts towards what is beyond its formulations and rites, in which alone the Supreme Truth resides." He became keenly aware of the limitations of Christian monasticism, at least with respect to its actual practice in the modern world:

---

14 Abhishiktananda, *Ascent to the Depth of the Heart: The Spiritual Diary (1948-1973) of Swami Abhishiktananda (Dom H. Le Saux)* (hereafter *Diary*), ed. R. Panikkar (Delhi: ISPCK, 1998), entry dated 6.1.56, p. 136.

15 Abhishiktananda, *Diary*, entry dated 7.1.54, p. 88.

Monastic profession withdraws the Christian from the world but binds him still more closely to the Church on pilgrimage (*viator*). Passage from one yoke to another. *Sannyasa* transcends all yokes of *maya*, all rights as well as all obligations . . . [and] sets free from all rites and all Canon Law. *Sannyasa* cannot be Christian.[16]

From this vantage point Abhishiktananda finds himself in a harrowing dilemma:

From now on I have tasted too much of *advaita* to be able to recover the "Gregorian" peace of the Christian monk. Long ago I tasted too much of the "Gregorian" peace not to be anguished in the midst of my *advaita*.[17]

I remain Christian so long as I have not penetrated into the "Darkness"—supposing that some day I penetrate that far. But is it still compatible with the profession of Christianity even to admit the simple possibility of something beyond Christianity?—Will I get out of this by distinguishing two levels? But even the possibility of another level is contradictory to Christianity. What then?[18]

However, he is able to take some comfort in the following reflections:

Even in the context of Christian theology, each one will be judged on the conformity of his life with the ideal he has glimpsed in his own depth, and not with the ideal of some other person, or of some particular religious sect. . . . The best can easily be the enemy of the good.[19]

In the years between these journal entries of 1953-54 and his death in 1973 Abhishiktananda became ever more implacably pledged to *sannyasa* but found a way in which to harmonize it with Christianity. His conceptual reconciliation of *sannyasa* and Christian faith hinged on the idea that, in its deepest sense, Christian faith was a call to the

16 Abhishiktananda, *Diary*, entry dated 9.1.54, p. 89.

17 Abhishiktananda, *Diary*, entry dated 27.9.53, p. 74.

18 Abhishiktananda, *Diary*, entry dated 26.1.54, p. 89.

19 Abhishiktananda, *Diary*, entry dated 7.4.54, p. 90.

"leap into the void" to which *sannyasa* also summoned the renunciate. There is also a growing awareness of the "two levels"—in traditional-ist parlance, the outer, exoteric dimension of formal religious diver-sity, and the inner, esoteric level where there is to be found a formless unity, what Schuon called "the transcendent unity of religions." Abhi-shiktananda also moved towards the view—seemingly impossible in 1954—that the Church in India might play a providential role in bring-ing *sannyasa* into the universal Church. By the early '60s, when Abhi-shiktananda came to write *Saccidananda*, we see him venturing both a theological and an experiential synthesis of the two perspectives. He was also now able to see more clearly that no religious form, whether Christian, Hindu, or some other, had an ultimate value but that all, in the Upanishadic metaphor, were like the taper with which the fire is lit; once the fire is ablaze, the taper can be jettisoned.[20]

Sannyasa in *The Further Shore*

Much of what has been said already indicates the main contour lines of the ideal of *sannyasa*. But here it is worth dwelling on Abhishiktanan-da's most cogent exposition, in *The Further Shore*. The call to *sannyasa*, he tells us, is in the first place inspired by *viveka*, the ability to discrimi-nate between the permanent and the transitory, the first requisite of the seeker of knowledge of the Real (*Brahma-vidya*). But he is at pains to make the distinction between "enchanting ideas which may inspire profound meditation or learned discussion among the initiated" and the actual raw and sometimes traumatic experience of non-duality which snatches one out of habitual modes of understanding.[21] The *san-nyasi* has but one desire, for God Alone, but not as a *deva* or celestial being who might confer favor:

> His desire for God is the desire for One who is beyond all forms, for communion with the One-without-a-second, for a joy which is beyond all sensible delights and a bliss from which has disappeared all distinction between "enjoyer" and "enjoyed."[22]

20 Abhishiktananda, *Saccidananda: A Christian Approach to Advaitic Experience* (Delhi: ISPCK, 1984), pp. 42-43.

21 Abhishiktananda, *Further Shore*, p. 3.

22 Abhishiktananda, *Further Shore*, p. 5.

Furthermore,

> *Sannyasis* are their people's oblation to God, their most precious
> *yajna*; they are the true human sacrifice (*purushamedha*), victims
> consumed in the fire of *tapas*, their own inner oblation.[23]

In *The Mountain of the Lord*, Abhishiktananda had emphasized the
role of the acosmic as witness to the Absolute:

> These acosmics are no less present to the world than are those who
> have been cast into the great stream of life, but their presence is at the
> very point from which this stream comes forth. They bear witness to
> the absolute, the *kaivalya*, to the Unmoving, *acala*, and do so on be-
> half of this world, while apparently remaining on its fringe. They are
> like the pivots of this world, holding it steady by their own stillness
> within the Unmovable.[24]

The Further Shore sketches the outlines of the renunciate's way of
life with respect to the needs of the body (food, clothing, shelter), various abstinences (from idle gossip, worldly affairs, intellectual debate,
unnecessary reading, and the like), the refusal to be seduced by the
temptation of "gregariousness, activism, and exteriority," the practice
of austerities such as fasting and silence. In his later years Abhishiktananda increasingly stressed that the final goal of the *sannyasi* was to
be "acosmic"—without name, place, possessions, without social and
religious obligations, "as dead to society as the man whose corpse is
being carried to the burning-*ghat*,"[25] without desire of any kind, and as
if unborn. In the words of the *Katha Upanishad*,

> He neither dies nor is born, the one who knows.
> From where does he come? What will he become?
> Non-born, eternal, primordial, always himself![26]

---

23 Abhishiktananda, *Further Shore*, p. 14.

24 Abhishiktananda, *Mountain of the Lord: Pilgrimage to Gangotri* (Delhi: ISPCK,
1990), pp. 44-45.

25 Abhishiktananda, *Further Shore*, pp. 13-14.

26 *Katha Upanishad*, quoted in Abhishiktananda, *Guru and Disciple* (London: SPCK,
1974), p. 113.

He found the acosmic in the Christian mystics:

[T]he Carmel—at least as it is idealized in my vision of it—is perhaps
what comes closest in the Church to India's deepest aspirations: the
acosmics of the Desert Fathers; the "Flee, be silent, remain at rest" of
Arsenius; the *nada* of St. John of the Cross; above all, the "establishment of oneself beyond oneself" of Tauler and Eckhart. That is what
the Christian monk should live out in company with his advaitin
brother, if he wants truly to complete in Christ the intuition of Being
contained in the *Saccidananda* of the India of the rishis.[27]

In almost the last of his journal entries Abhishiktananda reflects
on the "terrifying demands of non-possession in *sannyasa*," not only
the absence of possessions but rather the *impossibility* of any possession because there is no longer anyone who could be the possessor. He
now understands anew that this poverty, inner as well as outer, is really
the "radical starting point" of *sannyasa*.[28]

Abhishiktananda was not so naive as to be unaware of the pitfalls
which surrounded *sannyasa*, nor of the many abuses sheltering behind
the ideal. Not the least insidious of the possible snares was what Chögyam Trungpa called "spiritual materialism"—the appropriation of
"spirituality" by the ego for its own ends. Abhishiktananda regrets the
kind of snobbery and elitism which has sometimes betrayed the ideal
of *sannyasa*:

The *sannyasi* has no place, no *loka* . . . so if there is a class of Sannyasis, it is all up with *sannyasa*! They have renounced the world—
splendid! So from then on they belong to the *loka*, the "world" of
those who have renounced the world! They constitute themselves a
new kind of society, an "in-group" of their own, a spiritual elite apart
from the common man, and charged with instructing him, very like
those "scribes and Pharisees" whose attitude made even Jesus, the
compassionate one, lose his temper. Then a whole new code of correct behavior develops, worse than that of the world, with its courtesy titles, respectful greetings, order of precedence, and the rest. The
wearing of the saffron becomes the sign, not so much of renunciation, as of belonging to the "order of swamis."[29]

27 Abhishiktananda, *Letters*, letter dated 26.10.59, p. 123.

28 Abhishiktananda, *Letters*, letter dated 5.7.73, p. 383.

29 Abhishiktananda, *Further Shore*, p. 33.

The true *sannyasi* must, in the end, paradoxically, renounce renunciation itself, or to put it more precisely, *sannyasa* entails the renouncing of the renouncer: "'I have renounced'? The only one entitled to pronounce it without telling a lie is no longer capable of uttering it."[30] In this sense *sannyasa* "carries within itself its own abrogation." And here, by way of an aside, it is worth noting that the usual translation of *sannyasa*, "renunciation," is not altogether adequate. Raimon Panikkar draws our attention to this when writing, "The holy ascetic of Indian religiousness does not represent exclusively, and often not even mainly, an ideal of moral renunciation, but rather that of an authentic, naked, and pure life."[31]

What of the relation of *sannyasa* to religion?

> Whatever the excellence of any *dharma*, it remains inevitably at the level of signs; it remains on this side of the Real, not only in its structure and institutional forms, but also in its attempts to formulate the ineffable reality, alike in mythical or conceptual images. The mystery to which it points overflows its limits in every direction. . . . All *a priori* deductions and speculations fall short of discovering the Spirit in itself beyond the level of religions. It can only be reached existentially, that is, by piercing to the very heart of the religious experience itself. . . . In every religion and in every religious experience there is a beyond, and it is precisely this "beyond" that is our goal. *Sannyasa* is the recognition of that which is beyond all signs; and paradoxically, it is itself the sign of what for ever lies beyond all possibility of being adequately expressed by rites, creeds, or institutions.[32]

The crucial point here is that it is only through a *penetration* of religious forms—a very different matter from an impious iconoclasm in the manner of a Krishnamurti and other such self-styled savants, which announces itself as being "above" forms—that the nameless reality can be reached by those prepared to pay the price of self-annihilation (i.e., the disappearance of what the "self" is imagined to be). The writings of Bede Griffiths on this matter, not surprisingly, are in complete accord with those of Abhishiktananda. Here is a passage from Fr. Bede's *The*

30 Abhishiktananda, *Further Shore*, p. 34.

31 R. Panikkar, "The Monk According to the Indian Sacred Scriptures," *Cistercian Studies*, 9:2-3, 1974, p. 253.

32 Abhishiktananda, *Further Shore*, p. 26.

Marriage of East and West:

> A *Sannyasi* is one who renounces the world to seek for God, but his renunciation goes far beyond what is ordinarily understood by the "world.". . . A *Sannyasi* renounces the whole world of "signs," of appearances. . . . The Church also belongs to the world of "signs." The doctrines and sacraments of the Church are . . . signs of the divine reality. . . . The *Sannyasi* is called to go beyond all religion, beyond every human institution, beyond every scripture and creed, till he comes to that which every religion and scripture signifies but can never name.[33]

This states the "position" the *sannyasi* occupies *vis-à-vis* religion clearly enough. But certain misunderstandings inevitably arise at this point. Bede Griffiths again echoes Abhishiktananda when, drawing on his own experience of *sannyasa*, he goes on to write,

> Yet when we say that the *Sannyasi* goes beyond religion this does not mean that he rejects any religion. I have not felt called to reject anything that I have learned of God or of Christ or of the Church. To go beyond the sign is not to reject the sign, but to reach the thing signified. . . . As long as we remain in the world we need these signs, and the world today cannot survive unless it rediscovers the signs of faith, the "Myth," the "Symbol," in which the knowledge of reality is enshrined. But equally fatal is to stop at the sign, to mistake the sign for the ultimate reality. . . . This is essentially idolatry. . . . The *Sannyasi* is one who is called to witness to this Truth of the reality beyond the signs, to be a sign of that which is beyond signs.[34]

*

Abhishiktananda sometimes reproached himself for failing to live out absolutely the ideal of the acosmic to which he aspired, feeling that he lacked the courage to take "the final step."[35] Hence the joy he felt at the *diksha* (initiation) of his disciple, Marc Chaduc; the disciple had out-

---

33 B. Griffiths, *The Marriage of East and West: A Sequel to "The Golden String"* (London: Collins, 1982), p. 42.

34 B. Griffiths, *Marriage of East and West*, p. 43 (italics mine).

35 See R. Panikkar, "Letter to Abhishiktananda," pp. 444-445.

stripped the master in his commitment to *sannyasa*. Abhishiktananda himself still owned some books and a few other paltry possessions, maintained his tiny hermitage at Uttarkashi, and cherished the human contact of his family and friends. His letters and writings testify to certain contradictory impulses in Abhishiktananda's attitude to acosmism, and it would no doubt be easy to find certain inconsistencies in his "theoretical position." However, it would be impertinent to launch any kind of "psychoanalysis" to explain the contradictions, just as it would be foolish to gather together various passages from his writings to establish his intellectual inconsistencies. What can be said without fear of contradiction is that Abhishiktananda never ceased to explore in himself all of the possibilities of his vocation, painful though this sometimes was. Further, whatever his real or imagined failings to live out *sannyasa*, he gave us a magnificent vision of what the ideal, in its highest reaches, might actually entail.

Whilst it is impossible not to admire Abhishiktananda's aspiration to become an acosmic, it is also difficult to disagree with Raimon Panikkar who believed that Abhishiktananda had surrendered to a "certain absolutistic interpretation of monasticism" and who found Abhishiktananda's failure to realize the ideal in his own life a mark of his human warmth. Panikkar believed that monasticism's "irresistible tendency" towards "absolute acosmism," the attempt to "break all boundaries, the limitations of the body, matter, and mind as well as of the spirit," its aspiration to transcend the human condition, to be both "not human" and "not Christian"—and the latter because the Incarnation stands for the "divinization of the concrete, the limited, and even of matter and the body."[36]

*

In the very last of his published writings, *Sannyasa-Diksha* (the last of the five articles written for the Sivananda Ashram monthly) Abhishiktananda writes with a rhapsodic intensity which surely makes it one of the most heartfelt affirmations of *sannyasa*. It shines with the wisdom

---

36 R. Panikkar, "Letter to Abhishiktananda," p. 444. See also *Mountain of the Lord*, pp. 51-57. The notion of acosmism is discussed in some detail in J.G. Friesen, *Abhishiktananda's Non-Monistic Advaitic Experience*, PhD thesis (Pretoria: University of South Africa, 2001), pp. 294ff.

wrested from his long pilgrimage and gives us his final, profound word on this "sign beyond signs." It is worth quoting at some length.

> *Sannyasa* confronts us with a sign of that which is essentially beyond all signs—indeed, in its sheer transparency [to the Absolute] it proclaims its own death as a sign. . . . However the *sannyasi* lives in the world of signs, of the divine manifestation, and this world of manifestation needs him, "the one beyond signs," so that it may realize the impossible possibility of a bridge between the two worlds. . . . These ascetics who flee the world and care nothing for its recognition are precisely the ones who uphold the world. . . . They go their way in secret. . . . But [the world] . . . needs to know that they are there, so that it may preserve a reminder of transcendence in the midst of a transient world. . . . The sign of *sannyasa* . . . stands then on the very frontier, the unattainable frontier, between two worlds, the world of manifestation and the world of the unmanifest Absolute. It is the mystery of the sacred lived with the greatest possible interiority. It is a powerful means of grace—that grace which is nothing else than the Presence of the Absolute, the Eternal, the Unborn, existing at the heart of the realm of becoming, of time, of death and life; and a grace which is at the same time the irresistible drawing of the entire universe and its fullness towards the ultimate fullness of the Awakening to the Absolute, to the *Atman*. This sign, this grace is supremely the *tarana*, the raft by which man passes over to the "other shore.". . . Finally, it is even the *taraka*, the actual one who himself carries men across to the other shore, the one and only "ferryman," manifested in manifold ways in the form of all those rishis, mahatmas, gurus, and buddhas, who throughout history have themselves been woken and in turn awaken their brother-men.[37]

Contemplative Monasticism, *Sannyasa*, and the Church

The more Abhishiktananda was gripped by *sannyasa* the more he identified with the apophatic and eremitical traditions within Christian monasticism in both its Latin and Orthodox branches, turning often to the Desert Fathers of Egypt and Syria, to Pseudo-Dionysius, and to the Rhenish mystics, and cherishing the Carthusian and Carmelite Orders in the contemporary Church.[38] He also came to see St. Francis

---

37 Abhishiktananda, *Further Shore*, pp. 42-43.

38 Abhishiktananda, *Towards the Renewal of the Indian Church* (Bangalore: Dharmaram College, 1970), p. 130, and *Prayer* (London: SPCK, 1974), pp. 32-33.

of Assisi as the exemplary Christian *sannyasi*. No longer did he see an "abyss" between Christianity and *sannyasa*:

> The profession of a Christian monk certainly implies, at least in its roots, the full renunciation and radical transcendence which shines out so clearly in the tradition of the Hindu *sannyasa*. . . . Above all, the call to solitude which, beginning in the fourth century, carried off so many Christians to the deserts of Egypt and Syria, and then a thousand years later, to the great forests of Central and Northern Russia, was certainly no less radical than the call of Hindu *sannyasa*, and in its extreme form implied separation from all ecclesiastical associations and even from the sacraments. This call to solitude—alone with the Alone, alone with the alones of the One who is Alone—is still heard by Christ's disciples.[39]

Indeed, he hoped that

> The Indian Church will in the end bring to the universal Church an authentically Christian *sannyasa* as the crowning of monastic life. Thus the Church will recover after centuries the purest traditions of the Desert and of the Hesychast movement, and at the same time drink deep at the inexhaustible sources of the Hindu ideal of renunciation in a life devoted to God alone.[40]

One of the links which Abhishiktananda now perceived between the two traditions of his "double belonging" was contemplation. Indeed, in *Towards a Renewal of the Indian Church*, he writes

> That supra-mental awareness of the Spirit within and the inner communion with Him should be considered the most important thing in the life of the individual and of the Church here below. Unless such a conviction is widely disseminated, nothing worthwhile will be achieved in the Church.[41]

This was not an idle jotting in his journal but a statement in a memorandum for participants in the forthcoming All-India Seminar

---

39 Abhishiktananda, *Further Shore*, p. 29.

40 Abhishiktananda, *Prayer*, p. 33.

41 Abhishiktananda, *Renewal of the Indian Church*, p. 7.

of the Roman Catholic Church. In other words, we can take this as Abhishiktananda's considered position in his later years. Whilst this form of awareness was to be encouraged in all Christians it could best be nurtured within the contemplative vocations. At a time when many in the Indian Church were focusing on her social activities Abhishiktananda was adamant that contemplation must be at its very heart. He urged

> The establishment and the fostering of religious houses engaged in pure and real contemplation in silence and solitude, inside and outside. It is only from such centers that genuine contemplative life . . . can radiate and spread in the Church. . . . Let it be remembered, however, that it is not primarily of so-called contemplative institutions that the Church is in need of above all, but contemplative men and women.[42]

He goes on to write of the two formidable contemporary challenges that the Church faces—Western atheism and Eastern spirituality. Not just the Indian but the whole Church must meet the challenge of "interiority and spiritual depth put to her by Hinduism,—by the Spirit, as we would confidently affirm, through Hinduism."[43]

> The Church here finds herself confronted, not with materialistic and secularist tendencies as in the West, but with a religious tradition deeply contemplative and spiritual. . . . Hence the necessity for the Church, both for the sake of her own spiritual awakening and for the achievement of her mission and witness in India, to take into account the essentials of the Indian contemplative tradition, to integrate them into her own patrimony, and to develop them under the guidance of the Holy Spirit to the best of her ability.[44]

Elsewhere Abhishiktananda refers to the crisis facing Christian monasticism as it "gropingly seeks to find a path forward, avoiding on one side a sterile medievalism, and on the other, a modernism which loses all sense of mystery."[45] He looks forward to the day when there

42 Abhishiktananda, *Renewal of the Indian Church*, p. 8.

43 Abhishiktananda, *Renewal of the Indian Church*, p. 11.

44 Abhishiktananda, *Renewal of the Indian Church*, p. 55.

45 Abhishiktananda, *Further Shore*, p. 47.

might be a creative fusion of the tradition of the desert ("harking back to John the Baptist and the great Elijah, the typical monk-prophet of the Old Testament"), and the Indian tradition of *sannyasa* which flowed forth from "the primeval rishis of India."[46]

No doubt Abhishiktananda would have shared Raimon Panikkar's melancholy sentiments when he addressed the Second Asian Monastic Congress (Bangalore, 1973):

> The contribution of Christian monasticism in Asia to the Church at large is minimal, not to say practically nil. Christian monasteries, where they exist, have been almost "air-lifted" *ante litteram*, so that they become enclaves, colonies of Western Christianity. In spite of strenuous effort, immense goodwill, and even holiness, the history of monasticism in Asia is a sad page in the life of the Christian Church.[47]

The two friends were deeply concerned with making the Church in India not a colonial outpost but a channel through which the spiritual riches of India could flow into the Universal Church. In this enterprise they believed the monk had a crucial role to play. One of the many recommendations Abhishiktananda makes to the Indian Church is the development of an authentic Christian *sannyasa*. In *Renewal of the Indian Church* Abhishiktananda actually envisages the emergence of three types of Christian *sannyasis*: 1. pure contemplatives, men and women, both *jnanins* and *bhaktis*, who may be solitaries or living in small groups, preferably in India's holiest places; 2. preaching *sannyasis—ordo predicatorum*—who, between periods of extended silence, would develop a Christian *satsang*; 3. itinerant *sannyasis*, Christian *parivrajas*, who would recapture the "selfsame spirit that animated Francis of Assisi and his first companions," going from "village to village in utter poverty, living on alms, singing their love for the Lord, and calling all to share in their radiating bliss."[48]

In Abhishiktananda's view (shared by Thomas Merton and many others) the monk was peculiarly well placed to act as a bridge between

---

46 Abhishiktananda, *Further Shore*, p. 47.

47 R. Panikkar, "The Contribution of Christian Monasticism in Asia to the Universal Church," *Cistercian Studies*, 9:2-3, 1974, p. 74.

48 Abhishiktananda, *Renewal of the Indian Church*, p. 76.

East and West.[49] The monastic ideal was deeply rooted in both hemispheres, and the actual spiritual experience of the monk could bypass doctrinal differences to bring the followers of various *dharmas* together. This because "the only real meeting-point between men concerned with the ultimate is in the center of the self, in 'the cave of the heart,' which is where the monk abides."[50] Monks felt a natural and spontaneous affinity:

> There is indeed a "monastic order" which is universal and includes them all. . . . It is enough that they should thus recognize each other whenever they happen to meet, and in fact those that do infallibly respond to each other. Despite all differences in observance, language, and cultural background, they perceive in each other's eyes that depth which the One Spirit has opened in their own hearts.[51]

As David Steindl-Rast (himself a Benedictine monk) has observed,

> Monks and nuns the world over speak the same language, as it were. In the things that really matter, they are often much closer to each other across religious boundaries than they are to lay people in their own respective religious groups.[52]

There are many stories about the spontaneous bond of which Abhishiktananda speaks. Three examples come readily to mind: the meetings of the Dalai Lama with Thomas Merton and Bede Griffiths, and Abhishiktananda's first encounter with Swami Chidananda. Of that company of Christian monks who saw in the monastic ideal a vital link between Eastern and Western spirituality one may here mention not only Frs. Monchanin and Bede Griffiths, but also such figures as Aelred Graham, Thomas Merton, William Johnston, and David Steindl-Rast. It is also a striking fact that amongst the many Eastern teachers and gurus who have made an impact in the West, some of the

---

49 See J. Conner, "The Monk as Bridge between East and West" in *The Other Half of My Soul: Bede Griffiths and the Hindu-Christian Dialogue*, ed. B. Bruteau (Wheaton, IL: Quest Books, 1996).

50 Abhishiktananda, "The Depth Dimension of Religious Dialogue," *Vidjayjoti*, 45:5, 1981, p. 208.

51 Abhishiktananda, *Further Shore*, p. 27.

52 Quoted in J. Royster, "Dialogue in Depth," p. 76.

most revered and widely-loved have been monks—the present Dalai Lama, Thich Nhat Hanh, and Shunryu Suzuki readily come to mind

Further Reflections on Monasticism

We conclude with a few reflections about monasticism and its place in the modern world. From Thomas Merton:

> Let us face the fact that the monastic vocation tends to present itself to the modern world as a problem and as a scandal. In a basically religious culture, like that of India, or of Japan, the monk is more or less taken for granted.[53]

But, in truth, as Frithjof Schuon reminds us, "a world is absurd exactly to the extent that the contemplative, the hermit, the monk, appear in it as a paradox or as an 'anachronism.'" It is the monk who can save us from our idolatry of "the age" because he "incarnates all that is changeless, not through sclerosis or inertia, but through transcendence."[54] It is in this sense, as well as in many others, that the monk is, in Abhishiktananda's words, the true and ultimate human oblation, his individuality consumed in God. One of the charges leveled by humanists, slaves to an ideal of utilitarian activism, is that monks are useless, perhaps worse, a breed of social parasites. In considering this shallow and impudent attitude we can do no better than turn again to Schuon:

> When anyone reproaches a hermit or a monk for "fleeing" the world, he commits a double error: first, he loses sight of the fact that contemplative isolation has an intrinsic value independent of the existence of a surrounding "world"; second, he pretends to forget that there are forms of flight which are perfectly honorable: if it is neither absurd nor shameful to do one's best to escape from an avalanche, it is no more so to run away from the temptations or even simply the distractions of the world. . . . In our days people are very ready to say that to flee the world is to shirk "responsibilities," a completely hypocritical euphemism that conceals spiritual laziness and a hatred of the absolute behind "altruistic" or "social" ideas; people are happy to ignore the fact that the gift of oneself to God is always a gift of oneself

---

53 T. Merton, *The Silent Life* (New York: Farrar, Strauss & Giroux, 1957), p. viii.

54 F. Schuon, *Light on the Ancient Worlds*, p. 105.

to all. It is metaphysically impossible to give oneself to God without this resulting in something good for the environment; to give oneself to God—though it were hidden from all—is to give oneself to man, for this gift of self has a sacrificial value of an incalculable radiance.[55]

No one in the East still attuned to their own religious tradition could conceive of the reproaches to which Schuon alludes, let alone take them seriously. It is a measure of the spiritually sterile climate in which many Westerners live that such prejudices can be harbored by so many. The monks and nuns of Christianity and Buddhism, the Hindu *sannyasi* and *parivraja*, the Taoist recluse, the Zen master, the Tibetan *naldjorpa*, the Sufi contemplative, remind a forgetful world, as their predecessors have done through the ages, of the highest spiritual ideals by living as a "sign beyond signs," showing us a bridge not only between the East and West but between the manifest and the Absolute. There is no higher vocation.

In his writings on *sannyasa* Abhishiktananda refers more than once to the Vedic figure of the *kesi* ("hairy one"), the one who has gone beyond all forms, all dualities, even beyond *sannyasa* itself. In his last year Abhishiktananda seems to have attained something of the state of the *kesi*. Here is how he describes it in *The Further Shore*:

> The *kesi* does not regard himself as a *sannyasi*. There is no world, no *loka*, in which he belongs. Free and riding the winds, he traverses the worlds at his pleasure. Wherever he goes, he goes maddened with his own rapture, intoxicated with the unique Self. Friend of all and fearing none, he bears the Fire, he bears the Light. Some take him for a common beggar, some for a madman, a few for a sage. To him it is all one. He is himself, he is accountable to no one. His support is in himself, that is to say, in the Spirit from whom he is not "other."[56]

---

55 F. Schuon, *Light on the Ancient Worlds*, pp. 102.

56 Abhishiktananda, *Further Shore*, p. 38.

CHAPTER 18

Across the Great Divide:
Some Christian Responses to Religious Pluralism

We in the West now realize that we have no monopoly of religious truth. We must in honesty change our attitude towards other faiths, for our watchword must be "Loyalty to truth." This changed attitude, however, does not weaken, but rather, instead, reinforces one's faith in God, for He is seen to be not a small or partial being but the Great God who is working throughout all times and places and faiths.

Rudolf Otto[1]

The essential problem that the study of religion poses is how to preserve religious truth, traditional orthodoxy, the dogmatic theological structures of one's own tradition, and yet gain knowledge of other traditions and accept them as spiritually valid ways and roads to God.

Seyyed Hossein Nasr[2]

Understanding, at least in realms as inherently noble as the great faiths of mankind, brings respect; and respect prepares the way for a higher power, love—the only power that can quench the flames of fear, suspicion, and prejudice, and provide the means by which the people of this small but precious earth can become one to one another.

Huston Smith[3]

Today different religious traditions are everywhere colliding, sometimes in violent conflict, often in mutual incomprehension. We find ourselves in an unprecedented and highly volatile landscape, characterized by both inter- and intra-religious strife and discord. The

---

1 R. Otto, "Parallelisms in the Development of Religion East and West" (1912), quoted in P. Almond, "Rudolf Otto and Buddhism" in *Aspects of Religion: Essays in Honor of Ninian Smart*, ed. P. Masefield & D. Wiebe (New York: Peter Lang, 1994), p. 69.

2 S.H. Nasr, *Sufi Essays* (London: Allen & Unwin, 1972), p. 127.

3 H. Smith, *The World's Religions: Our Great Wisdom Traditions* (San Francisco: HarperSanFrancisco, 1991), p. 390.

media flood us with apocalyptic scenarios envisaging "the clash of civilizations," new "holy wars," and "crusades" against "terrorists" or "infidels." A persistent motif is the highly charged confrontation of militant religious fundamentalism and the forces of modernity. The most conspicuous locus of these scenarios is the Middle East and the smoldering confrontation of "Islam" and "the West." Whilst the Middle East remains a highly visible powder-keg there are many other parts of the world where religion is seen, quite understandably, as an explosive and divisive force. To restrict ourselves to flashpoints where Islam is involved we might mention the on-going Hindu-Muslim hostilities in the Indian subcontinent, Christian-Muslim antagonisms in Africa, central and south-east Asia, or the acute social tensions arising out of the settlement of Muslim communities in the West. Since 9/11 the Western media have been awash with "news," "opinion," "commentary," "analysis," and the like, much of it issuing from politicians old and new, recycled CIA agents, defense personnel, so-called terrorism experts, and Cold War veterans. Much of this material might better be described as propaganda—the continuation of politics by other means, one might say—obfuscating rather than clarifying the issues at hand. Ideological heat and rhetorical excess is the order of the day! No doubt the same might be said for various media networks within the Islamic world.

Here I do not want to launch any analysis of the role of religious factors in contemporary geo-politics, nor indeed to explore the political infiltration of the religious domain itself, significant and interesting as these subjects are.[4] My subject, rather, is the inter-relations of the religions, considered from a trans-religious viewpoint and within the context of the modern encounter of "East" and "West." More particularly I want to focus on creative responses to this phenomenon by Christian scholars and practitioners, and to consider several critical intersections within the Christian churches and in the Anglophone academic world. Nonetheless, it is important to take note of the fraught political framework within which much contemporary discussion of inter-religious relations now takes place.

Any inquiry into the inter-relations of the religions, today and into the future, must take account of three modern developments: the radi-

4 For some discussion of these issues in the immediate wake of 9/11 see R. Blackhirst & H. Oldmeadow, "Shadows and Strife: The Confrontation of Islam and the West," *Sacred Web: A Journal of Tradition and Modernity*, 8, December 2001, pp. 121-136.

cally altered situation, in the last two centuries, of religions *vis-à-vis* each other; the apparent triumph of anti-religious and anti-traditional forces in the West; and, thirdly, the consequent emergence of both religious fundamentalism (in both East and West) and religious liberalism (principally in the West). After briefly considering these developments I will turn to the question of finding a way towards an inter-religious *rapprochement* which might defuse some of these tensions and contribute to a more harmonious global community.

Since antiquity there has always been some intercourse in ideas and influences between the great religious civilizations; think, for instance, of Alexander the Great's conversations with the "gymnosophists," as the Greeks called the scantily-clad sages of the East. Or recall the ways in which the teachings of the Buddha were taken to the Far East. Nonetheless, each civilization formerly exhibited a spiritual homogeneity untroubled, for the most part, by the problem of religious pluralism. For the vast majority of believers in a traditional civilization the question of the inter-relationship of the religions was one which was either of peripheral concern or one of which they remained unaware. Martin Lings puts the matter this way:

> Needless to say our ancestors were aware of the existence of other religions besides their own; but dazzled and penetrated as they were by the great light shining directly above them, the sight of more remote and—for them—more obliquely shining lights on the horizons could raise no positive interest nor did it create problems. Today, however those horizons are no longer remote; and amidst the great evil which results from all that has contributed to bring them near, some good has also inevitably stolen its way in.[5]

The last few centuries have witnessed radical changes making for a "smaller" world, for "the global village"—the spread of new technologies of transport and communication, the unprecedented migrations of peoples, international economic and political developments which pay no heed to national and cultural boundaries, and the emergence of various dangers which now threaten humankind as a whole. The homogeneity of Christian civilization has long since been ruptured, and Europe has itself been the agent for the disruption and extirpation

5 Martin Lings, *Ancient Beliefs and Modern Superstitions* (London: Allen & Unwin, 1980), p. 70.

of traditional cultures the world over: the juggernauts of imperialism, "modernization," and "globalization" have created a world riven with new tensions and antagonisms.

Closely related to many of these developments is the ascendancy, in the modern West and increasingly in other parts of the globe, of a modernist worldview. "Modernism" is an umbrella term which covers the assumptions, values, and attitudes of the reigning worldview, the outlook shaping the temper of the times—discussed in earlier essays in this volume. Although its historical origins are European, modernism is now tied to no specific area or civilization. Its symptoms can be detected in a wide assortment of inter-related ideologies and intellectual movements, sometimes cooperatively co-existing, sometimes at loggerheads, but always united by the same underlying principles. Scientism, rationalism, relativism, materialism, empiricism, positivism, historicism, psychologism, individualism, humanism, existentialism, atheism—some variants of the modernistic thought which prevails in the liberal-secular West—are all ramifications of the same underlying worldview. Behind the proliferating ideologies of the last few centuries we can discern an ignorance of spiritual realities and an indifference, if not always an overt hostility, to the eternal verities conveyed by religious traditions. In this climate it is not surprising that so many Western commentators are anxious to seize on anything which can be exploited to further discredit the claims of religion. Nor is it surprising that many people in the non-Western world should have sometimes reacted violently to the depredations of modernity, witnessing as they do the rapid corruption or destruction of the institutions, customs, and values vouchsafed by tradition.

Within the religious domain itself we can discern two extreme reactions to the ravages of modernism. On the one hand, the emergence of an aggressive *fundamentalism*—that "blind lunge towards simplification," as George Steiner described it—characterized by theological literalism and exclusivism, an often sclerotic exoterism and religious xenophobia; on the other hand, a religious *liberalism* wherein "anything goes" as long as it lays some claim to an ill-defined "spirituality." Each of these symptoms of an underlying spiritual malaise are on full display in much of the modern West whilst it is the former phenomenon which is most evident in parts of the Islamic world. These two developments seem to be antagonistic but, while they are mutually exclusive, from a certain point of view they are actually two sides of the same counterfeit coin which has only come into circulation because of the canker of modernity. They both stand as formidable obstacles to any authentic inter-religious dialogue and ecumenicism.

Altogether these developments pose very real threats to the religious traditions of both East and West. It is all too easy to envisage developments entailing: (a) the *erosion* of religion by modernism, signaled by popular indifference, apathy, and "tolerance," and by a more active animus towards religion in the prevailing "orthodoxies" of the Western "intelligentsia";[6] and/or (b) the *violent destruction* of religious traditions by external forces (imperialism, modernization, globalization, ideologically-fuelled repression, and the "narcissistic fanaticisms" of unbridled nationalism, in which religious institutions all too often become entangled) and from within (internecine and inter-religious warfare); and/or (c) the *dilution and corruption* of religion by an ersatz "spirituality," bogus syncretisms or an insipid religious universalism, those "false idealisms" which "annex and adulterate religion."[7] Indeed, it would be sanguine to imagine that these processes are not already well advanced in many quarters. In this context, the question of the relationships of the religions and the imperatives of mutual understanding take on a new urgency for all those concerned with fostering a harmonious world community.

Hitherto I have painted a rather bleak picture of the contemporary situation—but there are also grounds for hope. It may be that in the West we are in a period of what historian William McLoughlin has called an "awakening":

> Awakenings—the most vital and yet most mysterious of all folk arts—are periods of cultural revitalization that begin in a general crisis of beliefs and values and extend over a period of a generation or so, during which time a profound reorientation in beliefs and values takes place.[8]

---

6 One sign of this anti-religious bias is the steady proliferation of "critiques" of religion by writers such as Richard Dawkins and Christopher Hitchens, following in the wake of figures such as Marx, Nietzsche, Freud, Bertrand Russell, and suchlike or, to trace the pedigree back further, the *philosophes* of the eighteenth century. An anti-religious posture is almost *de rigueur* in many university departments in the contemporary West—even in many Religious Studies departments.

7 F. Schuon, *To Have a Center* (Bloomington, IN: World Wisdom Books, 1990), p. 30.

8 McLoughlin quoted in R. Wentz, "The Prospective Eye of Inter-religious Dialogue,"

Between the World's Parliament of Religions in Chicago in 1893 and in Melbourne in 2009 there have been many initiatives aimed at promoting reciprocal understanding between the adherents of different religious traditions. A variety of attempts to create international cross-religious institutions have come and gone in the intervening century while individuals and religious groups continue to search for common ground where the suspicions and enmities of the past might be dissolved. Today there is a veritable "religious dialogue" industry in the West, with any number of conferences, seminars, symposia, workshops, retreats, and the like. There is no doubt that much of the ignorance and prejudice of past eras has been dispelled and that those so disposed are now much better situated to appreciate traditions other than their own. Despite the resurgence of various forms of religious fundamentalism and a hardening of exclusivist attitudes in some places we may rest assured that amongst religious folk in the West, particularly amongst the well-educated, there has been a growing acceptance of the validity of the non-Christian traditions and more widespread attitudes of respect and openness. Amongst scholars and theologians, clergy and religious, an awareness of Eastern traditions has penetrated quite deeply—one might say that the psyche of contemporary Christianity has been profoundly and irreversibly affected by the presence of both Islam and the East. One sign among many is the revision of the Roman Church's posture during Vatican II, evident in the decree *Nostra Aetate*. The comparative religionist Geoffrey Parrinder echoes many other thinkers when he suggests that the encounter with the East is "one of the most significant events of modern times," amounting to another Reformation within the Christian world.[9] Nonetheless, the question must be asked whether we are very much closer to finding a philosophical/metaphysical basis for inter-religious harmony, one that can take us past high-minded intent, neighborly good will, and the repudiation of the grosser forms of ignorance, prejudice, and suspicion.

Let us turn to some developments which have aimed to promote deeper inter-religious understanding. Our discussion will primarily concern the responses to the Eastern traditions of Christian thinkers and practitioners, sensitive to religious pluralism, who wish to engage

---

Japanese Journal of Religious Studies, 14:1, 1987, p. 8.

9 Geoffrey Parrinder quoted in J.J. Clarke, *Oriental Enlightenment: The Encounter between Asian and Western Thought* (London: Routledge, 1997), p. 130.

in creative dialogue and for whom the new Eastern presence in the West presents itself as a challenge and an opportunity rather than as a threat to be repulsed. Whilst many Asian scholars and practitioners have studied in the West it is generally the case that most of the initiatives in inter-religious dialogue have come from the Christian side. This may be related to the keener sense in this tradition of some deficiency which might be remedied by creative intercourse with Eastern traditions. Dialogue may also be felt, perhaps subconsciously, as an atonement for the historical ignominies of triumphalist missionizing and Western colonialism, or as a counter to the embarrassing excesses of current day Christian fundamentalists.[10] More positively these out-reaching initiatives may derive from certain dynamic and frontier-seeking tendencies in Christianity and in the Western *mythos* generally. On the other side, the comparative reticence of Easterners in sponsoring inter-religious dialogue may stem from a post-colonial wariness of the colonizing and universalizing tendencies in Western thought. Then, too, there is the fact that many Asian adherents feel no dissatisfaction with their own tradition such as might impel initiatives in this direction. Those Asians who *are* enthusiastic proponents of dialogue have themselves often been exposed to a Western education. Of course, these are somewhat facile generalities to which one can find many exceptions. Certainly, many prominent Asian religious leaders and scholars—D.T. Suzuki, the Dalai Lama, and Thich Nhat Hanh are conspicuous examples—have readily engaged in serious inter-religious dialogue.[11] We can distinguish several distinct, sometimes over-lapping twentieth century movements which, in various ways, have been directed towards inter-religious understanding. Here is a loose schema:

10 See H. Coward, "Hinduism's Sensitizing of Christianity," *Dialogue & Alliance*, 7:2, 1993, p. 77. The oppressive sense of the West's often aggressive presence is evident in a passage such as the following in which Fr. Henri Le Saux is reflecting on Christian missionizing in India: "I am thinking of all the harm that is done to the Gospel here, when it is preached by people who have behind them all the prestige, money, science, and technology of the west" (Letter dated 24.10.66, in *Swami Abhishiktananda: His Life Told through His Letters*, ed. J. Stuart (Delhi: ISPCK, 1989), p. 186).

11 We cannot here consider the significant resistances and reactions *against* the Eastern religions within the Christian churches (nor in the other Occidental religions). However, mention might be made of the re-affirmations of Christian exclusivism by theologians such as Karl Barth, Hendrik Kraemer, and Pope John-Paul II. We might also note the imperviousness to any Oriental influences of fervid evangelical movements thriving in many Western countries.

1. The growth of *comparative religion* as a discipline amongst whose practitioners one frequently finds an allegiance to the development of a "true cosmopolitanism," a "global culture," or a "planetary humanism" which re-visions the world community, leaving behind the religious and cultural provincialism of the past, and which provides a frame in which the different religious traditions may find new modes of creative co-existence and mutual enrichment. Thus, for instance, Mircea Eliade: "The history of religions can play an essential role in this effort toward a planétisation of culture; it can contribute to the elaboration of a universal type of culture."[12] (In this context one may also mention such scholars as Joachim Wach, Joseph Kitagawa, Huston Smith, Ninian Smart, Wilfrid Cantwell Smith, Klaus Klostermaier, W.T. Oxtoby, Eric Sharpe, Arvind Sharma, and Diana Eck.[13])

2. The emergence within the general field of comparative religion of *comparative mysticism* as the arena in which the formal and institutionalized differences of the various religions may be at least partially reconciled, sometimes under the rubric of the perennial philosophy (Rudolf Otto, W.T. Stace, Aldous Huxley, William Johnston), and of *comparative philosophy* (East-West Philosophy Conferences, Sarvepalli Radhakrishnan, John Hick), *comparative theology* (Henri Dumoulin, Karl Rahner, Hans Kung, Paul Knitter, John Cobb), and *comparative psychology* (William James, C.G. Jung, Joseph Campbell and the Eranos constellation, Ken Wilber), all of which compare and contrast and/or synthesize Eastern and Western understandings within a particular theoretical framework or field of practice.

3. The creation of *supra-religious universalist movements* which seek to synthesize or syncretize elements from many different religions and which claim to offer a new global "super-religion" or "spiritual way" which subsumes the religious differences of the past, and which often draws on "esoteric" doctrines from different traditions (Theosophy, neo-Hindu Vedanta, Baha'i, some forms of "ecosophy"); sub-sets of this group include those who construct systems purporting to meld esoteric religion and modern science (Blavatsky, Gurdjieff, Rudolf

---

12 M. Eliade, *The Quest: History and Meaning in Religion* (Chicago: University of Chicago Press, 1969), p. 69.

13 For more information on these figures, and those subsequently noted parenthetically, see H. Oldmeadow, *Journeys East: Twentieth Century Western Encounters with Eastern Religious Traditions* (Bloomington, IN: World Wisdom, 2004).

Steiner), iconoclasts who lay claim to some sort of "spiritual" teaching (Krishnamurti), eclectic free-for-all "gurus" (Bhagwan Rajneesh), and New Age "teachers" with a vaguely "spiritual" orientation (Deepak Chopra, Eckhart Tolle)—but whether any of these types should come under the canopy of "inter-religious understanding" is, to say the least, highly doubtful!

4. The various attempts to establish *trans-religious international institutions and forums* such as the World Parliament of Religions, Francis Younghusband's World Congress of Faiths, Rudolf Otto's *Religiöser Menschhietsbund*, and the like, as well as organizations with more modest aims, such as the Fellowship of Reconciliation or the International Association for Religious Freedom.

5. The cultivation of *inter-faith religious dialogue*, usually about matters of doctrine and spiritual practice but often also encompassing cross-religious responses to problems such as social injustice, political oppression, or ecological calamity, conducted by religious adherents who remain faithful to their own tradition but who wish to share their ideas and experiences and to learn from participants of other religious faiths (Paul Tillich, Klaus Klostermaier, Thomas Merton, Raimundo Pannikar, Diana Eck, David Steindl-Rast, Thomas Keating; journals such as *Buddhist-Christian Studies*, *Dialogue & Alliance*, *Studies in Formative Spirituality*, *Ching Feng*, *Hindu-Christian Studies Bulletin*, *Inter-Religious Bulletin*, and *Studies in Inter-religious Dialogue*).

6. *Existential engagements in a bi-traditional spiritual practice* which is firmly anchored in a particular tradition (usually Christianity) but which self-consciously and reflexively incorporates teachings and disciplines from another tradition in an effort to revitalize or reform a spiritual life which has in some respects atrophied (Bede Griffiths, Henri Le Saux, "Christian Zen," Pascaline Coff), and *inter-religious encounters aimed at mutual transformation* (John Cobb, Ruben Habito, Frederick Streng).

7. *The traditionalist exposition of the "religio perennis"* and the explication of the metaphysical basis from which *both* the inner unity and the outer diversity of the religious traditions derive (Ananda Coomaraswamy, Frithjof Schuon, Titus Burckhardt, Marc Pallis, Seyyed Hossein Nasr; journals such as *Studies in Comparative Religion*, *Sophia*, *Sacred Web*, *Vincit Omnia Veritas*, *Eye of the Heart*).

*

From the maze of developments over the last century let me isolate one small but illustrative episode. In 1984 representatives of all the major religions gathered at St. Benedict's Monastery in Snowmass, Colorado, to "meditate together in silence and share their personal spiritual journeys"[14] as well as deliberating on those elements of belief and practice which their traditions shared. Out of this gathering and subsequent meetings, which proved less vaporous than many attempts at dialogue, emerged a list of points of agreement. It is worth considering this list as an example of the kinds of convergences which can be discerned by adherents working together in a spirit of cooperative fellowship and dialogue:

• The world religions bear witness to the experience of Ultimate Reality to which they give various names. . . .

• Ultimate Reality cannot be limited by any name or concept.

• Ultimate Reality is the ground of infinite potentiality and actuality.

• Faith is opening, accepting, and responding to Ultimate Reality. . . .

• The potential for human wholeness—or in other frames of reference, enlightenment, salvation, transformation, blessedness, *nirvana*—is present in every human person.

• Ultimate Reality may be experienced not only through religious practices but through nature, art, human relationships, and service to others.

• As long as the human condition is experienced as separate from Ultimate Reality, it is subject to ignorance and illusion, weakness and suffering.

• Disciplined practice is essential to the spiritual life. . . . Humility, gratitude, and a sense of humor are indispensable in the spiritual life.

Father Thomas Keating pointed out that each of the participants in this dialogue were long-standing practitioners with a firm grasp of their own tradition. Furthermore, they were able to discuss creatively their differences as well as points of agreement; indeed, as Keating observed, the open ventilation of differences created even stronger bonds than the discovery of similarities. Participants were also alert to the

---

14 T. Keating, "Meditative Technologies: Theological Ecumenicism" in *The Other Half of My Soul: Bede Griffiths and the Hindu-Christian Dialogue*, ed. B. Bruteau (Wheaton, IL: Quest Books, 1996), p. 115.

dangers of any facile admixing of spiritual doctrines and practices such as would compromise the integrity of the distinct religious traditions. Keating also suggested that this kind of dialogue can only usefully proceed in an atmosphere of trust where people are able to speak from the heart, and to share their spiritual *experience* rather than engaging in academic debate about doctrinal divergences.

Meetings of this kind, large and small, have been taking place all over the globe for many decades now and signal the search not only for some sort of inter-religious theological and philosophical understanding but for moral solidarity. In an age of rampant secularism and skepticism the need for some kind of inter-religious coalition also makes itself ever more acutely felt. The religious representatives at Snowmass were acutely conscious of the "violence, injustice, and persecution" to which religious sectarianism and bigotry have given rise and affirmed the obligation of the world religions to play a decisive role in the cause of world peace:

> [T]he world religions will have to give the witness of mutual respect and understanding to the world community if political, ethnic, and nationalistic divisions are to be overcome or at least held in check.

They stressed that such an agenda would not be served by any attempt to blur the differences between the traditions:

> While emphasizing our common values and uniting in social action, however, the world religions must at the same time accept their diversity and cherish the integrity of each other's traditional spiritual paths. Genuine dialogue on this level is the catalyst that would facilitate harmony and cooperation on all the other levels of ever-increasing global interaction.[15]

People of good will must surely applaud such initiatives which can only result in greater mutual understanding and the formation of a common front against those many forces in the modern world which count against the spiritual life as well as against the attainment of a more peaceful international order. Such endeavors also throw into sharp relief those impulses and attitudes within the religious traditions

---

15 T. Keating, "Meditative Technologies," pp. 122-123.

which obstruct the possibilities of creative dialogue. Of these the most recalcitrant is a blind clinging to the belief that one's own tradition is the *exclusive* custodian of the Truth and provides the *only* path to salvation/enlightenment. This kind of exoteric exclusivism constitutes a very partial view but is not altogether unjustified, often arising out of a fierce commitment to the Truth as its has been revealed by the lights to which one has been exposed: in the words of Swami Abhishiktananda, "Every *dharma* is for its followers the supreme vehicle of the claims of the Absolute."[16] In some respects exclusivism is to be preferred to a sentimental "tolerance" which actually holds fast to nothing whatsoever and which can easily cloak an insolent condescension on one side or, worse, an impious indifference to each and every religion on the other. "Tolerance" often signifies nothing more than a vacuum of any firmly-held beliefs or pieties. As Coomaraswamy remarked, "the very implications of the phrase 'religious tolerance' are to be avoided: diversity of faith is not a matter for 'toleration,' but of divine appointment."[17] Recall, too, Joachim Wach's telling observation that, "There is something pathetic about the modern historian of religion who uses strong words only to convince us that he has no strong convictions."[18] Nonetheless, global circumstances are now such that an obdurate commitment to any rigid exclusivism will, in the end, amount to a kind of suicide.

Klaus Klostermaier has borrowed Niels Bohr's principle of complementarity to argue against three earlier Christian models of religious pluralism (fundamentalist exclusivism, eirenic universalism, and fulfillment theory) and suggested four principles which, we can reasonably surmise, would be widely accepted by many contemporary participants in inter-religious dialogue:

1. The acknowledgement of real paradox in the relation between different traditions, e.g., the categories of one tradition cannot explain

16 Abhishiktananda, *The Further Shore* (Delhi: ISPCK, 1975), p. 25.

17 A.K. Coomaraswamy, "Sri Ramakrishna and Religious Tolerance" in *Coomaraswamy, Vol. 2: Selected Papers, Metaphysics*, ed. R. Lipsey (Princeton: Princeton University Press, 1977), p. 42.

18 J. Wach, *The Comparative Study of Religions* (New York: Columbia University Press, 1958), p. 8. One might also recall Frithjof Schuon's observation that "the Christian saint who fights Muslims is closer to Islamic sanctity than the philosopher who accepts everything and practices nothing" (*Logic and Transcendence: A New Translation with Selected Letters* [Bloomington, IN: World Wisdom, 2009], p. 158n).

the other, and vice versa. 2. The acceptance of true mutuality between religious traditions [i.e., each can illuminate the other]. . . . 3.
The firm refusal to reduce one religion to another. . . . 4. The admis-
sion of the fragmentary and "incomplete" nature of each tradition.
. . .[19]

This is but one of many recent models and is adduced only to indicate the general movement away from Christian exclusivism in what
might be called the international dialogue community. That Christian
scholars and dialogists have abandoned the condescending models of
earlier times is heartening. The kind of inter-religious dialogue exemplified by the Snowmass gathering is also certainly to be welcomed. As
Thomas Merton pointed out,

> [G]enuine ecumenism requires the communication and sharing, not
> only of information about doctrines which are totally and irrevoca-
> bly divergent, but also of religious intuitions and truths which may
> turn out to have something in common. . . . Ecumenism seeks the
> inner and ultimate spiritual "ground" which underlies all articulated
> differences. A genuinely fruitful dialogue cannot be content with a
> polite diplomatic interest in other religions and their beliefs. It seeks
> a deeper level. . . .[20]

However, of itself, this kind of dialogue cannot neutralize the negative effects of exoteric dogmatisms on whose survival the religious
traditions actually, and somewhat paradoxically, depend. For a resolution of this problem we must turn to the perennialist school whose
pre-eminent spokesman in recent times has been Frithjof Schuon.

*

Many years ago Ananda Coomaraswamy's claimed that

> the only possible ground upon which an effective entente of East
> and West can be accomplished is that of the purely intellectual (i.e.,

---

19 K. Klostermaier, "All Religions Are Incomplete: Complementarity as Theoretical
Model to Guide the Praxis of Inter-religious Dialogue," *Dialogue & Alliance*, 7:2, 1993,
p. 74.

20 T. Merton, *Mystics and Zen Masters* (New York: Farrar, Strauss & Giroux, 1967),
p. 204.

metaphysical) wisdom that is one and the same at all times and for all men, and is independent of all environmental idiosyncrasy.[21]

If the malignant possibilities outlined earlier in this article—the erosion, destruction, and/or dilution of the religious traditions—are to be averted we need a proper understanding of what Schuon has called "the transcendent unity of religions." Crucial to any recognition of this unity is the ability to distinguish the exoteric and esoteric dimensions of the great traditions, and thus to forestall the terrible excesses which can arise out of religious literalism. In the present circumstances, this passage from Frithjof Schuon's *The Transcendent Unity of Religions*, written more than half a century ago, takes on a new resonance:

> The exoteric viewpoint is, in fact, doomed to end by negating itself once it is no longer vivified by the presence within it of the esoterism of which it is both the outward radiation and the veil. So it is that religion, according to the measure in which it denies metaphysical and initiatory realities and becomes crystallized in literalistic dogmatism, inevitably engenders unbelief; the atrophy that overtakes dogmas when they are deprived of their internal dimension recoils upon them from outside, in the form of heretical and atheistic negations.[22]

It is precisely this insight which are so often overlooked by fundamentalist groups and movements, wherever they be found.

Exoterism consists in identifying transcendent realities with the dogmatic forms—and if necessary with the historical facts—of a given Revelation, whereas esoterism refers in a more or less direct manner to these same realities.[23]

At a time when the outward and readily exaggerated incompatibility of divergent religious forms is used to exploit all manner of anti-

---

21 A.K. Coomaraswamy, "The Pertinence of Philosophy" in *Contemporary Indian Philosophy*, ed. S. Radhakrishnan & J.H. Muirhead (London: Allen & Unwin, 1952), p. 160. Cf.: "I am in fullest agreement about the necessity of recognizing a common basis of understanding, but see no basis . . . other than that of the *philosophia perennis*. . ." (Letter to H.G.D. Finlayson, December 1942, in A.K. Coomaraswamy, *Selected Letters of Ananda K. Coomaraswamy*, ed. R.P. Coomaraswamy & A. Moore Jr. [New Delhi: Oxford University Press, 1988], pp. 285-286).

22 F. Schuon, *The Transcendent Unity of Religions* (Wheaton, IL: Quest Books, 1993), p. 9.

23 F. Schuon, *Logic and Transcendence*, p. 123.

religious prejudices the exposure of the underlying unity of the religions is a task which can only be achieved through a *trans-religious* and *esoteric* understanding. The open confrontation of different exotericisms, the vandalism visited on traditional civilizations everywhere, and the tyranny of profane ideologies all play a part in determining the peculiar circumstances in which the most exigent needs of the age can only be answered by a recourse to traditional esotericisms wherein we find the *sophia perennis*, that timeless and immutable wisdom which informs all religions. Moreover,

> The need to recover a vision of the Center becomes ever more urgent for Western man as the illusory world he has created around himself in order to forget the loss of the transcendent dimension in his life begins to reveal ever more fully its true character. In such a situation, the response cannot, of course, come from anywhere but sacred tradition in all its authentic forms.[24]

The *philosophical* (or more precisely, *metaphysical*) question of the inter-relationship of the religions and the *moral* concern for greater mutual understanding are, in fact, all of a piece. We can distinguish but not separate questions about *unity* and *harmony*; too often both comparative religionists and those engaged in "dialogue" have failed to see that the achievement of the latter depends on a metaphysical resolution of the former question. A rediscovery of the immutable nature of man and a renewed understanding of the *sophia perennis* must be the governing purpose of the most serious comparative study of religion.

> Human nature in general and human intelligence in particular cannot be understood apart from the religious phenomenon, which characterizes them in the most direct and most complete way possible: grasping the transcendent—not the "psychological"—nature of the human being we thereby grasp the nature of revelation, religion, tradition; we understand their possibility, their necessity, their truth. And in understanding religion, not only in a particular form
> . . . but in its formless essence, we also understand the religions, that is to say, the meaning of their plurality and diversity; this is the plane

---

24 S.H. Nasr, "The Spiritual Needs of Western Man and the Message of Sufism" in *Sufism: Love and Wisdom*, ed. J-L. Michon & R. Gaetani (Bloomington, IN: World Wisdom, 2006), p. 179.

of *gnosis*, of the *religio perennis*, where the extrinsic antinomies of dogmas are explained and resolved.[25]

These words, written some years ago, are all the more compelling in the current climate.

It has not been my purpose here to expound the fundamental tenets of a properly constituted perennial philosophy, a task undertaken in several other places.[26] Interested readers are directed to the works of the great perennialists—René Guénon, Ananda Coomaraswamy, Frithjof Schuon, Titus Burckhardt and Seyyed Hossein Nasr, to mention only the most authoritative—who have explicated the metaphysical foundations of the "transcendent unity of religions," thus allowing us unequivocally to affirm the "profound and eternal solidarity of all spiritual forms"[27] and to "present a singular front against the floodtide of materialism and pseudo-spiritualism"[28] which threatens all integral religions.

*

Hitherto we have focused primarily on Christian initiatives to sponsor inter-religious understanding. However, it should not go unremarked that Islam in general and Sufism particularly have a special role to play in cultivating inter-religious concord and amity, not only because Islam belongs to both East and West but by virtue of the fact that the Descent of the Koran is the last in the great cycle of Revelations, that Muhammad is the Seal of the Prophets, and that, necessarily, at the heart of Islam there is a profound message about the mystical convergence of all integral traditions. Furthermore, Sufism is peculiarly well-equipped to help repair some of the damage wreaked on the Christian tradition over the last few centuries. Muhammad Ibn Arabi and Mowlana Jalaluddin Rumi are the most profound exponents of the *sophia perennis* within the Islamic tradition, and each actualized within himself the

---

25 F. Schuon, *Light on the Ancient Worlds: A New Translation with Selected Letters* (Bloomington, IN: World Wisdom, 2006), p. 125.

26 See H. Oldmeadow, *Frithjof Schuon and the Perennial Philosophy* (Bloomington, IN: World Wisdom, 2010).

27 F. Schuon, *Transcendent Unity of Religions*, p. xxxiv.

28 F. Schuon, *Gnosis: Divine Wisdom* (London: John Murray, 1959), p. 12.

transcendent unity of religions. Well-known to Sufis everywhere is the noble passage in which the Shaykh al-Akbar declares:

> My heart has opened unto every form; it is a pasture for gazelles, a cloister for Christian monks, a temple for idols, the Ka'ba of the pilgrim, the tables of the *Torah* and the book of the *Qur'an*. I practice the religion of Love; in whatsoever direction its caravans advance, the religion of Love shall be my religion and my faith.[29]

Rumi had Christian and Jewish disciples, and taught that adherents of different religions should be viewed with the same eye. It is said that people from five faith backgrounds followed his funeral bier and his mausoleum, the Green Dome in Konya, is today a place of pilgrimage for many thousands of wayfarers of differing religious affiliations. As Professor Nasr noted some years ago, "All attempts at a profound *rapprochement* with the other religions made by Muslims today can and should be based on the rich foundations prepared by Ibn Arabi and Rumi."[30] It is only the *sophia perennis* which they extolled that can lead us to that light of which the Koran speaks, "the light that is neither of the East nor the West," towards which we are beckoned by the great mystics of all traditions, the light that moved the mystic poet to utter those immortal words,

> I am neither Christian nor Jew nor Parsi nor Muslim. I am neither of the East nor of the West, neither of the land nor sea. . . . I have put aside duality and have seen that the two worlds are one. I seek the One, I know the One, I see the One, I invoke the One. He is the First, He is the Last, He is the Outward, He is the Inward.[31]

But, given the emergence of Islamic fundamentalism, often overtly hostile to Sufism, as well as the intransigence of the spiritually sterile

29 *Tarjuman al-Ashwaq*. (This passage has been frequently translated, with many small variations.) The gazelles signify different spiritual states. See F. Schuon, *Understanding Islam* (Bloomington, IN: World Wisdom Books, 1998), pp. 36-37.

30 S.H. Nasr, *Three Muslim Sages: Avicenna, Suhrawardi, Ibn 'Arabi* (Cambridge: Harvard University Press, 1964), p. 117.

31 Rumi quoted in W. Stoddart, *What do the Religions Say about Each Other? Christian Attitudes towards Islam, Islamic Attitudes towards Christianity* (San Rafael, CA: Sophia Perennis, 2008), p. 76.

ideologies of the modern West, no one should imagine that the way forward will be easy. If Sufism is, in Nasr's words, "to serve the world about it like a crystal which gathers the light and disseminates it to its surroundings" it must "remain strictly traditional and orthodox from the point of view of the Sufi tradition" but at the same time "address the world around it in a language which that world understands."[32] The same might be said of any traditional esoterism. It is only in the radiant light of the *sophia perennis* that we can celebrate and cherish our differences as well as affirming our common humanity beneath Heaven.

32 S.H. Nasr, "Spiritual Needs of Western Man," p. 205.

SOURCES

The essays in this volume first appeared in the following books and journals, to whose publishers and editors we are indebted for permission to reproduce them here. Only minor corrections have been made to the originals, though in some cases footnotes have been drastically curtailed.

1. "'Melodies from the Beyond': The Spiritual Heritage of the Australian Aborigines"
First published as "Melodies de l'au-dela: Perspective schuonienne sur la religion des aborigènes d'Australie," in P. Laude & J-P. Aymard (eds.), *Les Dossiers H: Frithjof Schuon* (Lausanne: L'Âge d'Homme, 2002), pp. 307-319.

2. "Metaphysics: East and West"
First published as "The Comparative Study of Eastern and Western Metaphysics: A Perennialist Perspective," *Sophia: International Journal for Philosophy of Religion, Metaphysical Theology and Ethics*, 46:1, May 2007, pp. 49-64.

3. "Shankara's Doctrine of *Maya*"
First published as "Shankara's Doctrine of *Maya*," *Asian Philosophy*, 2:2, 1992, pp. 131-146.

4. "'The Last Blade of Grass': The Bodhisattva Ideal in Mahayana Buddhism"
First published as "'Delivering the Last Blade of Grass': Aspects of the Bodhisattva Ideal in the Mahayana," *Asian Philosophy*, 7:3, November 1997, pp. 181-194.

5. "'Grass Upon the Hills': Traditional and Modern Attitudes to Biography"
First published as "Traditional and Modern Attitudes to Religious Biography," *Religious Traditions*, 7-10, 1984-1986, pp. 105-118.

6. "Joseph Epes Brown's *The Spiritual Legacy of the American Indian*"
First published as a book review, *Sophia: The Journal of Traditional Studies*, 12:2, Fall/Winter 2006, pp. 189-194.

7. "The False Prophets of Modernity: Darwin, Marx, Nietzsche, and Freud"
Based on a talk given at a conference on "Tradition and Modernity," sponsored by *Sacred Web*, Edmonton, October 2006. First published as "Tradition and the False Prophets of Modernism: Darwin, Marx, Nietzsche, Freud," *Sacred Web: A Journal of Tradition and Modernity*, 18, Winter 2007, pp. 47-70.

8. "Frankenstein's Children: Science, Scientism, and Self-Destruction"
First published as "Science, Scientism and Self-Destruction," *Sacred Web: A Journal of Tradition and Modernity*, 14, Winter 2004, pp. 87-92.

9. "Computers: An Academic Cargo Cult?"
First published as "Computer Technology: An Academic Cargo Cult?" *Research and Development in Higher Education*, Vol. 15 (Churchill: HERDSA, 1992), pp. 225-232.

10. "Frithjof Schuon on Culturism"
First published as part of "Humanism, Psychologism, Culturism," in *Frithjof Schuon and the Perennial Philosophy* (Bloomington, IN: World Wisdom, 2010), pp. 251-256.

11. "The Past Disowned: The Political and Postmodern Assault on the Humanities"
First published as "Disowning the Past: The Political and Postmodernist Assault on the Humanities," *Quadrant*, March 1992, pp. 60-65.

12. "Eckhart Tolle's *The Power of Now*"
First published as a book review, *Psychology and the Perennial Philosophy: Studies in Comparative Religion* (Bloomington, IN: World Wisdom, forthcoming).

13. "Ananda Coomaraswamy and the East-West Encounter"
First published as part of the Introduction to *Light from the East: Eastern Wisdom for the Modern West*, ed. Harry Oldmeadow (Bloomington, IN: World Wisdom, 2008), pp. vii-xi.

14. "Frithjof Schuon on Eastern Traditions"
First published as "Eastern Traditions: Hinduism, Buddhism, and the

Heritage of the Far East," in *Frithjof Schuon and the Perennial Philosophy* (Bloomington, IN: World Wisdom, 2010), pp. 138-150.

15. "*Ex Oriente Lux*: Eastern Religions, Western Writers"
Based on a talk given in the Winter Lecture Series at St Paul's Cathedral, Bendigo, September 1998. Not previously published in this form though some of this material appears in *Journeys East: Twentieth Century Western Encounters with Eastern Religious Traditions* (Bloomington, IN: World Wisdom, 2004), pp. xiv-xv, 3-6, 20-31, 80-82, 245-247, 267-268, 324-325.

16. "Huston Smith, Bridge-Builder *Extraordinaire*: A Tribute"
First published as "Huston Smith, Bridge-Builder *Extraordinaire*: A Tribute," *Sophia: The Journal of Traditional Studies*, 16:1, Winter 2010, pp. 73-80.

17. "Swami Abhishiktananda on *Sannyasa* and the Monk's Vocation"
First published as "The Monk's Vocation and *Sannyasa*," in *A Christian Pilgrim in India: The Spiritual Journey of Swami Abhishiktananda* (*Henri Le Saux*) (Bloomington, IN: World Wisdom, 2008), pp. 101-117.

18. "Across the Great Divide: Some Christian Responses to Religious Pluralism"
First published as "Crossing the Great Divide: Some Christian Responses to the Modern Encounter of Religions" in *Religions/Adyan*, 0, 2009, pp. 160-173.

Sectional epigraphs come from the following works by Frithjof Schuon: *Understanding Islam* (Bloomington, IN: World Wisdom, 1998), p. 26; *Stations of Wisdom* (London: John Murray, 1961), p. 47; and "No Activity Without Truth" in *The Sword of Gnosis*, ed. Jacob Needleman (Baltimore: Penguin, 1974), p. 39.

ACKNOWLEDGMENTS

It is a pleasure to acknowledge my debts of gratitude to:

the late Ranjit Fernando
Joseph Fitzgerald
Michael Fitzgerald
Ali Lakhani
Richard Lannoy
Patrick Laude
Rose Mazza
Clinton Minnaar
Seyyed Hossein Nasr
Diana and Russell Oldmeadow
Arvind Sharma
Wolfgang Smith
Mary-Kathryne Steele
Roger Sworder
William Stoddart
James Wetmore
Stephen Williams

BIOGRAPHICAL NOTE

HARRY OLDMEADOW is Coordinator of Religion and Spirituality Studies in the Arts Program, La Trobe University, Bendigo, Australia. A recognized authority on the Perennialist or Traditionalist school of comparative religious thought, his works include *Journeys East: 20th Century Western Encounters with Eastern Religious Traditions* (2004), *The Betrayal of Tradition: Essays on the Spiritual Crisis of Modernity* (2005), *Light from the East: Eastern Wisdom for the Modern West* (2007), *A Christian Pilgrim in India* (2008), *Crossing Religious Frontiers* (2010), and *Frithjof Schuon and the Perennial Philosophy* (2010). Over the last decade he has published extensively in such journals as *Sacred Web* and *Sophia*.

INDEX

For a glossary of all key foreign words used in books published by World Wisdom, including metaphysical terms in English, consult: www.DictionaryofSpiritualTerms.org.
This on-line Dictionary of Spiritual Terms provides extensive definitions, examples, and related terms in other languages.

Other Titles in the Perennial Philosophy Series by World Wisdom

Singing the Way: Insights in Poetry and Spiritual Transformation,
by Patrick Laude, 2005

The Spiritual Legacy of the North American Indian:
Commemorative Edition, by Joseph E. Brown, 2007

Sufism: Love & Wisdom,
edited by Jean-Louis Michon and Roger Gaetani, 2006

The Timeless Relevance of Traditional Wisdom,
by M. Ali Lakhani, 2010

The Underlying Religion: An Introduction to the Perennial Philosophy,
edited by Martin Lings and Clinton Minnaar, 2007

Unveiling the Garden of Love:
Mystical Symbolism in Layla Majnun and Gita Govinda,
by Lalita Sinha, 2008

What Does Islam Mean in Today's World:
Religion, Politics, Spirituality,
by William Stoddart, 2012

The Wisdom of Ananda Coomaraswamy:
Selected Reflections on Indian Art, Life, and Religion,
edited by S. Durai Raja Singam and Joseph A. Fitzgerald, 2011

Wisdom's Journey: Living the Spirit of Islam in the Modern World,
by John Herlihy, 2009

Ye Shall Know the Truth: Christianity and the Perennial Philosophy,
edited by Mateus Soares de Azevedo, 2005